ALSO BY THOMAS BELLER

Seduction Theory: Stories

The Sleep-Over Artist

How to Be a Man: Scenes from a Protracted Boyhood

J. D. Salinger: The Escape Artist

Lost in the Game: A Book About Basketball

Degas at the Gas Station

Thomas
Beller

Degas at the Gas Station

ESSAYS

Duke University Press   *Durham and London*   2025

© 2025 Thomas Beller
All rights reserved
Printed in the United States of America on acid-free paper ∞
Project Editor: Liz Smith
Designed by Dave Rainey
Typeset in Freight Text by Westchester Publishing Services

Library of Congress Cataloging-in-Publication Data
Names: Beller, Thomas, author.
Title: Degas at the gas station : essays / Thomas Beller.
Description: Durham : Duke University Press, 2025.
Identifiers: LCCN 2025006493 (print)
LCCN 2025006494 (ebook)
ISBN 9781478033035 (paperback)
ISBN 9781478029571 (hardcover)
ISBN 9781478061786 (ebook)
Subjects: LCSH: Beller, Thomas. | Beller, Thomas—Childhood and youth. | Authors, American—20th century—Biography. | Authors, American—21st century—Biography. | LCGFT: Essays. | Biographies.
Classification: LCC PS3552.E53364 Z46 2025 (print) | LCC PS3552.E53364 (ebook) | DDC 813/.54—dc23/eng/20250717
LC record available at https://lccn.loc.gov/2025006493
LC ebook record available at https://lccn.loc.gov/2025006494

For Elizabeth, Evangeline, and Alexander

From my place at table I would suddenly see through one of the east windows a marvellous case of levitation. There, for an instant, the figure of my father in his wind rippled white summer suit would be displayed, gloriously sprawling in mid-air, his limbs in a curiously casual attitude, his handsome, imperturbable features turned to the sky. Thrice, to the mighty heave ho of his invisible tossers, he would fly up in this fashion, and the second time he would go higher than the first and then there he would be, on his last and loftiest flight, reclining as if for good, against the cobalt blue of the summer noon, like one of those paradisiac personages who comfortably soar, with such a wealth of folds in their garments, on the vaulted ceiling of a church while below, one by one, the wax tapers in mortal hands light up to make a swarm of minute flames in the mist of incense, and the priest chants of eternal repose, and funeral lilies conceal the face of whoever lies there, among the swimming lights, in the open coffin.

—Vladimir Nabokov, *Speak, Memory*

Contents

xiii ACKNOWLEDGMENTS

1 The Misunderstandings

1 Introduction: The Misunderstandings
15 The Frozen River, Part I
18 iPod on the Tracks
21 The Stuff of Life
26 *The Bad News Bears* and *Breaking Away*
34 The Kinks at the Garden
46 The Lost Glove
49 On Moving Out
66 A Visit to the Library
71 The Laundry Room
77 Us and Them
85 The Topographical Soul
89 Negative Space
99 The Purple Krama

2 The Rights

- 107 Loose Teeth
- 111 Degas at the Gas Station
- 115 Thanksgiving Panic
- 121 The Pink Comma
- 127 How I Found My iPhone in New Orleans
- 134 The Two-Thousand-Dollar Popsicle
- 140 On Finding a Spot
- 146 Saying Goodbye to Now
- 151 Remembrance of Snows Past
- 160 Repeat, Memory
- 164 The Perils of Precocity
- 169 Drain You
- 173 Her Party
- 178 Napoleon on the Back Stairs
- 186 The Egg Cream in Mid-Manhattan, 1982
- 197 Somebody's Mother Is Waiting in the Lobby
- 203 That Time My Band Opened for Blur
- 209 Death of a Movie Theater
- 216 A Few Words About Jerry Stiller
- 220 Loitering with Intent at *Manet/Degas*
- 226 The Rights
- 237 Evacuation
- 243 The Frozen River (Reprise)

ACKNOWLEDGMENTS

I would like to thank the following individuals and institutions for their insight and support in the writing of this book: Sasha Weiss, Michael Agger, David Remnick, Mira Jacobs, Connie Rosenbloom, Frank Flaherty, Andrew Blauner, Adam Sternberg, Elaina Richardson, Yaddo, Lorin Stein, Hava Beller, Daniel Beller-McKenna, Edmund White, the Louisiana Board of Regents ATLAS grant, the Guggenheim Foundation, Whitney Donnhauser, Jennifer L. Sigler, Tana Wojczuk, David Daley, John and Melissa Gray, Owen Mazon, Alexander Compagno, Jonathan Ames, Tom Lowenstein, Nicholas Lemann, everyone at Duke University Press (Laura Sell, Cameron Ludwick, David Rainey, Chad Royal, Liz Smith, Chris Robinson, Alejandra Mejia), the Dutch translator and linguist Jan de Jong, a close reader of my work for thirty years. An especially deep bow of gratitude to my editor, Dean Smith, and agent, Rob McQuilkin. Special thanks to Nicholas Hamburger for his sensitive and perceptive notes on the manuscript, and to Phillip Lopate for believing in this book all along. And to Elizabeth Beller for everything.

Grateful acknowledgment is made to the publications in which some of the essays in this book first appeared, often in a somewhat different form:

New Yorker: "How I Found My iPhone in New Orleans"; "On Finding a Spot"; "The Two-Thousand-Dollar Popsicle"; "Saying

Goodbye to Now"; "Remembrance of Snows Past"; "Repeat, Memory"; "The Perils of Precocity"; "Drain You"; "Her Party"; "Napoleon on the Back Stairs"; "Somebody's Mother Is Waiting in the Lobby"; "That Time My Band Opened for Blur"; "Death of a Movie Theater"; "A Few Words About Jerry Stiller"

New York Review of Books Daily: "Negative Space"

Babble.com: "Loose Teeth"; "Degas at the Gas Station"

Guernica: "The Purple Krama"

New York Times: "iPod on the Tracks"; "The Stuff of Life"; "On Moving Out"; "The Kinks at the Garden"; "The Lost Glove"; "Loitering with Intent at *Manet/Degas*"

Paris Review Daily: "The Laundry Room"; "The Topographical Soul"

Tablet: "Us and Them"

Threepenny Review: "The Frozen River, Part I"; "A Visit to the Library"

Salon: "Thanksgiving Panic"

Harvard Design Review: "The Egg Cream in Mid-Manhattan, 1982"

Some of these pieces were included in anthologies: "The Kinks at the Garden" appeared in *The Show I'll Never Forget: 50 Writers Relive Their Most Memorable Concertgoing Experience*, edited by Sean Manning; "Negative Space" appeared in *Central Park*, edited by Andrew Blauner; "The Rights" appeared in *What I Would Tell Her*, edited by Andrea Richesin.

Introduction

The Misunderstandings

One day, more than twenty years ago, I won a luxury cruise. I won by opening a fortune cookie at a party for a travel magazine. When the big tray of oversize fortune cookies was presented to my table, I had initially waved it away, taking a pass. Everyone around me took one, but I didn't want to engage in what I was sure was a charade. The young woman holding the tray was wearing the black pants and shirt of the catering crew; her face was pale and very smooth. She looked like Jim Morrison, I remember thinking, which I found jarring—Jim Morrison encouraging me to take the giant fortune cookie. I took one just to be agreeable and cracked it open along with everyone else.

I examined the slip of paper within.

"It says I won a cruise," I said.

I assumed this was a tease, and that I had won a *chance* to win a cruise. I looked at the young woman. Her face became blank and a bit soft.

"Wow. You won the cruise," she said in a stunned manner. It dawned on me that I had not won a chance to win; I had won.

Over a year went by without my taking the cruise. Part of the delay was a mild indifference bordering on contempt for the idea of a cruise, but mostly it was that there was no one with whom I especially wanted to go. Finally, I received a "use it or lose it" ultimatum from the magazine's marketing department.

As it happened, I had recently met someone for whom I wanted to do something impressive. I didn't know what, exactly. A gesture. When I called Elizabeth to suggest we take a cruise together and said I had one picked out, I neglected to mention the giant fortune cookie. "I would like to invite you," I said, as though I had bought a pair of tickets for us, or was prepared to. For many people, the idea of paying for a vacation is reasonable, even obvious, but for me, it was a kind of absurdity. I was in no position to buy tickets for a cruise; I was a freelance writer. When I traveled, which I sometimes did, it was on assignment, usually for the travel magazine at whose party I had won the cruise.

"A cruise?" said Elizabeth warily.

I played it straight. She agreed.

It would begin in Nice and end in Rome. We made plans to fly to Rome, travel through Italy, and spend a weekend with Don and Helen Meyers, old family friends who had a place in Saint-Paul de Vence. Then we would descend to the port in Nice and commence the cruise. Elizabeth insisted on paying for the Rome part of the trip. I didn't say anything about the fortune cookie, again. Was this an example of bad manners? I am still pondering.

It was an intense time. We were brand new. We met at a wedding. She was friends with the groom. I was friends with the bride. It was the second time I attended her wedding. The first was to a close friend of mine, Rob Bingham, who had died six months later. There was a lot going on at that second wedding party, a lot of currents. I had glimpsed Elizabeth during the wedding but did not actually meet her until the afterparty.

By the time we got to Nice a couple of months later, we were on some kind of rocket. A matrimonial aura hovered over us. It felt meaningful that I was bringing her to Don and Helen's place; I wanted to show this lovely woman to old friends of my mother and my late father. I suppose I was seeking their approval, though I didn't think about it that way at the time. They were delighted with her.

Taking me aside on the first afternoon, Helen whispered, in her thick Viennese accent, "Buy her jewelry." Their pleasure in Elizabeth was, I couldn't help but feel, shadowed by a certain impatience with me.

Don and Helen were both psychoanalysts. Intellectuals. Also, Francophiles, as was the case with many of their generation who were in some way shaped by World War II. At some point in the 1980s, they bought a glamorous villa overlooking the Mediterranean in the South of France.

The summer after college, I had rolled into their Vence house in a rather bedraggled state, having spent a couple of months traveling on my own in Europe. The trip culminated in a strange few days in the Greek Islands that ended with me getting off a boat in Athens with no money other than one random credit card that happened to have fallen out of my wallet just before I lost it along with my passport.

I finally made it to Don and Helen's place a week later, and they fed me and housed me for a couple of days, leaving me rejuvenated by the sense of shelter and the conversation. I was in good spirits when I got on the train to Paris and my flight home. Helen drove me down the steep mountain and came with me to the platform. The most vivid image of the whole trip might have been Helen in a white and yellow striped dress standing on the platform waving at me as my train pulled away while I waved back.

Don and Helen had met my father at the Columbia Psychoanalytic Institute, but Helen's connection to my father preceded their actual meeting—both of them were refugees from Vienna, though Helen came from a nicer neighborhood, she often added.

I knew enough, by the end of college, to sense that there was a special resonance about goodbyes in train stations in Europe if you were someone whose escape from Europe involved a train. Beyond that, I had a fleeting moment of seeing the scene through her eyes: Here is the son of her dear friend and colleague, who died about a decade earlier, going on the train to Paris and the rest of his life in better shape than when he had arrived a few days earlier. While she stood waving to me in her capacious yellow and white striped dress, and big sunglasses, and I waved back, I had the fleeting but pleasurable notion that I was going to be all right, in part because I thought whatever happened to me, I could always roll into Don and Helen's lives for a night or two to recuperate. I suppose I should mention that there was a long history of this, dating back to the day of my father's funeral, when I was nine. I spent that first night at their house. Sometime later, they bought the house in France, high on a mountain in Vence, with a pool and elegant cypress trees dotting the view of the faraway sea.

It was to this glamorous house on a mountain overlooking the coast of southern France—Nice, Cannes, and Cap d'Antibes—that I brought Elizabeth, for a couple of days before we embarked on our cruise. And it was there, surrounded by various shades of Matisse blue, that I asked Don and Helen a question about my father whose answer has resonated all the way into the pages of this book. I had not realized that it was urgent until the moment I asked it: "Why didn't my father ever publish anything?"

My father, Alexander Beller, had been a psychoanalyst. This is a division of the medical profession in which literary production, though not required, is an indication of advancement, or at least ambition. Don and Helen had published articles and edited books. Why not my father?

I don't know when my father's lack of production as a writer started to bother me, but by the time of this visit, it had started to seem conspicuous. As a child, I knew my father wrote. When I woke in the middle of the night to go to the bathroom, the trip from my bedroom to the bathroom took me past the entrance to his study, where he would invariably be sitting, bathed in lamplight, at the "French Desk," as my mother calls it, an antique from another century with a smooth, subtly uneven surface of dark chestnut wood and curving legs, which my parents bought while traveling together in Europe sometime before I was born.

There he sat at this stately desk in the middle of the room, wearing his tortoiseshell glasses, a cigarette maybe smoldering between his fingers or in the ashtray, pondering his formidable Olivetti if he wasn't busy emphatically stabbing at its shiny black keys. From this evidence, I knew that he wrote. I just didn't know what.

At some point, many years later, when I was in psychoanalysis myself, I decided to try and find some of his writings. I was aware that many of his friends and colleagues had written articles, if not books, and assumed he had, too. But this was not the case. He'd never published anything, I discovered, which was particularly strange as there was a prize in his name at Columbia for best writing by a graduate of the Psychoanalytic Institute. This detail, in particular—giving a prize for writing in the name of someone who'd never published—had come to seem . . . perverse.

It feels utterly remote now, the lost land of psychoanalysis, newly ascendant in postwar America, and now largely submerged beneath heaps of psychology and pharmaceuticals. But this was the world in which my father and his friends lived and worked. I know a few things about it, if only through osmosis. For instance, the time Don and Helen came to visit me at summer camp, which their son Andy also attended, and over lunch inquired about my dreams. I shared with them an image in which I was shooting baskets at a hoop, only instead of a ball, I was picking up and throwing globs of white foamy stuff that traveled from my hands uncertainly.

"This is clearly a dream about sperm," declared Helen. Her thick Viennese accent might have made such a proclamation funny, but my father had the same accent, so, for me, the effect was one of poignancy.

In that same conversation I mentioned climbing up and coming down a slide. Don, cheerful, gentle, and encouraging where Helen tended to be sharp-elbowed and blunt, explained to me in his broad American accent how things such as slides and roller coasters—things that go up and down—could be seen as sexual imagery.

Now I was a grown-up, bobbing up and down in their pool as I posed my question about my father: "Why didn't my father ever publish anything?"

Elizabeth was on a lounge chair just beyond the edge of the pool, as were Don and Helen. It was an odd angle from which to ask a question about my father and writing. But it gave the velocity of their response an added impact.

"None of us were publishing at the time your father died," said Helen. "We all started publishing a few years later."

At that time, in the early 1970s, they explained, there were all sorts of rigid hierarchies within the psychoanalytic community. There were insiders, and outsiders. My father and Don and Helen Meyers were all members of the Columbia Psychoanalytic Institute. This was the outsider group.

"We were intimidated," Don said, "by the New York Psychoanalytic Institute." That was the insider group. "We were, you know, terrified of the establishment. If he had lived a few more years, he absolutely would have started publishing along with the rest of us."

When I say there was a matrimonial aura around Elizabeth and me, I mean that we were besotted, in love, in a state of fiery combustion, mostly in good ways, but also that I had the feeling of a new era about to dawn in my life. I had been in several relationships that had developed for some length, and even ripened toward marriage, only to move beyond ripe to be discarded. Sometimes I did the discarding, sometimes I was discarded, usually a bit of both. That I was hearing this information about my father's silence with regard to publishing in Elizabeth's presence only added to the feeling that I was entering a new world. The world of marriage and family. And how, from the perspective of this new world, I would begin to have some insights into the old world from which I came.

I was familiar with the New York Psychoanalytic Institute, having been employed there, very briefly, during a high school summer. The job involved boxes of books. The chief librarian, who was new, had just taken over from the just-retired chief librarian, Liselotte Bendix Stern, who was my step-grandmother.

Lilo had met my grandfather, the psychoanalyst Max M. Stern, at the New York Psychoanalytic Institute. My mother's father was a brittle, tall German of some formality whose writing was, and remains, well represented "in the literature." I both can and cannot imagine their courtship in the context of his use of the library, which was just a few blocks from where he lived and practiced psychoanalysis. When I was seven, they married. When I was fourteen, Lilo retired. Her replacement made every effort to be tolerant of the step-grandchild of her predecessor, whom she'd hired to unpack all of these boxes. But the whole thing lasted only two days. I unpacked a box of books but put them on the wrong shelf. Or had I failed to unpack some other box of books? It is all a somewhat hazy blur.

When I returned, many years later, to the New York Psychoanalytic Institute, it was as a supplicant. I wanted to be taken on as a patient by a training analyst at a "sliding scale." It was like applying to college or graduate school, except one had to advertise in particular not one's triumphs or small aptitudes but the ways in which one was flawed, self-impeded, and in need of help. The whole thing was quite arduous, though perhaps a necessary preparation for psychoanalysis itself.

Once I got in and underway and a couple of years had passed, I decided to go to the New York Psychoanalytic Institute to see if my grandfather or father had published anything I could read. Which is when I found the many articles and reviews by my mother's father, Dr. Max M. Stern, and even a book, posthumously published, over which he had labored the last few decades of his life. *Repetition and Trauma*, it was called. Looking up his writings in the *Psychoanalytic Quarterly* of the 1950s and '60s, I discovered a voice much more droll than the severe Germanic voice of the man I thought knew. Meanwhile, I found nothing by my father.

My father, Alexander Beller, born and raised in Vienna in the shadow of the Prater and its famous carousel, had a lilt in his voice that I recognized as irony long before I knew what the word meant. He was warm. Distracted, preoccupied, often absent while at work, but warm and loving when he was around.

My maternal grandfather, Max, born and raised in Frankfurt am Main, Germany, did *not* have a lilt in his voice. Nor did he seem at all warm. They were very different people. But—strange as it is for me to put it this way—they were the men in my life.

My father died of cancer when I was nine and he fifty-two. My grandfather died seven years later, at eighty-two. Later in life I learned from my mother that the two men had never got along very well, and simply accommodated one another. Perhaps, during the seven years of my adolescence when my grandfather was alive and my father wasn't, I may have embodied that conflict. My grandfather and I didn't speak for two of these years, after a huge fight at his house. I had cursed (at Passover). He had told me not to. I invoked freedom of speech. Not in his house, he said. Then I'll just leave, I said.

Back and forth. Never did we break into chuckles over the absurdity of it all. Stern. Could there have been a more appropriate last name? The severity of that round forehead, that lean face, accentuated by a white goatee that echoed the medieval wood carvings and German expressionist art filling his apartment. Just thirteen at the time, I became tearful and finally stormed out of his apartment. My mother, her face thin-lipped and severe, followed behind, lending me tacit support.

The living room of my grandfather's Park Avenue apartment was the stage on which our family visits unfolded, and at its center was a round table that spun, like a giant lazy Susan. Pouring tea as we faced him on the nubbly brown couch, we would gently rotate the table for careful stops at West, South, East, and, finally, North. But what if one had been... less careful? Our teatime visits existed in tension with my temptation to spin the table when it should not be spun.

The living room had a plush cream carpet, paintings on the walls, and a good many ancient artifacts from Greece and Rome in alabaster white—a head missing some of its nose, a female body, curvaceous and tiny, missing everything but the torso. But it was the African art, those fierce, forbidding masks, that best reflected the atmosphere of severity that surrounded my grandfather, along with the almost petrified, reddish wood sculpture of a large Virgin Mary extracted from a medieval church somewhere in Europe. This leaned slightly back toward the wall, in the corner of the living room behind the stereo equipment, which was itself piled on a side table at the end of the long brown couch on which he alone sat.

We reconciled when I was fifteen, my grandfather and I. He came into the foyer much more stooped than I remembered him, lifted his head up, and then further up, his bright blue eyes looking shocked and, I guess, delighted at my height, which I got from him, possibly the only time I ever saw him express delight. He brought me over to the glass vitrine in which small ancient artifacts had been arranged in rows on the shelves. Every time I visited, he said, I could choose one to take home. I scanned the shelves, trying to calculate the most valuable one, but then I gave in to a more basic impulse and chose a small metal figure of an enraged warrior shaking a stick in the air. A trinket that at the time felt like a triumph.

My parents had married in this apartment. My father was forty, nearly ten years older than my mother. After the wedding he walked six blocks to his office on East Seventy-Fourth Street. It was in a neighborhood where all the shops were prefaced by the word *Carlyle*—Carlyle Photo, Carlyle Chemists, the Carlyle Hotel—and saw some more patients. Their honeymoon took place the following weekend, when they drove down to Washington, DC.

I report these forensics almost as an act of pantomime in which I demonstrate that the raw data of facts and dates give only an illusion of intimacy with a time and place, while mainly achieving a kind of narcotizing effect on feeling or understanding. Like a narcotic, the facts are addictive, once you get used to dealing them out and using them.

The difficulties between Alexander Beller and Max M. Stern, in fact, predated my father's discovery of Dr. Stern's daughter.

Psychoanalysts, as part of their training, must be analyzed by a training analyst, and my father was to have his future father-in-law as a training analyst. My father spent a session on my grandfather's couch. The relationship did not take. Afterward—he must have stood up from the couch and left the apartment, thinking he would never return—he sought out a different training analyst. But a few years later he returned and got married in that very apartment, in the living room, just down the hall from the waiting room and the office with its ill-fated couch.

I wonder what my father felt when he returned to that address with Max M. Stern's daughter on his arm, to stand under a chuppah in the living room, a doctor getting married to a doctor's daughter. A psychoanalyst marrying the daughter of a psychoanalyst. A member of the Columbia Institute of Psychoanalysis getting married to the daughter of a member of the New York Institute of Psychoanalysis.

Years after my visits to the library where my step-grandmother had once worked, and where I had, too, for a couple of days, and years after that scene in the pool in the South of France—years, in fact, after Helen had died—it dawned on me that in seeking out an analyst, I had gone to the place associated with my grandfather, the cold one, and not to the place associated with my own beloved father, sanctified in the way that fathers who die too young are, at least at first, for their survivors.

I rushed with this question to Don, this time on dry ground, in the city. Had I betrayed him?

"Not at all," he said. "Your father and Helen were both snobs. They would have wanted you to go to the New York Psychoanalytic Institute."

It wasn't this fact, or *only* this fact, that assuaged my worry and unburdened me, but the humor and warmth with which it was conveyed. Which was just like him. Late in his life, Don came to a party for my J. D. Salinger book as a kind of guest of honor. His aunt Fritzi had been best friends with Salinger's older sister, Dorothy. Fritzi had brought Don along to meet her when he was a psychiatric resident in the hopes he might have some insight for Dorothy about her troubled younger brother, Jerry. Amid this crowded book party, Don took a seat in a grand old chair in the corner, whereupon the host rushed up to him and said, "Oh no!—You can't sit in that chair!"

"Why not?" Don said.

"Because . . . it's not long for this world."

He shrugged. "Neither am I."

But back to Provence, if you'll indulge me. For it was here, bobbing up and down in Don and Helen's swimming pool with the entire coast of France spread out below us, all of the Mediterranean it seemed, the incredible blue of the sea melting into the blue of the sky, and Elizabeth my not-yet-bride-to-be comfortably nearby, that I resolved the question of my father's publication, or lack thereof, which really was a question about his silence. Which, in turn, was another way of lamenting the fact that he had died too soon, had not seen me grow, had not been able to help with that, had not seen the long period of adventures and misadventures come to this most satisfying juncture, and now was not present to gaze upon Elizabeth and myself as we were set to embark on, among other things, a cruise. This is when Don mentioned, as though in passing, that as a kid I used to walk backward.

"Why?" I asked.

"No one knew," said Don.

Sometimes unrelated facts, purely for the timing of their arrival, feel paired: My father was publishing no more nor less than any of his peer group when he died; it's just that he died young. And when I was little, I walked backward.

This small biographical fact seemed, if not significant, then ripe for metaphor. What did it mean? That I was contrary? That I had been born with a genetic propensity for nostalgia? For looking back at the landscape that I had just left, as opposed to the one I was about to enter? That I was a descendant of such people? One generalization about the Jewish diaspora, after all, is that there is a lot of looking back, along with a lot of escaping and fleeing.

What does it mean that a kid walks backward? Does it mean that I preferred not to know where I was going? That I had—*have*—an innate need to make things complicated? Was it sheer contrariness? Any of it was plausible. All of it. I asked my mother, who stated flatly that none of it was the case to begin with. Never had there been such backward walking.

Was she in denial? Or were Don and Helen, those beneficent figures of my youth, being in some way malevolent, or at the very least careless? I let this paradox simmer for a while, circling back to it now and then, asking my mother again from time to time. Who knew? Perhaps her take on it all might have changed since the last conversation.

Maybe there was no walking backward, just as maybe there would be no meaningful metaphor if there were. But I have to say, I like it, because it made sense to me that a child who enjoys walking backward would one day grow up to be a writer who draws from life, who writes books about the very act of looking back.

Many of these essays recount confrontations or predicaments that a more cautious person would have avoided. They were written over a period of time during which I got married, and we had a child, and then had another. Concurrent to these events, I moved from New York City to New Orleans, with a pit stop in rural Virginia. All of it normal enough on the face of it, yet within each one of these episodes, I found my way to the sort of Clouseau-esque fiascos one usually dodges with a little foresight—again, not a strong attribute in a kid who may have liked to walk backward.

One often fails to grasp how much a friend, lover, or family member has affected you until they are gone. It turns out that this is true of places as well. Many of these essays are propelled by a kind of separation anxiety. From a city, a neighborhood, an apartment, and also from possessions with which one may be separated only to be reunited.

Losing things is a big part of life, but so is finding them.

The walking backward riddle lingered on until once, when I brought it up yet again with my mother. After her affirming, yet again and with utter confidence, that I had never made a habit of walking backward, she added, "Unless it was in baseball or something like that."

This is when I remembered that five days after my father's funeral, I had my tenth birthday party under the auspices of Don and Helen, who had organized a baseball game. Some other kids, older kids, who were children of other psychoanalysts, were also present. I have a dim memory of it having been nice, a fun afternoon of feeling special, as one would want a kid to feel on their birthday, even though there were so many ways that being special could now be construed as a bad thing, for I was now part of that special province of the fatherless.

And it suddenly came to me, if dimly, that during that baseball game I may indeed have run the bases backward. I won't say I recall doing it. But it suddenly seemed plausible, something at the edge of memory.

The riddle was solved. There was no riddle. So I *didn't* walk or run backward as a matter of course; nor was there a habit to which one might trace a significance. On the other hand, I may have done it once. Enough to register memorably for Don and Helen. A kid running from home to first base backward in those exciting moments after smacking the ball good. And from first base onward, moving forward but looking back and . . . oh, it's almost too easy to say, or maybe it's too difficult, finding his way home.

The Misunderstandings

The Frozen River, Part I

Growing up next to the Hudson River, I wondered how strong the ice was when it formed along the shore in winter, whether it could bear a person's weight. I wondered about this while leaning against the window of our apartment from which, if I put my right cheek against the glass, I could see the river clearly enough.

A bright blue sky. Choppy water the color of gunmetal. The buildings of New Jersey a toy-like abstraction on the far shore. In the foreground, on the near shore, below the park and past the West Side Highway, the snowy ice arranged itself in giant geometric shapes extending thirty or forty yards out into the river. The feeling of wind whipping just on the other side of the window, gusts of wind so strong they sometimes rattled the window frames. The outline of tree branches far below, tipped by frozen buds from which, one day, life once more would spring. And up above, in white briefs and a white undershirt, standing in an apartment so warm and bright that the chill of a windowpane felt refreshing against my cheek, I surveyed the ice.

When he was diagnosed with blood cancer, my father was told he had six months to twenty-five years to live. That was the spread, two to twenty. He had lived for about eight of them by the time he got truly sick and had to begin an emergency round of chemo. Six months later he was gone.

In the years after my father died, my Uncle Kuno would sometimes visit us from Philadelphia and spend the night on the living room couch. My uncle had bristly hair that he wore on the longish side, with a somewhat flamboyant side part, and intelligent, attentive eyes. He dressed well, and in his wake there was always the fragrance of cologne. But the sense of finery around him transcended what he wore or how he looked or smelled. It was manifest, most of all, in the deliberate pace with which he spoke, moved, looked at the world, looked at me. Uncle Kuno's visits to our New York apartment had an element of multitasking, I now realize. He was visiting the wife and child of his late brother, and so fulfilling a duty. It was also true, though, that he was in New York for professional reasons and needed a place to spend the night. He could have afforded a hotel—I can almost hear the slight indignation in his voice, a sudden rise in pitch that was almost musical, at the suggestion he couldn't—but these overnight visits combined his obligation to check in with his younger brother's wife and son with his innate sense of thrift. And there was his sister, Berta, who lived just a bit farther uptown. He could have stayed with her. But she was a famously contentious woman. He would have spent a large sum to avoid her couch. And here we were anyways, so he didn't have to.

My mother would put out a spread of cold cuts from Zabar's and brew a pot of coffee, actions reserved for the presence of special friends or dignitaries. This wasn't a question of formality or etiquette for my mother, or not entirely; she did this out of a genuine personal warmth, and also an idea of how life should be lived. Nevertheless, I read these gestures of hospitality through the lens of a child sensitive to hierarchy, the sensibility of a prince who has lost his patrimony.

Other than these languorous picnics at the kitchen table, and the sight of my uncle lying on the couch in the morning as I went to school, I saw little of my uncle on these visits, at least little that I recall. His presence in the house was signified mainly, for me, by his toiletries bag, a beautiful leather object within which were housed any number of delightful mysteries. He always used my bathroom, and this toiletries bag sat on the black porcelain shelf beneath the mirror. I was able to inspect it after school in his absence, plucking out the fancy German electric razor, matte black with a tight coil cord, and the three silver discs that did the cutting that gleamed in the soft afternoon light. There were many little bottles containing mysterious and fragrant liquids of different textures and colors, the glass clinking gently as I removed them and put them back, one at a time.

Now, remembering the pleasure of these inspections, I am suddenly overwhelmed by sadness as I see myself at the age of ten, eleven, twelve, looking so curiously into my uncle's toiletries bag. From my earliest years, I had now and then playacted with my father's things—slathering my face in shaving cream and pretending to shave while standing beside him at the bathroom mirror, or wearing his shoes and tromping through the apartment with them—and this continued in those first years after his death, when his clothes were all still there. I say "his," though in a way they no longer were. By this, I mean that with my father no longer there, the thrill of imitation had by necessity evolved into the thrill of usurpation. Which was, in fact, no thrill at all. Now these items were just artifacts, and I wore them brazenly, carelessly. Maybe I understood that his clothes fitting me when I was eleven meant that I would only outgrow them, that their utility was finite. But I was also reacting, I think, against what happens in many homes after such a death, when it becomes a kind of museum to the departed.

There is one scene in Riverside Park that stands out from the rest of my boyhood. An afternoon game of pickup tackle football on the ratty lawn between the playground and the highway. I was wearing a pale blue oxford shirt from Brooks Brothers that had belonged to my father. I wasn't that athletic, but I was big enough, and ran the ball with ferocity. They called me "Little Larry Csonka," at least one kid did, once. Anyway, after a run up field and a tackle, I got up from the ground and noticed that one of the buttons had popped off the shirt. Upon seeing this, I burst into inconsolable tears. When I finally managed to explain that the shirt had belonged to my dead father, someone said, quite reasonably, "Then why are you playing football in it?"

iPod on the Tracks

I was bounding down the stairs into the subway, three steps at a time, hoping to make the train. The stairs were wet. The air was cold. It was a day of harsh weather, a gusting snowstorm, but I had my iPod and was experiencing everything dreamily. I was getting married in a few months. Which is not to say anything had changed, really. We lived together in the same apartment, the two of us and Elizabeth's aged cat.

To say it is a new iPod is only half of it. I had sent it in for repairs, and its return had been delayed. Weeks turned into months. By the time it arrived, it felt like a reunion. And this was but the second day of its second act.

The subway doors were still open, thank God. I was listening to a Chopin prelude and moving fast. I took the last few steps in a giant jump, sidestepping a man in a wheelchair who was shaking a cup of change. The sounds of the piano filled my head. I was going to make this train.

Then I felt a brief tug on my ears, and silence. The iPod had fallen through a hole in my coat pocket and, hitting the concrete at a reckless angle, skidded across the platform like a bright white puck. There was a sharp thwack as it slammed into the side of the subway car and then fell into the crack between platform and subway, all the way down to the tracks. The whole moment had the brisk finality of a goal in air hockey.

Everyone facing the open subway door, and a number of people standing behind them, watched the iPod drop down to oblivion. Then they looked up at me.

The man in the wheelchair sprang to his feet. A miracle?

"What you drop?" he demanded. "I get it for you. No problem."

I turned my back. I couldn't let them see my despair. I waited for the doors to close. But the doors did not close.

"I go down there for you?" the man said. One of his eyes was gray and cloudy.

"It's all right," I said. "I can get it."

"I go for you!"

The train was still there. It was being held in the station. I turned to face the people in the car.

"I can see it," one of the men on the train said. "It's safe."

I went over and peered down through the crack. There it was on the black, grimy subfloor, a narrow frontier of plastic bags and furtive rodents.

"If you go and tell them, they'll get it for you," someone else said helpfully. It was a sympathetic crowd. The guy in the wheelchair had by now returned to his wheelchair, his body language suggesting it was a seller's market. I would come around. Or not. All the same to him. I took out my wallet, hoping to see a ten. Five would seem too cheap, and twenty profligate. But no. I could not pay a man in a wheelchair to do my dirty work, even if his actual need for the wheelchair was now dubious.

I waited until the train was gone, and the two that immediately followed were finally gone. The iPod lay on the floor of the tracks. The tunnel was dark and quiet. I stared down into the narrowing blackness to make sure nothing was coming, and then down again at the tracks. My knees were a little loose, like someone about to jump off a diving board.

New York is a vertical town, the emphasis being on things that rise up, and the New Yorker's panic-stricken need for accomplishment—the need to go up—is matched by a kind of vertigo that comes with being constantly aware of the distance below. I took a breath and hopped down, then quickly grabbed the iPod, its whiteness now streaked with grime. I stood there a moment rubbing it clean, rubbing it dry, petting it, really, as if it were a small animal that had gotten itself into trouble but was now safe. I dropped it in a more reliable pocket, planted my hands on the filthy platform, and began to hoist myself up.

Only I didn't make it, bonking my shin, and fell back down. On the next try, no problem. But in the few seconds between these two tries, I felt a pang of awareness. There I was on the tracks. Tracks I'd stared down at all my life. Always it had been rats, the third rail, and garbage investing that space with its faint air of horror, but it turns out that the most powerful feeling while down there was simply . . . being lower than, *beneath*, everyone else. Looking up into all those knees, I wanted only to rise.

Back on the platform, I brushed myself off. An older woman, well dressed, looked at me as though I were the Loch Ness Monster.

"You get it?" yelled the man in the wheelchair, still shaking his change cup.

"Yes!" I yelled back. I thanked him profusely and for some reason pushed ten dollars into his cup. Perhaps for giving me courage, even if it had arrived only via shame.

The iPod, though now scuffed, worked fine. When I got to the restaurant where I was having lunch, I washed my hands several times in rapid succession, channeling Lady Macbeth, or maybe Howard Hughes. Long after my hands were surely already clean, I kept rinsing and soaping and rinsing and soaping long after my hands seemed perfectly clean.

The whole episode should have been a fleeting moment, something barely remembered, but that evening, getting into bed, my then-fiancée Elizabeth said, "What happened to your leg?"

I looked at my shin. There was a small cut, no more than a tiny red line, and a little bump.

I explained about the iPod, gratified to see her amusement as I described it skidding across the platform, all the faces in the subway car turning toward me, and the fellow in the wheelchair jumping up to help. Then her face darkened a little. There were three months to the wedding.

"You didn't actually go *down* there, did you?"

"It's just—I couldn't bring myself to hire the guy in the wheelchair," I said.

"You went down on the tracks?"

When I said I had, she got worked up. This really bothered her.

"You're not alone anymore!" she said, and then asked me to promise I would not jump down onto the subway tracks in the future. I promised. She shook her head.

"I ought to put some of your sperm in the freezer," she said.

The Stuff of Life

I only wanted it to be over, even as I dreaded its arrival. For weeks I walked around in a clenched state of anticipation, unaware of how tense I had become.

"An adventure or an exile?" I asked myself. I couldn't decide.

I had gotten a temporary teaching job in Roanoke, Virginia; we weren't moving out, a subletter had been found. Much of the furniture and many books were staying. But we were taking a lot with us, too, including stuff for the baby we were expecting.

A few days before the big move—for what would be a one-year stint—I was walking out of Rice, on Mott Street, when I saw a couple of guys carry someone's possessions out of a nearby apartment and into a truck. There was no sign of the person who was moving. Yet here before me was a parade of their stuff packed in clear plastic crates—Tupperware for your whole life, really.

"Souvenirs only reminded you of buying them," wrote David Berman in his poem "Governors on Sominex."[1] I have wanted to argue with the sentiment, or at least discuss it, especially the word *only*. It's such an ambiguous line.

A box of underwear paraded by. Then sheets, a lamp, chair, papers. I stood there, transfixed. I thought of that Raymond Carver story in which the guy re-creates his living room in the front yard, only it's all for sale. It occurred to me that high among my concerns about moving was who might be around to see our own possessions paraded out the front door and into the truck.

On one end of the spectrum was the slightly blind billionaire who lived next door. Having a billionaire as a neighbor brings many peculiarities with it, but these are greatly compounded when he is about your age and, as I have been told, legally blind. The only manifestation of this blindness I ever saw was when I would now and then venture a hello as we passed on the street. My hello was invariably met with serene and total indifference.

"It's because he's legally blind!" I would tell myself, unable to resist feeling slighted. A year would go by, I would try again, with the same result. I wondered if the occasion of my departure would finally elicit an acknowledgment.

At the opposite end of the spectrum, though geographically just across the street, was Shienbaum, who always wanted to talk, and with him it was I who did my best to avoid conversation. Perhaps I was for him what my billionaire was for me. Anyway, I was worried Shienbaum would be there on his stoop when we moved, watching.

Shienbaum had been occupying his tiny studio apartment—rent controlled, bathroom in the hall—for forty years. He spent a lot of time on the stoop. He had a salt-and-pepper beard and walked with a defiant, rather bearish strut, as though at all times ready for a fight, even when simply going around the corner to get a coffee, practically the only act in which I had ever seen him engaged.

Once, back when I'd first moved to the block, I saw Shienbaum out in the world in a restaurant, the one time I saw him beyond the stage set of the stoop and the deli around the corner. He was dressed up, on a date. I watched as he leaned toward the woman across from him with what looked like an expression of tenderness, his neck straining against the dress shirt he had worn for the occasion. Later, when he went to get his coat, he marched over as though he were going to attack the coat stand, as though, fuming with rage at this coat stand for years, he had finally had enough. That was the only time I saw him with a woman.

I finally gave in and made small talk with Shienbaum, mostly because I had made friends with his friend Josh. As a reward, he hectored me for years with unwelcome remarks, yelled from across the street, such as, "Hey, Doctor! What happened to your Knicks?"

It was such an old-school kind of annoyance, I endured it. Plus, it's nice to be called a doctor. But then the day after the 2004 election, Shienbaum, a communist, had glanced at my Kerry button and said, "Too late for that."

I exploded and he exploded, and we cursed each other right there on the street. It ended with his remark, "I never liked you anyway!" the childishness of which I found oddly touching for some reason. Regardless, I didn't want him to see me moving.

"You're leaving here for some redneck town where you don't know anybody?" said Udi, the mover, as he picked up yet another astonishingly heavy box of books as though it were a tissue. "Why do you do this?" He turned toward the door and then gestured with his bald head at the window overlooking my block in the West Village. "Now *this*," he said. "This is living!"

It turned out that this tough if chatty Israeli had left New York five years earlier and now lived in Florida. "In a redneck town," he lamented, "no one to talk to. My wife wants to move back to Brooklyn. But we have a kid."

"So, what's all this about a redneck town!" I said. "You're projecting!"

"Maybe," he said. "Maybe not."

We checked our fraternizing when Udi announced that we had much more stuff than we had contracted for and that their fee had to be doubled. I had a meltdown; he called his office; we worked it out.

Downstairs, the other mover, Carl, was loading the boxes from the sidewalk into the truck on the corner with the same remarkable grace with which Udi had carried them down four flights. With Carl, thankfully, the exchange was less fraught. Seeing my "Vassar Basketball" T-shirt, he asked if I'd played there. When I said I had, he told me he'd grown up in Poughkeepsie and had gone with his best friend to the Vassar campus bar every night as a senior in high school.

Carl was a good-looking black guy, in excellent shape, and he communicated what a feast this high school adventure among the college kids must have been with just the slightest flicker of tone.

He looked around at my corner, West Eleventh and West Fourth, noted the crowd at Tartine, where I usually had breakfast, and then let his eyes graze the patina of the old brownstone on the corner before moving on to the newly renovated one across the street. He nodded with the connoisseur's gaze of a man who has seen a lot of places. Carl lived in Atlanta, he told me, but he hadn't been there in weeks.

It turns out the moving business is a bit like the Merchant Marine. Crews get on their trucks and set off for weeks. They sleep in motels, or on the truck, or not at all, rarely seeing home as they travel the high seas of the interstate highways, moving other people's stuff.

Finally, everything was packed. "Take care of my stuff," I called out, in what I hoped was a tone that sounded hopeful, and not simply pleading.

They got into the cab of the truck and looked out the window at me and laughed in a manner not entirely encouraging. We were buddies now, in a way. I had admired the economical force of their movements. We had talked about life. They had sized up the way I was living and seemed to judge it all as interesting, if overpriced.

They had also parked beneath the deliciously lush, low-hanging tree on the corner with the one branch that time and again had been threatened by huge, boxy moving trucks like this one. I had been so worried that the truck that finally broke the branch would be mine. But Udi and Carl had been careful, and I saw, as they pulled away, that the branch was still mercifully intact.

We had been at our new place, at the edge of the Hollins University campus, in Roanoke, Virginia, for two days before the pink truck showed up bright and early, with Udi and Carl in it, looking sleepy.

"Nice place you got here," said Udi, and I confess his approval pleased me enormously. They unpacked everything into our neat little bungalow, and then Udi marched down to the corral to look at the horses. We lived next to a horse corral, you see. With horses in it. A fact I repeated to myself frequently, and corroborated by looking out the kitchen window. This helped me adjust to the new reality.

It took some time to grasp where I was. Hollins itself was a mystery, though it echoed my own alma mater somewhat, a plush little jewel box enclosed within a slightly depressed city. But then, that could describe any number of academic institutions.

One night, early on, I took a walk by myself at midnight. The school sits on a ridge, above which loom gorgeous mountains. From the hollow below came the invisible whoosh of the interstate. At night, though, the mountains vanish, and there above the interstate are all the bright signs of corporate hospitality that generically dot interstates all over the country, and which unfailingly unnerve me. Gone, the reliable comfort of being inside the fort, within the protection of the city walls.

To my right, down a hill, was the white fence of the horse corral, and within it, the shadowy movement of the hooved beasts.

I veered down into the darkness, a half-eaten apple in hand, clucking and making little whistle sounds. The horses moved toward me, only to stop ten feet away. After a bit more clicking and whistling, the white one came forward, sniffed the apple, and then with a great flapping of lips, snorted it out of my hand.

The summer in the city, for me, ended that night, in the dark, with a sliver of moon above and three shadowy horses standing beside a fence next to their trough. Two drank and grazed, and one stood by while I stroked its long muscular face, its huge nostrils dilating hypnotically as soft, warm breaths pulsed out into my hand. Its inquisitive eye stared at me for a full minute before it gave another snort and pulled away into the dark.

Note

1. David Berman, *Actual Air* (Open City, 1999), 9.

The Bad News Bears and *Breaking Away*

The Bad News Bears was released in movie theaters in April 1976. It was a surprise hit. One possible reason for its success was that it was a summer of weak competition, in box office terms. The two other successful movies of the summer of 1976 were *That's Entertainment, Part 2*, a movie composed of snippets from lots of old movies, and *All the President's Men*. Another possible reason for its success were people like me: I saw *The Bad News Bears* ten times. This in itself was not so unusual. *Jaws* had come out a year earlier. *Star Wars* would come out the year following. It was suddenly customary for people—eleven-year-old kids, especially—to see movies over and over in the cool darkness of a movie theater.

Repetition is connected with ritual and, by extension, with reassurance. Babies and little kids, upon seeing something that amuses or pleases them, will call out, "Again!" At least mine did. But at the age of eleven I wasn't all that little. And, I assume, the audience for the movie went beyond eleven-year-olds and their parents. Is it possible that there was some feeling of the tectonic plates moving deep down beneath America that made people yearn for the reassurance of seeing a tried-and-true movie again and again?

In my own life there was nothing metaphorical about the moving of those tectonic plates. The earthquake had struck in 1975, with the death of my father. One obvious reason for my interest in the movie, then, was that Walter Matthau reminded me, a little bit, of my father. Not in any explicit way—my father wasn't the cranky, alcoholic ex–minor league baseball player who drove around Los Angeles with his pool cleaning equipment in the back of his Cadillac convertible played by Matthau. He was a doctor, trim, somewhat athletic, even. But there was something about the coloring of Matthau. The dark helmet of hair. The fatalistic humor. Am I just talking around the word *Jewish*? Maybe. But it went beyond that. At any rate, one possible explanation for my intense interest in the movie was the echo of my father in Matthau.

I was told my father was very handsome—by my mother, of course, but others too. A woman named Jane Moss, who knew him from college at the University of Iowa. "Terribly handsome," Jane told me, "and shy." Her roommate was in love with him, she said. They'd had a falling out over it. Her roommate was engaged to be married to another man. But she was in love with my father. And she was an anti-Semite. This came out in pieces over the course of years—first that she had gone to college with him, and then that she knew him. And then years later, when it occurred to me to ask her direct questions. And even now, years after those conversations, new information arrives by virtue of it dawning on me that my father and Jane were in college during World War II, for example.

Jane was wispy, white-haired, ethereal, lovely. Every year or so I would call her, ask her questions, wanting to hear the story again. She'd been in a sorority, she explained, and her roommate had blackballed a girl who wanted to join because she was Jewish. Furious about this, Jane quit the sorority.

I forgot to ask Jane one important detail about this roommate who was in love with my father in spite of the fact that he was Jewish—and an immigrant, no less, a refugee!—in spite of the fact that she was engaged to someone else: Namely, had my father had the slightest idea of this girl's love for him? Had they interacted in any meaningful way? Or was my father simply a crush?

So, he was shy, and handsome. There are photographs that attest to the latter, one from his early twenties, another from later, in his forties, a full-on adult with the weight of responsibility visible in the lines of his forehead. Handsome, yes. But it's mostly the monkey-like qualities I see; for me he is always making a face, cross-eyed, making me laugh, the thick black hair a bit low on his forehead, like one of the lower primates. As far as I know he never made a point of exercising. He wore elegant suits, drank coffee with a certain style, smoked cigarettes, read the newspaper, sometimes all at once. The whole package—the coffee, cigarettes, suits, newspapers—surely a legacy of his youth in Vienna. He was a European guy.

He left Vienna when he was just sixteen years old, or so I thought for most of my life until I began to look into it and discovered that he was just fifteen when he left. And relieved as he may have been to make it to America, he was never an American. It's so tempting to think of his having escaped the Holocaust as some sort of triumph. But can there be any feelings of triumph when society—your society, speaking your language, in your country, your city, your neighborhood, your neighbors!—had tried to murder you? Had made you kneel in the street to scrub the sidewalk with a toothbrush? And that you had been forced to flee your apartment on the long narrow street at the end of which was a newsstand where you always bought candy for your friends? This detail about my father sharing his candy was one of the pearls I wrested from my otherwise unforthcoming uncle, my father's older brother, when he was ninety-two, just before he died.

At some point in my childhood, when I was around seven, and after what seemed like years of interminable drives through the boring countryside, my parents bought a country house, and it was there that I witnessed my father exercise in the manner of a country farmer. I was always eager to help. Once the two of us set about attacking weeds along the side of the house, each of us with a big scythe. We stood near each other, madly whacking at the weeds, cutting clear the whole side of the house. This image has stayed with me vividly, intact from the moment it happened—the silence, the cadence of our swinging arms, the thwacking sounds, the steady breathing. Only now, a father of a boy who is seven, do I wonder: Why were there two scythes? Had he bought them with the idea we might have such a moment?

I never knew he was sick. Not until that last year.

I defend my parents' decision to withhold this bad news from the third member of the household on the grounds that, after the initial bad news, when he was diagnosed with cancer, and the ensuing round of chemo and radiation, he did get better. Maybe he was a little less robust than he might have otherwise been, but . . . better. He had a good seven or so years after that.

And, surely, if the man was well enough to scythe for an hour in the summer heat, then he didn't need to advertise his illness to his son. This factual omission extended as well to his professional life. He was a doctor, a psychoanalyst. His social life was composed largely of people who were his colleagues at the Columbia Psychoanalytic Institute, where he taught. He didn't tell anyone there, either.

I am not inclined to second-guess this choice, which was surely a product of the time in which he lived, when cancer was an almost unmentionable condition. I look at my own children and think of what it must have been like for my parents to live with such knowledge. I feel pity for him, a very strange thing to say about a man I last saw when I was nine years old, a father in every important way—a protector, one who returned from trips to other cities bearing gifts, the mystery of his combs, pipes, cigarettes, his razor, the thick white shaving cream on his face, the peering into the stock market tables in the newspaper, someone my mother loved with an intensity that she must have thought, on some level, could keep him alive.

Pity that he had to look at me knowing he had this secret: that he might not live to see me grow up. But that doesn't fully pinpoint what it is I pity him for. It's the degree to which he would have been able to fathom the pain his child would feel at his loss. He would have been all too capable of gaming it forward, seeing the possibilities for turmoil that arise when a kid loses their parent, their father. Sometimes I wonder to myself why he worked so hard, spent so much time in his office, and didn't make as much time as possible to spend with me while he could. The answer, I think, has to do partly with the conventions of the era, when fathers were not expected to spend a lot of time with their kids. But perhaps some of it had to do with precisely this feeling of poignancy that seeing me would have engendered in him. Were I in his position—and maybe that is the phrase with which adulthood commences—I would look at me, the kid, with tenderness and anguish, thinking of everything they would have to deal with in my absence.

I am not inclined to second-guess the way he lived with his cancer for the seven or so years he had it. Nor do I doubt the wisdom of my parents' decision not to tell me about it. And I also accept Elizabeth's theory, that I must have been absorbing the truth through osmosis.

But then, of course, it happened. In 1975. The earth opened and swallowed my father, literally. Everyone around the grave threw a flower into it. Broke it at the stem. I chose one already broken for fear I would be stuck struggling with a flower stem, unable to tear off the bloom. Later, from the top of a steep and very beautiful hill where he is buried, everyone came down to the road except my mother and a friend of my father's named Arnie. After a while Arnie helped her off her knees, and they, too, slowly made their way down.

It was just my mother and me now. Which is how it came to pass that the following year I saw *The Bad News Bears* for the first time with my mother, of all people. In those first couple of years after my dad died, I was constantly dragging my mother to things that she would not have otherwise gone to. Baseball games, for instance. And certain movies, some that were less appropriate, not for her, but for me, for *us*, such as *Barry Lyndon*. I am tempted to say that her judgment was a little clouded by the overwhelming responsibility of raising me alone. It was hard to know where to draw the line. Also, she was a foreigner, unaccustomed to American life on some basic level though fluent enough in its New York, émigré permutation. There was no father who could be consulted when I made demands. No other adult who could play bad cop to her good cop, or vice versa. Just my incessant requests to go do things and see things.

Now that I am raising two kids with the help of a very present, alert wife, I think it may be that the position of parent is one that requires a constant struggle for balance and perspective in the face of the barrage of pleas, needs, and requests of the child, particularly if your children are as willful as mine are, as willful as I once was. I suppose just about all children are born geniuses of lobbying and negotiation.

So, she took me to see *The Bad News Bears*. I loved it. To my surprise she enjoyed it, too, so that when I asked to see it again, it didn't seem all that hard for her to agree. She may even have seen it with me a third time. After that, I was on my own. At a certain point the movie was playing in only one theater in the city, a place across town, on Third Avenue. I negotiated rights to make the pilgrimage solo on the cross-town bus—for by then I had exhausted my supply of friends willing to see the movie—provided I came straight home afterward. I sat in the theater by myself, eagerly imbibing the whole spectacle, laughing and feeling some other hard-to-name feeling. It was a private communion. I was rooting for the Bears, for Matthau. Identifying with them. But what exactly was I identifying with? Being bad at baseball? Being fat or an immigrant or full of self-pity for one reason or other. Or, in the case of Tanner, a kind of mini Archie Bunker, simply seething with anger at everyone always?

I found a clue as to what quality I might have been responding to when, years after the fact, I read the *New York Times* critic Vincent Canby's review. "At 12 she has a peculiarly unsettling screen presence," he wrote of Tatum O'Neal, "looking, as she does, like a pretty child but possessing the reserve of someone who has been through the wars." About Jackie Earle Haley, the delinquent, athletic biker kid who is, in essence, O'Neal's love interest, he wrote, "There is something about him that makes you suspect he may actually be an aged munchkin, exiled from the land of Oz for crimes that must remain unspeakable." Both of these fanciful descriptions evoke qualities that, at the dawn of my own delinquent years of exile, must have resonated.

When the sequel, *The Bad News Bears in Breaking Training*, came out a year later, I went and saw that one eleven times. It's true you can't go home again, but this came very close. *Breaking Training* was pretty terrific in its own right; it was written by Paul Brickman, who went on to discover Tom Cruise in *Risky Business* and make many other movies, though it lacked Walter Matthau, replaced in the role of coach at first by a tyrant ("Never assume," he scrawled out on a blackboard in front of his blinking team, "or you will make an ass out of *u* and me") and then a young, athletic coach played gamely by Bill Devine. It featured some amazing footage from the Houston Astrodome, too, including a chase scene that made me scream with happiness every time I saw it. Mostly it featured all the same kids (minus Tatum O'Neal) and even had Jackie Earle Haley (about whom more in a minute). But without question, it was not as good as the first one.

The last couple of viewings, I recall, were made mostly with an eye toward beating my previous record of ten. I was keeping score. Once I got to eleven I could rest. They made one more movie, in 1978, *The Bad News Bears Go to Japan*. It was horrible. I barely lasted through one sitting. But for two seasons, 1976 and 1977, there was something going on with *The Bad News Bears* and me.

The 2005 remake of *The Bad News Bears* does not concern me, except that it was released not too long after I met Elizabeth, and prompted the original movie to rise to the surface of my consciousness. I asked her to watch it with me.

Though I was moved by the film while watching it with her, it didn't move me nearly so much as another film from around that same era, *Breaking Away*. The two movies share similar themes of castoffs and fatherless kids; their plots are both organized around a sport and its rituals; and both culminate in a contest between the underdog heroes and the seethingly entitled favored sons. There is a father in *Breaking Away*, a flustered, ineffectual father who sells used cars for a living. Played for comic relief, he is baffled by this son of his who attends college and, more perplexing yet, is suddenly obsessed with Italy and cycling. In the middle of the movie, at the part where the dad has a heart-to-heart with his son about how he had helped quarry the rock that built the university that was now the province of the asshole frat boys against whom his son was going to compete, I started to cry. Then I was sobbing.

I wept so copiously that there was time to laugh about it through tears, apologize, pull myself together, almost, only to break down again, with Elizabeth alternating between concern and affectionate amusement, stroking my back and shoulders while saying, over and over, with fluctuating degrees of alarm, "Oh honey." I sobbed some more, and it wasn't funny. And then it was funny again. This outburst was mysterious at the time and remains mysterious. My only thought was that I had experienced these two movies in the first sharp years of fatherlessness, and I was now watching them as I approached marriage and, out of sight but coming into view, fatherhood. And here was this well-intentioned father giving a pep talk to his son, talking to his college-age son as a peer, man to man, the kind of talk I never had with my dad.

The Bad News Bears begins as follows: We see sun-struck sprinklers pulsing over a Little League outfield. There are long shadows on the ground. Somewhere in suburban California it is early morning. This landscape is completely foreign to me, as a New Yorker, and yet the sunshine has an elegiac glow that is my favorite light, and the sprinklers are like a baptism, not that I have ever had this done. Seeing them, the viewer is enveloped in an almost narcotic glow as you settle in.

We see kids doing drills in the infield, prompted by an adult voice, a coach, in whose faintly heard exhortation one can sense all the micromanaging passion for winning that, in time, will come to be revealed as both deeply screwed up and also highly prescient about where the culture of parenting in America was, even then, headed.

Into this pastoral scene of modern irrigation and baseball training sweeps Walter Matthau, driving a big, old, shambolic convertible, well past its prime but, like its driver, still possessing more than a bit of charm. His face, while not exactly handsome, nevertheless has a certain charisma to it, a monkey-like instinct for comedy. Reassuring, too, for me, is the thick black hair that sits a bit low on his forehead. He reaches back to the cooler in the back seat and removes a beer. How often has Matthau played this character, the lovable slob? (See: *The Odd Couple.*) And though there is no evidence that his clothing is kept in the trunk, it would be no surprise, after seeing this fellow for five seconds, to discover that this is the case.

Having popped open the fresh brew, he pulls the tab off and chucks it over the side of the car. It lands on the pavement with a tiny but very audible *plink*. To say it was the plink heard round the world may be an overstatement, yet the whole ethos of an age, really, is contained in the sound of that flimsy piece of metal plinking against the impassive pavement. Hard not to call to mind the heavily creased face of a Native American man (who turned out to be Italian) in that public service ad against littering—hair in braids, a tear running down his stoic cheek. But the creases on Matthau's own leathery face remain dry as, with a degree of concentration unique to substance abusers setting up the day's first fix, he pours some beer off the top, and now produces a mostly empty pint of whisky with which he tops off the beer. All to the happy pulsating sound of sprinklers. Registering the first couple of sips as both medicine and ambrosia, he peers out at the unsoiled infield.

The Bears are hopeless, we soon learn, and so is Matthau. But then hope arrives. They improve. In the end the Bears lose the big game but get to pour beer all over themselves. And also drink it.

The real triumph of these kids is having rescued this man from his lethargy and boozy despair, just as he has somehow rescued the kids from their hopeless, self-loathing ineptness. Soulful imperfection is rewarded all around. Everyone on the Bears is a hero, and Matthau—not just coach, but surrogate father—has been resurrected.

Perhaps it was this feeling of paternal resurrection, or at least redemption, that had me coming back to the theater again and again.

The Kinks at the Garden

Not long after the night in question, the night of the Kinks, there was another visit to Madison Square Garden, to see the Knicks. Kinks. Knicks. Interesting to put the two words side by side—the two nights, like the meaning of the two names, have nothing in common. And yet some odd overlaps.

There was my own presence in the company of friends. There was Madison Square Garden itself. And there was the police officer, the sight of whom, at the Knicks game, would have turned my face white had it not already been painted the same.

It was Halloween, and I was dressed up in costume, as were a lot of other kids. Except I wasn't exactly a kid. I was sixteen, and tall enough to have made the varsity basketball team. I was vying for the last spot on the team with my friend Steve, the best athlete in the grade. In the end, it was my name posted on the varsity list. The sight of this list made me proud but also made me feel guilty. Steve was the last one to get cut; he was a much better athlete. This was widely seen as an injustice, but he was a good sport about it—a good enough sport to have invited me to this game, the home opener of the season.[1]

I wore a black tuxedo with a white shirt, my face painted in whiteface with red lipstick and a black fedora; I had worn a similar outfit the previous year with a top hat. But a top hat seemed too formal for the Knicks, too gothic, and it would block someone's view. All sorts of random costume was shoved in the closets of my house, remnants of my mother's career as a choreographer, and I found a fedora. I was a theater kid, although that year, literally a couple of weeks later, with the start of basketball practice, my life as a basketball person would begin for real, and for reasons both psychic and logistical, that would be the end of the theater for me.

I saw the cop standing at the doorway to one of the levels, glancing at people's tickets to make sure they weren't sneaking into better seats. Our seats were decent enough to begin with. This was our level.

I flashed my ticket, and his eyes went from the ticket to my face. Our eyes didn't meet so much as rake past one another. His face registered an apparently benign smile, and I thought I saw a raised eyebrow. To anyone else it would have seemed perfectly friendly.

"Shit, shit, shit!" I muttered as we turned in the direction of our gate. "That was him!"

"Who?"

Steve hadn't been with me at the Kinks concert, and I hadn't told him, or anyone else, about it.

My problem was not that the cop had recognized me, which I was sure he had. My problem was that, now that he had acknowledged our special bond, I felt I ought to do something. I hadn't expected to see him again, and yet here he was, a fat, turkey-like figure in his blue police officer's uniform and cap. Confronted with this opportunity, what should I do?

The answer was nothing other than to proceed to our seats. We got sodas on the way. And at some point during the first quarter, while Michael Ray Richardson ran around trying to get the ball to Bill Cartwright and Marvin Webster, Steve reached into his pocket and produced a joint.

The Kinks at the Garden. The school year was less than a month old. Four of us had tickets, which had come via one of our parents, who was an agent at ICM. They were free. We were excited, but there was something a bit casual about our excitement, too. Was this going to be the all-time greatest musical event of our lives? No. Were we especially psyched for the Kinks? Yes, but only sort of, by which I mean we didn't really see the Kinks at the time for what they were. We liked their big fat rock songs of the late seventies. Our musical taste could be summed up by the Zeppelin/Stones/Beatles/Who days on WPLJ. John Lennon was shot not that many blocks away from where we all lived; one of us actually lived *in* the Dakota. I used to walk past groupies camped out in front of the building on the way to his house. We were city kids; money was everywhere, sluicing around, untethered from reality, even though it was not in my possession.

I hadn't yet connected with the wistful, bitter, and very English flavor of Ray Davies's songs, such as "Celluloid Heroes," "Waterloo

Sunset," and on and on. The Kinks, for us, at this point, were "Low Budget," "Catch Me Now I'm Falling," "Destroyer," and "Lo-lo-lo-lo-lo-la." In the late seventies they were trying to do what all their British Invasion peers had done years earlier: be big in America. This very concert was the first time they had ever played Madison Square Garden.

A few weeks before the Kinks concert, a kid goes shopping with his mother. The softness in the summer air has been replaced by something crisper. Time for a new jacket to get ready for the new school year. The mom is a thrifty shopper. Morris Brothers, the local standby for clothes, is being bypassed, however, in favor of Alexander's, a huge emporium on the East Side. The kid's anticipation is mixed with guilt on account of his many other visits to Alexander's, about which his mother knows nothing.

For months, he had a scam going in the record department that goes like this: You can pay for the records right there at the record department, *or* you can take them to the registers on the ground floor. He takes them downstairs. Only instead of paying for them, he unwraps the record's plastic covering and approaches the security guard in the dark blue, pseudo-cop outfit, goes right up to him and says, "Excuse me! Excuse me, sir?" as loud as is reasonable, waving the record in front of the security guard. "This record has a scratch!" he says. "I just bought it and it's scratched!"

The guard is about to refer the kid to the record department, but the kid continues, "And I brought it back to exchange it for one that isn't. Only I came all the way from home and I can't believe I forgot my receipt! At home! So now I have to go all the way home and get it. All right?"

The kid would have acquired the new Kinks record, *Give the People What They Want*, in just such a manner. Except that a few weeks earlier, things had gone wrong. He had been flagrant and lazy, unwrapping the plastic covering and dropping it on the down escalator. He'd barely even made it to the security guard standing at the door to begin his monologue when two plainclothes store detectives grabbed him and pushed him through double doors that led to a back office. A backstage area: all the store's beckoning displays suddenly replaced by fluorescent lights, low-grade foldout party tables, a few desks, and a small jail cell. The kid spent some time sitting there in the small jail cell. At length, a thin-mustachioed man in a brown three-piece suit appeared, sat at a desk, and ignored the kid. After half an hour he opened the cell, gestured to the chair in front of his desk. Once seated across from him, he made the kid empty his pockets and produce all his money, a humiliating wad of dollars and coins. It wasn't enough for the records he had unwrapped.

"I'll need your parents' phone number," he said finally.

"They're not home."

"Then you might have to wait here until they *get* home."

The kid wrote the number of his friend Nick. It seemed possible that upon receiving such a call, Nick might grasp the situation and improvise. The man in the brown suit examined the number, and then looked at the kid. The kid began to apologize. He apologized at length. The man in the suit fingered the piece of paper with the phone number some more.

"This jail cell is a lot more pleasant than a real jail cell," he said finally. And then, his work done in ungrooming a potential criminal, the man in the brown suit let the kid go.

Now, with his mother, the kid is vaguely terrified that one of the guards or detectives is going to recognize him. Perhaps even the man in the brown three-piece suit himself. It is discomfiting how the mood of deceit overlaps with the mood surrounding his mother, which has often involved omission, concealment, but never outright deceit. Once a boat docked firmly to her pier, he now finds the ropes holding him there going slack, with all too much room in between him and the pier.

They look at jackets. He needs one for the fall. They try on this one and that one. She uses the word *windbreaker* and engages the salespeople in discussions on the subject of quality. He models and shrugs his shoulders and puts his hands in various pockets until they encounter something in deep navy blue that is a bit shiny, with no collar to speak of, with zippers on the pockets and an alligator on the chest. He does not own anything with an alligator on it and is pretty sure he doesn't want to. It is, for one thing, too intentional, would convey the "follower" overtones at school. Considered as one single protoplasmic organism, as opposed to individuals, the members of his grade are highly resistant to anything resembling personal evolution and reinvention, and already he has stirred some angry animal consciousness by making the varsity basketball team. To add to this transgression of the established order by buying something with an alligator on it might seem . . . actionable. No, this jacket would be asking for it. Still, he can't get over how cool it looks. How cool it feels. And the zippers on the pockets! His mother likes it, too.

"You look very nice in navy blue," she says. She's been going on about how nice he looks in navy blue his entire life. It is exhausting, but for once, he forgives her for this.

On their way downstairs, they pass the record department. Also on this floor is the typewriter department. His record-stealing ritual had involved making a pit stop at the typewriter department once he had his desired records. There was a practical aspect to this—the long, empty aisles of typewriters, all perched on shelves with pieces of paper in their carriages so you can try them out, are ideal for unwrapping the plastic coverings of the records. He usually stuffs them behind one of the typewriters, taking the opportunity to tap a few letters on the typewriter keys, blurting out some meaningless series of letters, sometimes whole words, and even brief spurts of narrative that are like news bulletins from that very moment.

"la la la bam a lam black betty Frankenstein," he might type. "And when I get home I will be home with the new record I am stealing a record!"

And now, he has the weird impulse to stop at the typewriter aisle and leave a little note: "I'm buying a jacket!"

When he gets to school the members of his grade do not seem to notice about his new jacket, which is fine with him. He's still into it; in fact, he wears it to the Kinks concert.

The seats were down on the floor of the Garden, which had been bisected into a front half and a back half. Ours were in the front half. Halfway through the first song, we and everyone else charged up the center aisle, and so came to be a part of that throng of people standing with their heads craned upward at the man singing into the microphone, playing his guitar. Under the spotlights, Ray Davies, in a blazer, a button-down shirt, and a bow tie, looked remarkably pale, part freaky professor, part aged yet still rebellious student. We leaped and jumped and waved our hands and marveled at how much spittle came flying out of his mouth as he sang. "Destroyer," "Give the People What They Want," "Art Lover," "Yo-Yo."

At some point, a man ran onto the stage wearing shorts only, the Union Jack draped over his shoulder like a cape. That the entire pantheon of AOR rock gods was English—Zeppelin/Stones/Beatles/Who, and Pink Floyd, and also Bad Company and Queen, and Bowie . . . everyone, really, except the Doors, Jimi, and Janice—was hard to grasp. It was just *there*, the English thing. It didn't really register that this might mean the musicians themselves came from and currently lived in an actual faraway place called England.

What would the Kinks have seen looking down from the stage that Saturday night? A bunch of bratty, excited kids rocking out, one of them particularly tall and in his brand-new, shiny, navy-blue Lacoste windbreaker, already trying to do that impossible thing of jumping up and down while at the same time not totally obscuring the views of the two or three rows of people behind him.

And then it was over. The house lights came up to a gradual dispersal, the anticlimax of it all kept at bay by the remaining buzz, the ringing in everyone's ears. The naked dude with the Union Jack, back among the mortals, was smiling in triumph. Davies himself had embraced him. One moment the place was filled with thousands, but now it emptied quickly. The four of us were walking out amid the many empty seats whose color scheme was red and orange and yellow and green, taking the longest possible route out. The concert had at once exhausted and energized us, fed us and stoked an appetite that needed appeasing. In short, we didn't want to leave.

Every exit was now manned by a police officer. When we finally trudged the length of the floor and up some stairs to an exit, the police officer there directed us elsewhere, to another, different exit. And so, we headed in that direction. Hefty men in T-shirts were already disassembling the stage. Otherwise, the four of us kids and the police now seemed the only occupants of the arena. When we came to the exit we had been instructed to leave through, the police officer there said we had to go to yet another exit.

"But we were told we had to come here," one of us said.

"Well, now you're told you have to go over there," said the cop.

One of us said something, and the cop said something, and there was a reply, and maybe another go around, or maybe not. Then the cop suddenly grabbed my arm rather roughly and shoved me in the direction in which he wanted us to go. It was a weird combination of shoving me while also holding on to my arm, as if my insolence was a kind of fruit and if he shook the tree hard enough, it would simply fall away. It didn't hurt, exactly, but I looked down to see his hairy fist clenching the shiny fabric of the sleeve of my new jacket, and this offended me.

"Hey!" I said. "Let go of my jacket!"

I tried to yank my arm free. But he was not a letting-go kind of cop. Now we were in a tug of war in which the item being tugged at was my arm—or, more specifically, my jacket's sleeve with my arm in it. This was very upsetting. I said let me go, let me the fuck go, fucking *let me go*. Then I got quiet. Or maybe I hadn't cursed. Maybe I didn't say a word, and it all happened in silence. I can't truly recall. I was taller than the cop, that much I remember. I was sixteen. I had just grown a lot. I had no muscles. When I picture it now, I see two figures struggling amid thousands of empty red, orange, yellow, and green seats, one tall and thin, the other short and stout, each dressed head to toe in blue.

Somewhere in the process of trying to yank my arm away, I had the idea to punch the guy in the face.

I am not good at throwing punches. I still vividly remember throwing a punch in the cookies and juice line when I was eight. Someone had cut the line. Or maybe *I* had cut the line. It was a soft, almost apologetic gesture to my classmate's chin. I remember thinking, "Why are you punching this kid if you're not actually going to punch him hard?"

The only actual effect of this punch, of course, was to enrage the boy. It's awful to relay this memory, as if I just *wanted* to get creamed in the cookies and juice line. And here I was now, repeating the same gesture toward much the same end.

When I look back at those years, especially the years just before, the bad junior high school years, I wish I had thrown punches, been angry, physical in my hostility, let off steam, demarcated territory, tried to make a stand. I wish I had been more disciplined, run up the long staircase from the field to the locker, lifted weights, used my excitement after seeing *Rocky* to do more than drink a glass of raw eggs a couple of times. But I never did. Never threw a punch through those years. This was a kind of poorly timed debut.

My fist reached a face, the softness of a cheek. He flinched. Then his arm became very straight and he shoved me against the low wall behind me. I believe I flailed at him a bit more, screaming over and over, "Get off my jacket!"

All over the Garden, the little dots of blue that had been positioned next to the exit tunnels suddenly began to converge in my direction. I went slack. I was quiet. My three friends stood off to the side, silent, poised, expectant. The little dots of blue got closer and became visible as men with stern faces and big hands. One of them put my right arm behind my back, while another pushed my head down so I was doubled over at the waist.

In this position, I was marched forward, down some stairs, while I began to ready my apology. I wondered if I would be given a talking to. Or was I in more trouble than that? Maybe something like the little jail cell at Alexander's.

What came next provokes in me a kind of sick delight. "You stupid idiot!" I want to snap at that kid. "What did you expect? This is not shoplifting and these are not department store rent-a-cops!"[2] I want to reach into my memory to smack the kid myself, if only so he would have some frame of reference for what was to come.

After a few steps, me in this doubled-over position, several bodies around me, something like a thunderclap occurred—first a low rumbling, then a scary darkness, and finally a sharp cracking sound that reverberated through my head and my whole body. I had no idea what had happened. I was still moving down the flight of stairs. Then it happened again, and I understood that a knee, someone's knee, had just crashed into the side of my head. Then there was a sharp jabbing to the ribs and a punch in the lower back.

I could vaguely make out the shrill cries of outrage and fear coming from my three friends. But they were far away. I was still moving. At the bottom of the stairs, I was turned left. I walked some more. I had forgotten all about my jacket.

Now I was back in some restricted area, and my first thought was that this is where they must keep the elephants when the circus comes to town.

The memory of this episode seems so outlandish, now, I am sure I'm embellishing. And yet I do recall the bare light bulb hanging down from a very high ceiling, along with fluorescent lights up above and a table, like a kind of picnic bench, where some of the cops had gathered as if at leisure, as though they were about to tuck into ice-cream sundaes, while a couple of other cops stood on either side of me and held my arms as if I was about to be crucified.

Part of me protests that this detail must be imagined. Was I actually made to stand with arms outstretched? But that is what I remember, my being held, arms out, while the cop I had punched took off his jacket, which had many gold buttons, folded it on the bench, and rolled up his sleeves. I stared at those hairy, thick forearms rather than at his face as he came up to me and smacked me on the side of the head. Not the face but the side of the head, somewhere between the ear and the cheekbone. He did it again. And once more. Beginning to enjoy himself, I suppose. In between assaults he made conversation with some of these other cops who were not cops.[3] But, then, why did they have badges? Cigarettes were smoked. While I was being smacked around I was crying and also making a speech. "This is America!" I protested. "I am a citizen! I have my rights!" All this in a grand soliloquy of sobs, total wetness, blubbering civics.

My discourse on America and my role in it, and the police's role in it, went into hysterical fever pitch at the sight of the baseball bat. I was sobbing heavily now in fearful, helpless anger. They poked me in the side with the bat, until eventually they lost interest. Then they all sat around smoking while I stood there sniffling. Finally, I asked when I could go home. I'd like to report that someone told me to shut up, but I don't even remember what was said.

The amazing thing about it all was that before the torture scene commenced, my jacket was removed. Was it neatly folded on a chair? I can't quite remember, but in the end I was allowed to pick it up and it was fine, actually, oddly pristine considering all that had just come to pass.

Led through the bowels of the Garden, following the path of the elephants, I was eventually pointed in the direction of a ramp twisting circularly down. I now recognize this as the kind of spiraling entrance or exit ramps of parking garages across the land, but at the time this was an architectural novelty to me, its cylindrical passage only adding to the dreamlike quality of the experience.

I followed the ramp downward until I found myself on the street, where my friend Peter Sultan was waiting. My friends had split up to fan out around the Garden, figuring, as he later put it, "that they would spit you out eventually." I was so grateful to see him. He put his arm around my shoulders while I wept. Still palpable is the forgiveness and comfort in his arm around me. He was just so cool-headed and decent about the whole thing.

By the time we met up with the others, I had calmed down. We all agreed that what happened was totally fucked up. And that none of us would talk about it with our parents or anyone else.

While my face swelled a bit, there were no bruises, as such, and I was later told that the beating I got was a kind of "police special" whose purpose was to leave no marks. This was why they kept hitting me in the side of the head, rather than my face itself, and why they kept banging my ribs. No one at school noticed and, more importantly, neither did my mother. How that happened I have no idea, as she was generally very attentive. I must have gone into a deep Sunday hibernation in my room, is my only guess. The whole thing receded pretty quickly.

A few weeks later, I went to that Knicks game with Steve in my Halloween costume, and saw the same cop whom I had punched, the same guy who'd then beaten the crap out of me. After the initial sickening adrenalin rush had subsided, and we took our seats, we got around to taking those surreptitious hits of Steve's joint. You could smoke cigarettes in the Garden back then, but still it seemed absurdly audacious, looking back. But that was what Steve was like then, and me, too, I suppose.

I exhaled a plume of smoke into the Garden's basketball ether—then, as now, the sports arena with the warmest, most lamplit glow—and sat back, feeling comforted by the sense of our smallness amid the big open space of the Garden. The men on the bright floor below were exerting themselves. All we had to do was sit and watch.

I slid down in my seat and pulled the fedora lower over my brow, going undercover. In the next few minutes I was filled with good feeling. I remember this moment with a peculiar clarity. The memory of it sits beside the memory of Ray Davies's pale, spotlit face all clenched up, his bow tie so tight it's as if a hand is strangling him as he belts a high note into the microphone, spittle flying. Just then, sitting at the Garden, I felt like an alien, but also pleasantly invisible. The rush of the drug filled my upturned head as I lifted my gaze from the court to the mutedly colorful, multipaneled ceiling of Madison Square Garden, one of the only places in New York that doesn't change.

Notes
1. I was dubious that I had remembered this detail correctly. A home opener on Halloween? But the Knicks home opener of the 1981–82 Knicks season was a Saturday, and Halloween. The whole story in this piece is so outlandish, and for that reason I have fact-checked it with various sources, in spite of my feeling that the vagaries of memory should be allowed some latitude in the art of essay and memoir. The late David Carr, beloved media columnist for the *New York Times*, wrote a book called *The Night of the Gun* in which he fact-checks and reports on his dim memories of his years as a heavy drinker and addict. I objected to this technique when I read the book. It flattened Carr's otherwise lively prose. The testimonies of his old drug and drinking buddies in which they tell him stories about himself, some of which he remembers, much of which he doesn't, felt to me mundane. What was missing was the strange magic of memory. I don't mean factual embellishment, but the energy and yearning that comes with the act of writing down recollection. The energy Carr might have put into recounting his dim memories was instead put in service of this documentary technique. Yet here I am acting on a similar impulse to corroborate my memory. Carr wrote his book in his fifties, my age now. Maybe this is what happens at a certain point in life, when one's faith in one's own memory begins to wobble and a sense of incredulity at what you know happened rises up to challenge your own version of the facts.
2. To my amazement, it turns out this is exactly what they were.
3. After a version of this piece appeared in the *New York Times* in 2006, twenty-five years after the events described, a stern letter was sent to the *Times* by the New York City Police Department. My references to

"police" were an issue, as were illustrations accompanying the piece that had officers with "NYPD" on their badges. The *Times* published the following editors' note:

> A first-person essay on Nov. 26, about the author's recollection of a violent encounter with uniformed authorities after a Kinks concert at the Madison Square Garden arena in 1981, incorrectly implied that officers from the New York Police Department were involved. After the essay appeared, the department contacted The Times and said that it did not assign officers to work inside the Garden in 1981. It said that it does not do so now, and that with rare exceptions, police officers do not enter the arena. Madison Square Garden officials say they employ private security workers for events inside the arena and issue uniforms to those workers. The author has since said that he assumed the workers were police officers because of their uniforms and badges. The assumption should have been checked with the Police Department and Madison Square Garden officials before the essay was published.
>
> Also, two accompanying illustrations of uniformed police officers should not have included the New York Police Department insignia on the uniforms.
>
> The essay also erroneously stated that a police officer was checking tickets during a New York Knicks game later that year. Madison Square Garden employs ushers who check tickets; police officers do not do so.

"Editors' Note: Essay Published on Nov. 26, 2006," *New York Times*, December 10, 2006, https://www.nytimes.com/2006/12/10/nyregion/thecity/editors-note-essay-published-on-nov-26-2006.html.

The Lost Glove

It began when I was walking down the street and several people called out at once, "You dropped your glove!" And just like that I was swept up in one of the unseen subterranean currents of the city, that of lost and found, which holds you longer than you'd expect. It holds you and spins you around and around. I looked down behind me, and there was my glove on the sidewalk.

I picked up the glove and thanked each of the three people who'd intervened on my behalf.

An hour or so later, I walked into a Starbucks and saw, on the floor, a wad of cash. I picked it up. A ten and a five. Not a fortune, but no insubstantial sum, either.

"Is this yours?" I asked the man who was standing at the cream and sugar counter, next to where the cash had lain. He said it wasn't.

Another person said he thought the money belonged to a woman who had just left.

"Which way did she go?" I asked.

"To the right."

"Describe her."

"She was with a kid."

Out the door, to the right—I moved quickly, and soon I saw a woman with a little girl. Right before I caught up with them, they turned into a Barnes & Noble, and I followed.

Just as I came up behind the woman, the girl dropped her pink hat. It fell to the floor like a weightless little cloud. This seemed proof enough that between the two of them, they couldn't hold on to anything.

"Excuse me!" I practically shouted. They stopped and turned. I pointed to the girl's hat. And then, seized with feelings of chivalry and perhaps excitement at my imminent gesture of altruism, I bent down and picked it up for her. The woman said thank you.

Then, holding out the crumpled bills, I asked, "Is this yours?" The woman looked confused, glanced down into her purse, then again at the bills. "Fifteen dollars?" she said.

"Yes."

"I think it is," she said with a smile. The little girl in the pink hat hardly took notice. Perhaps this sort of thing happened all the time, I thought. Perhaps people run up to her mother and return things she has dropped every day.

All this would have been no more than a bit of random city choreography were it not for the fact that a couple of days later I went home and realized that my wallet was not in the pocket of my coat. Deep panic. A lost glove is annoying, but a lost wallet is a statement. It means that you have misplaced your identity, your money and your credit cards, along with various gift certificates accumulated over various holidays and birthdays given to you by your mother. What does it mean to be so careless with love and money?

I tore through the apartment and then emptied every pocket in my coat. Just a half hour before, I had rushed out of a deli with my wallet and loose dollar bills in one hand, a sandwich in the other. I now had the sandwich but not the wallet. Maybe in my moment of haste, I had pushed it into what I thought was a pocket, but was in fact thin air, and it had fallen to the street.

Picturing my wallet lying on the street, I wanted to rush outside to look for it. Then I thought, "No, don't do that. It's crazy to think it's lying in the street. Keep looking in here."

But barely a minute went by before I was standing in front of the open refrigerator. There comes a time in all searches for objects lost at home when one capitulates to the irrational urge to check the fridge. You realize that rationally, there is no way that whatever you are looking for is in the refrigerator. But it isn't anywhere else, and . . . what's the harm in looking?

No sooner had I seen the fridge light blink on than I slammed it shut and raced outside. What's more irrational, looking for your wallet in the fridge, or on a city street?

I trotted back to the deli, eyes on the ground. I know there are worse tragedies than losing your wallet, but are there worse feelings than walking down a city block in New York looking at the ground fully understanding how deluded it is to think that your wallet, containing eighty bucks and credit cards and driver's license and gift certificates from your mother, will be simply lying on the street untouched?

But there, in front of the deli, right in the middle of West Fourth Street, wet and flattened by how many tires, lay my wallet.

But it wasn't over. The next day I sat in a diner on Prince Street and watched placidly as a tall man strode confidently down the street, chin aloft as *his* wallet slipped out of his back pocket. A woman walking in the opposite direction picked it up. I leaped to my feet, not sure which of them to address, the loser or the finder. I went after the guy.

"Hey!" I called. He didn't hear me, or ignored me. He was wearing a big black puffy down jacket. I slapped him on the back, quite hard.

"Hey!" I said again, full of self-recognition. It was all I could do to refrain from adding, "Idiot!"

After I explained what had happened, I went back inside, returned to my seat, and watched out the window as the man explained himself to the woman. She handed him his wallet. Smiles all around. Her gesture seemed to bring me full circle to the dropped glove; the cycle complete. And for a while after that, I didn't lose anything.

On Moving Out

1.

I sit alone in a room. A beautiful place in the West Village of which I have been exceedingly proud from the first day I moved in. I am tempted to call this my room, but that's inaccurate. For one thing, it's not just mine—I have a wife and a baby, and we had a glorious summer here. For another thing, it's a rental in a building with no rent stabilization and, for most of the time I lived here, no lease. "My room," at any rate, is a phrase from childhood, unseemly at my age. My childhood room still exists, uptown, at my mother's place, revised but still recognizable. This room is certainly not that one—it's my adulthood room, I suppose.

It's the room where I achieved a kind of independence. Not my first apartment, but the first place where I carved out a home away from the Upper West Side. For all the people who have traveled great distances to live in New York City, a twenty-minute subway ride to a different neighborhood may not seem like a big deal. But to me it was.

I found the apartment by accident, having heard about it from a friend. I took one look and then sat down with landlords, who occupied the bottom two floors of the brownstone, to tell them I wanted it. I'll call them John and Harriet. We sat around their round, wooden kitchen table, a kind of interview, though it was also more relaxed than that, civilized, even. I didn't know for a fact, at that time, that they had raised their now adult children in the house, but I sensed it.

"We just want to get to know you a little," said John. He was a retired lawyer. White hair, lean face, red cheeks, a face redolent of old New England, including a touch of the Ichabod Crane insanity, but friendly.

"We'll see a lot of each other," said Harriet, dryly. "Not that you'll come to our parties, or we'll come to yours."

There was a Cheeverish, gin-flavored sense of pride in the remark about parties. I nodded my head in understanding. Close, but not intimate. The New York proximity.

The interview ended with warm handshakes and a sense of mutual recognition and trust. I thought the place was mine, but they said in passing that I should go meet their realtor, Bill. "He's handled our affairs for years."

It seemed like a formality, an extension of the family feeling, and I left feeling the elation of the newly hired. A place to live is not a job. But they are both identities, in a way, or part of one, and you generally need one in order to have the other.

I didn't yet have a job, as it happened, and after five minutes with their realtor, Bill, it seemed like I wasn't going to have the apartment, either. He was a tall, loose-limbed man who sat folded behind his desk chewing his lips while he looked over my application in his tiny storefront office on Waverly Place. The window was crammed with affably leafy plants. By the time I left that interview I felt the window should have been filled with cactus—so pointed were his questions, designed to draw blood.

"So you're a freelance writer," he said. "What happens if you stop getting work? What happens if you can't think of anything to write? If you're thirty days late with the rent, they slap a lock on the front door and you're out on the street. You need to get a real job."

"How many people with real jobs get downsized and laid off, right?" I countered. "I mean, what about you? What if all of a sudden your phone stops ringing?"

This failed to move him.

At the time I thought this man was a monster, but he was just doing his job, being a realtor. These were the facts of real estate life. Still, I wanted to choke him, and left trembling with rage and helplessness.

What upset me more than his hardball was the idea that the scene at the kitchen table with Harriet and John was just a sham. The reality was that they would abide by the letter of the law. It was a business transaction; never mind who attends whose parties or not. I did not for a moment think that my landlords were my parents—this was my own apartment, after all, and the whole point of it was independence—but in hindsight it is clear that I still expected to be treated as somebody's son.

2.

In thirteen years, you get attached to a place. The apartment itself is private, yours alone, but your experience of it becomes interwoven with, inextricable from, its surrounding neighborhood. An irrational sense of possessiveness takes root. This is your place. And if your neighborhood undergoes a transformation into a chic shopping mall in which *Sex and the City* tour buses run over the quality of life, as mine had, then the proprietary impulse will soon become tinged with righteousness. But then, we are always moving in over the bones of others.

As I prepared to move out, I remembered a scene I'd witnessed down by the Hudson River shortly after arriving in 1995. It was dusk, a cold autumn evening with a brisk wind. The place was deserted. The sky and the river reflecting it had moved beyond the pretty sunset moment to become forbidding, ominous, moody. Up ahead were two men talking: athletic, well-dressed, youngish if not actually young. As I approached them, they embraced. A hug. If they had let go after a moment, it would have meant nothing more than goodbye; but they did not let go.

It was unusual and kind of beautiful, these two solitary figures hugging against the darkening river, the cold wind whipping against them. When I got closer I heard them crying. It was like the sound of gently breaking waves, a cracking sob. It hit me like a slap in the face. They weren't hugging so much as clutching each other. The sound of grown men weeping profusely has always disturbed me; perhaps it has something to do with memories of grown men weeping at my father's funeral. Grown men shouldn't cry—and I don't mean that as some intolerant directive. They shouldn't fight, either. Grown men crying is too much to take, all that emotion pouring out through such an unlikely crack in the surface; to me anyway, it's deeply upsetting.

I had no idea what these two guys were crying about. My imagination went first to the notion that they were lovers and saying goodbye for the last time, but there was something so stark and mutually grieving about them, it led to other conjectures. What would two men be sobbing about at river's edge in 1995? Who knows. But thinking of it now, I remembered the remark a gay friend of mine made back then when I told him where I was moving. "Oh yeah," he said. "I heard that straight people live in the Village now."

3.

It was a tree-filled, quiet street when I moved in, or so I thought. I was on the fourth floor, treetop level. I put my single bed next to the window overlooking the street, the better to enjoy that exciting top-bunk feeling. My view consisted of the storage company across the street, Siegler Brothers, whose brick facade was a shade of sun-faded orange and brown that made my heart leap with pleasure, along with a set of old decayed fire escapes that I thought quite beautiful, too. It was my good luck, I thought, to be across from a building where no one lived, whose windows were always dark. On one side of Siegler Brothers was another brownstone, and on the other a small apartment building, unselfconsciously ancient looking, its brick a pleasing shade of maroon.

It was heaven, at first. Then I made two discoveries that jolted me. One was that Siegler Brothers, who, according to the faded sign on the building, had been in business since 1895, was not just a sleepy warehouse, but an active moving company from which a few guys, perhaps the Sieglers themselves, practiced their art of moving and storage. One element of this art involved the construction of crates, using a hammer and nail. This often began, as is the case with so much of the noisy labor required in the city, at about eight in the morning.

Another more existential problem presented itself in the windows directly across from mine. Shortly after I moved in, I sat at my desk facing the windows, intending to write. What I did instead of writing, in those first few moments at the desk, was what anyone would have done—I looked out the window. And there, directly across the street, sitting at a table, not facing me but in profile, sat another man about my age, clearly trying to write.

At first I wasn't sure what he was doing. I watched him stare at something on a table just outside the frame of the window. Then his arms lifted and his shoulders hunched over the unseen keyboard. After a minute of spasmodic concentration, he leaned back, seemingly relieved, after which the old expression of anxiety crept back over his face and he leaned forward again. Definitely a writer.

I was horrified, then furious. Who needs a doppelgänger across the street? We live in the age of the café as public office space, and though I like these places well enough to frequent them, the downside to this has been the necessity of seeing writers in the act of composition—the expression on their faces bearing a resemblance to a baby breastfeeding, or someone counting money, or, worse, a person absentmindedly picking their nose while driving. At any rate this doppelgänger was a nightmare. You sit down to write with the conviction that you have something unique to say, and right there, across the street, is another you with presumably the same conviction. Had I glanced across the street and seen someone crapping on the floor, I would have been less put off.

Why hasn't he drawn the shade? I thought. Or why hadn't I? I did not want to close my shutters. My place had three windows. Gorgeous light. I was not closing the goddamn shutters. And so, my system for avoiding the sight of this guy was to avoid sitting at my desk when he was at his.

A month or so later, he stood directly in front of me, at a party, smiling, a plastic cup of white wine in his hand. He wore a cap, but there was no doubt it was him.

"Hey, I know you," he said. "You're the guy who lives across the street!"

"I didn't need to know that," I said coldly. He looked mortified, understandably, and shrank away.

I noticed later that when I was sitting at my desk, he seemed to avoid his. A happy state of affairs as far as I was concerned. At night, his shades went down.

This ignoring of the doppelgänger across the street went on for four years. Then one day I looked out my window and saw the doppelgänger at his open window frantically waving at me and, simultaneously, yelling down at the street.

"Hey! Hey!" I heard him shout. "Get away from the bike!"

I opened my window and saw a guy with a heavy coat hastily walking away from my bike, which I kept locked to the streetlamp below. I ran downstairs. My bike lock lay broken on the sidewalk, but the bike was untouched. Instinctively, I hurried after the thief. He wasn't running, and I didn't run, either. I walked faster, closing the gap. I was contemplating what kind of violence to inflict. Having one's bike stolen is one of the great traumas. At least it has been for me. And one of the most painful aspects of it, as I had experienced it over the years, was the sense that one had no idea where the bike was, and who the thief was. This was a rare moment for redemption for all those past crimes.

After half a block the thief turned around and, seeing me on his tail, turned forward again very quickly. He did not break into a run, though. Instead he took off the black knit hat and shook out his hair. A large amount of luxurious brown hair tumbled to his shoulders. A moment later he unzipped his jacket.

By the time he got to the subway, he was almost in arm's reach. He went down the stairs, through the turnstile, and hurried through the open doors of a waiting subway car. I hurried after him. It was like a chase scene acted out by speedwalkers. He took a seat at the far end of the car. I went and sat across from him. A young kid, maybe sixteen. He looked toward me for a split second and, looking away, seemed to gasp with a kind of exasperation.

The sigh—it was a heavy, eye-rolling sigh—combined a plea for clemency with the kind of gesture kids make when they think their parents are being stupid. The subway car was fairly empty. The desire to kill this person was now severely complicated by the fact that he was on the uptown local heading—it seemed inevitable, for some reason—to an apartment on the Upper West Side that bore some resemblance to the one I had grown up in.

Perhaps this kid was merely an aspiring bike thief, and this was his first run, his first search for a bike to steal—he had the Freon, the hammer, all the tools, he's about to be in business, but instead he gets busted by an older version of himself, some guy who is twisted with weird anger. Who stalks him. The kid worries that he will be attacked, but in the end what happens is the guy insists on coming upstairs to tell his mother that her son has been freelancing as a bike thief in the West Village, at which point she invites him in and offers him tea. I let all this run through my head and then realize that for some reason the train is still in the station, the doors are open. We haven't gone anywhere. This all seems sufficiently poetic and weird to have been worth the effort, and without saying anything at all I get up and leave.

The guy across the street, whose name turned out to be Josh Gilbert, would become one of my closest friends, though even this act of goodwill was sufficient only to thaw the ice but not quite break it.

It was another year before we actually got to know each other when my girlfriend at the time started waving at him through the window whenever she saw him, or calling out, "Hi!" in the warmer months, when our windows were both open.

I had told her the whole convoluted history of my unfriendliness. How I couldn't abide seeing a guy directly across the street trying to do what I did. Perfectly clear in her own mind just how ridiculous this was, she started a charm offensive. My neighbor waved back at her. Eventually I started waving now and then. He waved at me. Finally, we had a lengthy conversation on the street, and soon, we began a litany of adventures in city life, most of which were tinged with the feeling of generosity, even rescue, established in the incident of the rescued bicycle.

Josh was a screenwriter who got into fights with everyone he worked with. He had a knack for complicating the basic gestures of city living in ways that made life both more difficult and more interesting. And he was always eager to find a reason to interrupt his work.

For example, the time I put a bag of my washed and folded laundry down outside the front door of my building, unlocked the door, and, lost in thought, went upstairs with the laundry still on the stoop. When I returned for it, the bag was gone. Josh accompanied me on a wide sweep of the neighborhood, freshly coated in a thin layer of snow, which just added to the sense of absurdity—two men wandering around leaving footprints as they searched for a bag of washed and folded clothes. I was as incredulous that I could do something so stupid and equally incredulous that anyone would steal another person's laundry, even if it had just been washed and folded by Frank the Laundry Guy on West Fourth Street. I kept insisting all was lost and lamenting all the T-shirts I liked that I would never see again, but Josh was adamant it would turn up. "Someone who takes a laundry bag is not going to go far!" he insisted, and sure enough we encountered a disheveled man inspecting my clothes outside the church a couple of blocks up on Waverly Place. The exchange was civil, even friendly, as Josh explained, pointing at me, "Those are actually this guy's clothes."

By then my apartment had accumulated too much history and personality to allow for me to write in it anyway; I was off in the city like everyone else, looking for some nook or cranny, a library or a rented desk or a café table, some place where I could try to collect my thoughts.

Josh and I became friendly and then friends, and finally very good friends, which means we survived a huge falling out early on and then regrouped in better shape. It came to seem like one of the great amenities of life, having a friend you could see from your window.

When I finally moved out once and for all, it was Josh who performed one of the true rubber-meets-the-road acts of friendship and helped me and the movers pack boxes of books while Elizabeth took care of the baby. Josh even took the movers out for dinner while I continued to pack at my excruciatingly slow rate. It's very hard to pack your own stuff, especially books. You can't help but look at every one.

The next day, after the movers left, after I'd wrenched out all the custom shelving, Josh came over with an extra broom and a coffee, and helped me sweep. It was a pleasant afternoon, and the apartment, once more just a well-lit room, glowed with a serene sense of possibility.

I had a broom; he had a broom. We swept for a long time, moving slowly in random circles around the room. There was no talking. The brooms made a pleasant shushing sound, as though to say, "It's all right. It's all right." It felt like something out of a silent movie, for some reason. Two men moving around an empty room, sweeping. Josh was sad that we were leaving. Shush, shush, shush. I was sad to be leaving. Shush. But it was going to be all right. In fact, kind of exciting. Shush, shush, shush. Long after the floor was clean, we were still sweeping, listening to those brooms' shushing duet.

4.

There is some ambiguity about why I left the apartment. At its heart is the unspoken question in people's eyes after you tell them about a breakup—did you leave or were you dumped?

I left the apartment on my own terms, and I was also, so to speak, dumped. Perhaps you could say I was hurried out the door toward which I was already heading. But that is what people who get dumped often say. The ambiguity is only half the story, though. The other half is the remarkable fact that a question pertaining to a love affair, or a marriage, could also pertain to an apartment. What could a relationship and an apartment have in common? Perhaps they are both things you inhabit and which come to reflect you back to yourself, for better and for worse.

Elizabeth moved in before we were married, before I had even proposed. She liked the place but didn't really enjoy *living* in it, if that makes any sense.

"It's your bachelor pad," she said. "Your place. Not our place."

I had an upstairs neighbor, Gordon, an architect who for years worked on renovations to his floor-through apartment, which he turned into a work of art, exposing ancient brick walls, sanding down layers of paint to reveal the cherry wood banister leading to his door. For a decade, our two bachelor lives evolved on parallel tracks, something that never really dawned on me until we both found ourselves married at approximately the same time, still in our respective apartments. We went upstairs for drinks one night, and in no time at all the women found their common theme. They got very loud and excited about it.

"Enough!" his wife said.

"I know, really," said Elizabeth.

"But this is, like, the most beautiful place in the world to live," I said. "And this apartment of yours is, I mean, a work of art."

"There are lots of beautiful places in the world to live," said his wife.

"Even in New York," said Elizabeth, whose departure from her bachelorette pad, in Gramercy Park, was not without some cost.

"You guys are living in the past," said Gordon's wife now.

"How is this the past?" said Gordon. "We're sitting here right now."

We looked at each other, he and I. They were right, of course. But so were we.

Elizabeth moved in with me on Eleventh Street not long after we met. She moved in somewhat reluctantly, sending her cat first as an ambassador, a kind of canary in the coal mine. There was an interesting synchronicity in our real estate lives—we both lived in these little jewel boxes nestled in jewel box neighborhoods—Gramercy in her case, the

West Village in mine. I insisted she move into my place, even though it was a fourth-floor walkup. It had to do with the neighborhood, and the light, and the trees.

What I did not try to explain was the sense of well-being that welled up in me as I turned off Seventh Avenue onto Eleventh Street and saw before me the lush tunnel of trees that funneled me down Eleventh Street to my home. I loved my neighborhood.

Shortly after Elizabeth moved in, however, she wanted to move out. I don't mean she wanted to leave *me*, but rather that she wanted us to move to another place. Not right away. But the feeling was there. For her, this would always be a transitional place. For me, this thought was a blasphemy, and leaving not a possibility I entertained.

I spent an enormous amount of energy building her a giant armoire to house her clothes. (It was Gordon who actually built it—designed it, too, for that matter. But I bought the materials and carried all the wood and held his tools and fetched him a beer now and then.) There was something unreasonable about this armoire, and not just because Gordon, being an innovative architect, had designed it to float off the ground. It was as though, by architectural ingenuity, I could make my place viable for us in the long term. This floating armoire was, literally, a kind of shrine to her nice clothes for which, after many weeks of waiting, she finally had a place. But it was also a kind of totem to my unreasonable hopes of sticking around.

5.

In the beginning it was the landlord's realtor. At the end it was the landlord's daughter, a lawyer like her father. These transitions are so hard to effect without abrasions. Just as it's hard to get all your stuff through the door without some nicks and dents, so too with your soul, or at least your ego.

"I'm going to be handling the building for my parents," came the voice on my machine. "There are going to have to be changes. We have to talk about your lease."

John and Harriet had raised the rents, but slowly, reluctantly. The staircase was a bit shabby, my apartment was never painted unless I did it, so this seemed appropriate. But it went beyond that—we didn't go to each other's parties, but we did see a lot of each other, and maintaining civil relations with the tenants was clearly important to them.

It was an arrangement that defied gravity, in a way—gravity, in this case, being the cold hard laws of real estate. There was turnover in the building, but not too much. For years Gordon and I had speculated on how long John would hold out as a landlord. That's how we phrased it, but what we were really talking about was how much longer he would live.

John would throw himself into the minutiae of the building with such commitment it was a kind of mania. Locating the proper destination for a stray piece of mail could occupy an afternoon. Taking out the trash was a major event. He would sometimes wait down at the bottom of the stairs to herald the news of the new Yellow Pages to his four tenants as they came in at the end of the day. Recycling night was a special occasion. He would work past midnight dragging out the carefully tied bundles of paper to the curb while clutching a small flashlight.

It was charming, I guess, but also a pain in the ass. To Harriet I was polite, chatty; close, but not intimate. John's boundaries, though, were more porous. In my first years in the building, he slowly drained a carafe of red wine every night, which he had shipped to him by the box (neatly cut up and tied together in string on recycling night). I would often come upon him tying string around the cardboard, his lips stained purple from the wine. I would sometimes return home late at night to find him staggering around with recyclables out on the sidewalk, the beam from his little flashlight veering wildly. One day he had a terrible fall on the stairs. He recovered and, to our surprise, stopped drinking. And he carried on.

He had a wonderful cheerfulness about him, John. In the last years he would greet me with great excitement every single time I saw him, shaking my hand as though I had just returned from a long journey even as I held the paper and a coffee I'd just grabbed from the deli. These same habits could seem sinister or strange when directed at Elizabeth, especially when accompanied by attempts to hug her.

He repeated himself. I can report to you that he went to school at Amherst College and had as a fraternity brother a man named Frisbee, who invented the object of that name. I heard this a hundred times, in spite of the fact that he never once saw me with a Frisbee.

One of his hobbies was something called "county counting." Harriet told me about it with a roll of the eyes. The goal was to visit every county in the United States and mail a postcard to yourself from the post office, thereby collecting the postmark of every zip code. For some reason this struck me as both heroically strange and also one of the loneliest things I had ever heard. It was something out of Kafka, or Borges, or maybe Edward Hopper. A box full of blank postcards you had mailed to yourself from all over the country.

Sometimes I would see him in the neighborhood, walking with his cane, his face preoccupied and drawn with the concentration of his journey, usually to or from the bank or Garber's Hardware. At first I always greeted him. But he liked to talk so much. If he caught you in the hallway, he would never let you go. I learned early on to say, "Gotta go!" and, if I hoped to get anywhere, turn my back on him while he was still talking. Eventually I took to observing him as he walked by, ready to assist if he fell, but keeping my distance. Amazingly, year after year, in spite of his teetering shuffle, he never fell, other than the one time on the stairs, so far as I know.

I can't help but note that these observations have some of the fraught impatience and concern with which one often regards parents. They had kids my age, more or less. And I had a parent their age, more or (in this case) less. Such are the intimacies of living in the same small building.

It was Harriet, in the end, who provoked the inevitable shift. Harriet, who was so much more fluent in negotiating the etiquette of landlord and tenant, upstairs and downstairs. So much more elegant. She gardened prodigiously in her backyard, took trips to Lincoln Center with friends, made small talk that ended curtly but politely. She also seemed to be the custodian of what I would call a middle-class ethos which, in the rapidly chic-ifying West Village, was coming to feel distinctly old guard. Part of this ethos, which Harriet and John shared, was not raising the rent—at all for the first years, and then only slowly, even if it was their legal right to charge whatever they wanted at the end of every lease, given how few units there were in the building. For many years there *was* no lease. It was Harriet who started to lose her mind. And then the daughter started making calls.

"Things are going to have to change," she said.

The phrase *power of attorney* drifted down the building's cool wooden staircase during stairwell chats with my neighbors. We all hated her.

"This woman is talking to me like I am ripping off her parents," Jeanie, my downstairs neighbor, a banker, said. "I said, 'I'll pay the new rent but, look, don't talk to me like I'm a criminal.' I mean, this woman doesn't *know* me."

"The sound of her voice on my answering machine makes me cringe," said Gordon. He played me her message, and it was true—her tone had the irritating quality of some very hungry person calling a takeout place that had not yet delivered dinner as arranged. Actually, it was worse than that, full of simmering accusation and irritation.

But to complain about someone's tone of voice, however valid the observation, is usually just an excuse to complain about what it is they are saying.

At one point in my discussion with her, I asked her if she was a lawyer.

"No," she said. "But I play one on TV." Her attempt at a joke. Then she mentioned her husband was a lawyer, as was her father. When she mentioned this it struck me that the source of her irritability might have had nothing to do with the tenants. She had three children of her own, after all, and three other siblings. How had the task of managing her parents' building, her childhood home, fallen to her? Had she asked for it? Had she deserved it?

I once had dinner with a friend who grew up in the neighborhood and mentioned in passing where I lived, and he lit up, saying that the sisters had been the great beauties of the neighborhood. Listening to her now, I had a hard time imagining that.

It seemed my landlord's children, or at least the managing daughter, were under the impression that their kindly parents were suckers, soft touches, and had for years and decades been squandering the family fortune by not keeping the rents at maximum market levels. In any event, everyone was to get a huge 100 percent rent hike now or move the hell out.

By the legal terms to which she was drawn, I suppose I would have some grounds to stand on, given that, in thirteen years, they never painted my place and that her father, in his zeal to manage errant letters, had let himself into our apartment a couple of times while we were there. In bed. At 8 a.m. Sleeping. But the larger principle that she was missing, I felt, was that for her parents there was value in a sense of neighborliness and community in the building—values that, I could tell, infuriated her. I could imagine her shouting at her soft-headed parents, "This neighborliness is being paid for by my children!"

It was as though the whole daughterly psychodrama was being played out within the narrow context of managing the rent increases for the four tenants in her parents' building. I did feel a twinge of sympathy for her, though, because within the sense of avarice that seemed to pulse its way through her remarks was the anticipation of her parents' death. I use that word *anticipation* in both the positive and negative sense—the excitement of the prospect of inheritance balanced against the terror of losing one's parents, a willed attempt at making one of these eclipse the other.

6.

When I took a teaching job in Virginia, we sublet the place from September to May. In the interval, Evangeline was born. We left Eleventh Street as a couple, and returned as a family. But if the place was more crowded with a crib, it was also cozier. Harriet cooed over the baby. Delighted, both she and John seemed to take a personal pride in my progression from bachelor to husband to father on their watch, especially John.

"She's wonderful," John had remarked, without invitation, upon first meeting Elizabeth. "Don't lose this one!"

If anything, I got more pressure to get married from them than from my own mother. Perhaps this was because it was their house that I was occupying.

The summer with a baby in the fourth-floor walkup was not without its difficulties. But when Harriet asked to see me about our plans, I took the baby down, and we sat in the garden while she wriggled on my lap. While Harriet made cooing noises at the baby, I announced that we would like to sublet one more time, through the following summer, before moving on. She was dubious, but the baby giggled, and she soon enough agreed.

Elizabeth was not too keen either—at issue was not just the size of the studio but the fact of the four stories we had to climb and descend each day with the baby, generally more than once. In my zeal to keep the place, I had promised to carry the baby up and down the stairs myself every time we came and went. And this I did. But no sooner had I secured the commitment from Harriet that we could come back the following summer than I threw out my back for the first time in my life.

It's hardly uncommon, before moving out of a long-held apartment for good, to sublet your place. A friend of mine, for instance, is moving out of his place of ten years to live with his girlfriend. Or, more accurately, he moved in with his girlfriend and is now subletting his old place before giving it up for good in the fall. Whenever he returned to pick up his mail and check on things at the old place—still legally his—he was filled with a sense of dread and even horror.

"Are you filled with dread remembering everything that happened there?" I asked him. "Or are you filled with dread at the prospect of leaving?"

"Both," he said.

The tenant for the second sublet did not work out too well. I'd found her on Craigslist. A West Coaster, she was effusive about the pictures and the location. Her fiancé was in business school in the city, she explained, and she had managed a transfer to New York to be near him. She told me a few things about her family, as well. I admit I paused for a moment when she sent, along with her deposit, a photograph of herself and her family. They looked perfectly nice—casual, sophisticated even, drinking red wine on a patio somewhere. The envelope was heavy paper stock. I felt like I had been invited to a fancy party, which is not really a welcome sensation when receiving a check from your tenant.

She arrived. I showed her the place, handed her keys, and walked away. Ten minutes later the phone rang. She was distraught. Her distress was, in part, that of someone not from New York encountering a New York apartment. But it also echoed complaints I had heard from Elizabeth. The hole in the bathroom wall, for example, or the need for a new coat of paint. We made a deal in the end—I lowered her rent so she could paint the place—but I was somewhat chastened that this neat, fastidious woman, not unlike Elizabeth in this one respect, had felt such affront at the whole place.

She lasted only a few months in my apartment. By the end she corresponded not on heavy paper stock but by email and was very evidently pissed off, as though the sublet had been some kind of fraud. Gordon told me that more than once, passing my front door, he had heard hysterical crying.

I wondered what had happened. But I didn't know her well enough to ask and, at any rate, she made it clear she wanted nothing to do with me.

I took this disruption badly until I realized it meant that for the winter break from teaching I would have my place back. The winter light in that place was remarkable, three long rectangles of sun appearing at 9 a.m. against the bookshelf of one wall, then slowly dancing in a trio across the wood floor until sometime after 3 p.m., when it would flash against the other wall briefly and then bow out. I was elated to once more be witness to this daily miracle, to again occupy my rightful place in the world. Elizabeth and I spent some time there in the afternoons, but never the whole night. The baby was up at my mother's, and so were we, really. So instead of living there, I used it to work. All my books were there. A table and chairs. Also, a bed. It was fantastic, at least at first.

But then one afternoon, alone, I worked for a while before lying down on the bed for a nap. The place held its marvelous stillness; even denuded of most of its furniture and artwork, it was still recognizable as itself—there were the bookshelves, the many books, the familiar cracks in the paint, the view through the windows of the trees, and the different shades of red brick across the street. I fell asleep.

Upon waking, I had the most disconcerting feeling. I've had the feeling of waking up and not knowing where I was, but this was different. I knew exactly where I was, but wasn't sure exactly *when* I was there. Dusk had come early, the sky dimming in a way particular to the season. Just a handful of months earlier, I had been living here, but that was summertime. This was winter, another world; it had been two years since I woke in this bed to see a similar sky.

What I experienced in those confused moments was not quite the cinematic scene of a jury of ex-girlfriends aligned before me, ready to extol or scold me, one at a time. But close. All the many years, the many layers of my life in that place, were all hovering, present, somehow visible to me in the dusky light. I blinked my eyes a few times, and they were gone. Or were they? My first thought was that Elizabeth had been right. This was my bachelor pad.

I had denied it, but now saw that denial for what it was. We had been living with ghosts. It made me question why I had been so reluctant to leave. What was I holding on to? Or whom? To these women who had spent time here? To old friends who, for all kinds of reasons, were no longer friends? To what extent does living with the past impede living in the present? Or living for the future?

I love things that hold their own history—places, objects, apartments, and most of all people—but for the first time I felt that this apartment's history might also be toxic. Had it thrown a curse on my tenant, whose engagement had blown up? The memories that loomed before me as I awoke from my nap were not, after all, entirely good.

And so that evening, in some fundamental way, I made my peace with moving out. I gathered myself, turned some lights on, and peered across the street to see if Josh was home. He wasn't. I sat there alone. After a little while, satiated with the sense of privacy and sensing its limits, I closed up shop and hurried uptown—that strange fate of someone whose childhood home remains that, long into adulthood—where the brightness of Elizabeth and Evangeline were waiting.

A Visit to the Library

I took the subway to the New York Public Library. I had been back in New York for a few days now, and the feeling of elation had not yet abated. Why this elation? Because I was home? I had a home in New Orleans, where I had a teaching job. Now we were visiting my mother, as usual, for the holidays, summer vacation. So, if I was now home, it was in the other sense—the home of my mother, of my late father, the home I had grown up in, preserved in amber.

Elizabeth and I and Evangeline, all of two years old, had piled into my old bedroom, now renovated. But the light and the mood were the same. And the view. Also the desk. My father's old desk (not the French Desk, but the one brought home from his office after he died, the wood a kind of chestnut blonde, the mood mid-century) was now crammed with baby stuff. Was that why I was elated? The convergence of old and new? Or was it being in the care of my mother, even as I now had others to care for? Maybe it was simply the excitement of being back in New York City.

Bounding out of the subway with that particular energy of parents of little kids who have some time on their own, I walked up Forty-First Street, turned left on Sixth, then right on Forty-Second Street. The library was now in my sights, my heart pounding with excitement, thoughts racing to identify important landmarks in my proximity. Up ahead on the corner, my first publisher. To my left, the old office of the *New Yorker*, where I had once had an office. But that office was an interstitial one—they had moved to it from the original space one block away, where the founders had toiled—and had brought with them an entire wall drawing by James Thurber. It happened shortly before my year as a staff writer. Then, not too long after I left, the Thurber drawing was again exhumed from behind a plate of glass and moved to yet another office, a glass tower on Forty-Second Street and Broadway, one block behind me. And later still they would move all the way to the bottom of the island, to another glass tower, the Thurber still under glass, a kind of cartoon shroud.

Thinking about that year and the sting of how it ended, I pictured a scene that took place on the corner of Fifth Avenue and Forty-Third Street, shortly after I started the job. I had been punched in the face. A car grazed my shin as it turned into the crowded crosswalk. I smacked it on the hood, the way I often did on my bicycle when I moved through the crowded streets with a proprietary air, as though the cars were errant cattle. Except I was not on a bicycle. I was a lucky dude on his lunch break from his new job as staff writer at the *New Yorker*. The car was a sports car, dark gray and new; its shiny bumper nudged forward an inch as I passed amid the swarm, touching my leg. I slapped it. Then a guy got out of the car. Short. Stocky. Wearing a ski hat. It was winter. He walked right up to me and punched me in the face. I wrestled with him, but never got a punch in myself. Afterward he got back in the car and drove away. I stood there straightening my jacket, wondering if I had been taught a lesson, though the exact nature of the lesson was ambiguous. Beyond violence begetting violence, it had something to do with good luck, I felt, and its propensity to regress to the mean.

I had also been punched in the face on Fifth Avenue and Fifty-Fifth Street during my egg cream summer. Fifth Avenue is the avenue on which I have most frequently been punched in the face.

I arrived at the side entrance of the New York Public Library. Past the security check—like so many precautionary measures against terrorism in New York City, an absurd Kabuki dance. ("Oh, there's a police car parked at the foot of the Brooklyn Bridge—turn the truck bomb around!")

Safely in the library, I raced to the elevators, eager to get upstairs, only to hesitate once more at the sight of the wooden telephone booths. Incredible objects. Beautiful. Caught between the satisfaction of seeing them now and the dread of their being carted away before my next visit, I began photographing them.

I had been in this building countless times, but my most memorable visits were when I was trying to research an essay about J. D. Salinger and went to look at his papers. Writing from the era when wooden phone booths were a fact of life, Salinger was the poet laureate of just this sort of semipublic, semiprivate space—restaurant bathrooms, too, or the waiting room at Grand Central Station—and there was a meta quality to these visits to research him in a place where the last of these repositories of solitude still lingered. And so I stood there now, an idiotic tourist taking a picture of the wooden phone booths, as if they were some seminal ruin in ancient Greece. Then I left for the bathroom.

Up the stairs, into the restroom, and then back out, the bustle of the city streets now transposed to the old marble floors of the library's second floor, where I suddenly caught a face I knew well: an old professor of mine who taught urban literature—Dreiser's *Sister Carrie*, Meriweather's *Daddy Was a Number Runner*, and *Last Exit to Brooklyn* by Hubert Selby. I'd always admired the ferocity and commitment of his lectures, his passion for literature, but for some reason kept my distance, as though he were a piece of unexploded ordnance. Still, I liked him. Maybe we had bumped into each other in just this manner sometime before, because after quite a few years had passed without seeing him, I was invited to his home, where he had gathered some of his favorite students, or maybe just the ones who would still talk to him, for a retirement party. A small gathering.

I called out now, and we greeted each other warmly, both of us with that surprised "What are you doing here?" look in our eyes.

One of those pugilistic, no-bullshit literary Jews for whom almost everything had a moral dimension, which inevitably got him in all kinds of hot water, my old professor had left the school at which I had taken his classes, or was fired, I never grasped the details, and had since been teaching elsewhere. But we didn't need to get into all that; nor did we need to ask each other why we were here. We were here for books, of course. And my pleasure in seeing him was greatly enhanced by the fact that, wandering through Midtown, I had been hoping to see someone I knew.

I asked a passerby to snap a picture of us in front of the men's room, so excited was I by this encounter, so relieved that this is still a city in whose crowds I could find a familiar face. In the photograph I am tall and pleased; he is short and laughing. Looking at it later, I would see that right behind us is a sign that says Men, with an arrow pointing to us.

We stepped out to Bryant Park for coffee, attained via a very exciting zigzag through stopped traffic on Forty-Second. My old professor bought the coffees; he insisted on it. On the way out the door, he reported that the cashier in the sandwich shop had asked if I was his son. He seemed kind of jazzed by this, and for a split second I thought, "It's because he has two daughters; he must have that eternal longing for a son." As the father of a daughter, I was troubled by this thought—was I projecting my own longing?—until his amusement at the cashier's comment, which he repeated, overtook this mood. It all felt funny and providential again, all the more so when we found an empty table in Bryant Park.

My old professor and I talked about Vienna, which I would soon be visiting. In fact, this was why I had come to the library—not only to confirm the reality that I was back in New York but also to pull out some books on the old Hapsburg capital. My professor found the Austrians repulsive, he told me. "At least the Germans are aware of their past," he said. "They commemorated it, built museums and statues. The Austrians, they never acknowledged that part of their history. It's as though their entire self-image is: We make the world's best chocolate. About their Nazi history, they have nothing to say."

My professor, a Holocaust survivor, had been spirited out of Germany at four months old, in 1937, he told me. Other than his parents and his maternal grandmother, most of his family died in the camps. As for his father's mother, it was assumed she'd died in the camps, because his father never heard from her. After the war, however, he was told she was still alive in Poland.

"My father started to make arrangements to get her a visa and bring her to New York," said my professor. "Then he got another call." There had been a postwar pogrom in the Polish town where she was living. It was the second night of Passover. "They came, dragged her and a bunch of other Jews outside, and shot them. So my father got another call. 'Never mind,' they said. 'You don't need the papers.'"

My professor went on to tell me that for the last ten years of his father's life, they did not speak. "My daughter married a guy who was not Jewish. And so he stopped talking to me. He was convinced that pretty much everyone who was not Jewish was a Nazi. He talked to my daughter, actually, but never to her husband, and not to me. The one time I ever had a chance to discuss it with him, he said, 'Why have you let her marry a Nazi?' And I said, 'Jim is not a Nazi! He wasn't even *born* then.' 'Well, his *father* was a Nazi!' 'His father wasn't born then either!' 'Then his grandfather was a Nazi! One day they will come and they will drag her out of the house and Jim will not do anything to stop them, I can tell you—because he is a Nazi.'"

My professor paused in his story, and at this moment, from the minnow-like density of the lunch crowds at Bryant Park, emerged one face, as though spotlit: a young woman, ridiculously Aryan-looking, and quite pretty. I stared at her for a moment. But then I stopped looking at her, out of respect for Elizabeth, who does not take such looking at all lightly, but who, as it happens, is a bit Aryan-looking herself.

"So, he was irrational," my old professor continued. "And it took me a couple of decades to connect that remark about Ellen being dragged outside to what actually happened to his mother."

Eventually, we walked back into the library, where my old professor had to use the restroom again. I took a few more pictures of a different set of phone booths before we said our goodbyes, and I made my way into that great cavern of a central reading room, that huge airy hall whose democratic atmosphere is always sharpened by the diffuse but unmistakable tang of body odor, which dissipates soon enough as you get used to it.

The Laundry Room

The streets are covered in snow. The wind whips harshly, a blizzard's aftermath, and in the basement laundry room of my childhood building, I find an old neighbor pulling clothes out of the dryer.

She is distracted when I say hello, stares at me without recognition. But then something clicks and a shaky stream of lucidity pours forth. She asks after my mother, Elizabeth, our baby girl. And I ask after her son, Garth, my old babysitter, who used to take me downstairs to their apartment on the C line.

The building has four lines of apartments—A, B, C, and D—and two separate elevator banks to service them. The C line, facing east, gets the least light. It shares the landing with the D line, which overlooks the river and gets the most. Through a door, down the service hallway, and through another set of doors, and you are on the A-B landing, which mostly faces north. Put another way, the D line is all river views, the B line is half river views, the A line has a view of the river if you stand on one side of the window, from which you can see a sliver of it, and the C line faces either east or into the air shaft. I grew up on the A line, "which has the best layout," my mother has remarked.

In the whole building, these days, there is a slight tension between the old guard and the new. Anyone who's come in during the last decade spent a fortune to be here. The old guard, while certainly not have-nots, come from a different world. They march with dignified postures in and out of the lobby, nodding to the doormen, indignant, almost, at what their apartments must now be worth, the strain of the contradiction between smugness and shame playing faintly across their faces.

Do the kids in the building today still wander from apartment to apartment? It used to happen a lot. I remember one night in Garth's apartment, seated under a single light bulb toward which rose, gleaming, a trombone held by his older brother, who was for some reason bald at a young age. It was magnificent, that honking sound, his bald head flush with effort as the light glinted off the beautiful burnished brass of the trombone. It hadn't occurred to me then that Garth was trying to keep me entertained; I merely felt swept along on a strange adventure through the building.

Garth is well, his mother tells me now, but her older son died at sixty. "A strangulated hernia," she says. "He refused to go to the doctor. *Refused!* It got to the point where Garth threatened to fly up from Florida and declare him insane, just so we could get him to the doctor. But that wasn't going to work."

I offer my condolences.

"I'm learning to live with it," she says. "We had him cremated, and afterward Garth and I went into the park and spread his ashes in all the places he liked." She gets the laundry out of the dryer and into the same red handcart she uses for groceries. She sighs, smiles, leaves.

I remain in the laundry room, absorbing the exquisite warmth of a big old building in winter, the boiler cranking steam up through the floors. I love this heat, and I love this silence and the groans that interrupt it, the mechanical hum. I sit there and think about the pianist. He also lived on the C line, three floors above the trombonist who refused a trip to the doctor.

The pianist was truly talented, played gorgeously. He taught students, too. Sometimes you'd hear him play a perfect phrase, followed by the uncertain attempt of the student. Other times he would play for long, unbroken stretches, recitals for an unseen audience of other people in the building. It was an amenity—not one you could include in a real estate brochure, but one that had been a part of the building's life for so long that you could forget how unusual it was, gusts of classical piano rising up the air shaft. The delicate curtain over the kitchen window would tremble with a breeze, the afternoon sun hitting at an angle. It was as if the notes themselves were moving the curtain as they entered.

The pianist was fragile, pale, with a weak chin, his expression always somewhat aghast. He lived with his parents. The father, slender, serious faced, wore a trench coat and a beret in winter, and got everywhere on a bicycle. The same was true for the pianist himself, including the beret. The mother, never seen, existed only in the abstract.

The parents died very quickly, one after the other. I am not sure exactly when this happened, sometime in the late 1990s, I think. At some point I noted that I hadn't seen the parents in a while, which I realized was years, and then confirmed with one of the doormen, who of course know everything, that the pianist was living alone. What prompted my question was the fact that the pianist had begun to get skinny. So skinny, he had to tie his belt in a knot. This should have been the first sign: He didn't buy a new belt, didn't even bother to puncture himself a new notch, just walked down the street drinking apple juice from a bottle, his belt tied up at his waist like a shoelace.

"At least he can still play," I said. But my mother, who knows about these things, said, "No, no, he's rushing; you can hear it. There is something unsettled about the way he is playing."

The notes, drifting up the air shaft, got faster and faster.

One day he showed up at our door. It was dinnertime.

"Hi," I said.

"Hi," he said. "How are you?"

"I'm good." I paused, uncertain where this was going. "Is there anything I can . . ."

"I just wanted to say hi, say hello, and tell you what a wonderful family you have."

Apparently he did this to other people in the building, too. For years his music had wound its way up the airshaft, through windows, up the back stairs, and now it was as though he were crawling after it, determined to meet the listeners. I would later learn, when I inquired with the doorman, that he focused on the famous people. The newspaper columnist, the actors. I was flattered to be on the list of those poked and prodded.

After the in-person visit, there were messages taped onto the front door, or slid under it. At first a short note of appreciation for something I had written. Then something less legible. He said that he was doing his own writing. Stories. Could he show me? In a moment of weakness, on the street, I said yes, and so under the door they were soon shoved, pages dense with tiny script, so well handled they were soft to the touch. Indecipherable lines. Here and there I could make out a word. *He.* Or, *She said.*

Finally, they declared him insane and managed to get him out of the building on a technicality. He hadn't signed some necessary documents relating the transfer of the apartment to his name. I got the information from the doorman. The day the moving truck appeared there was a current of outrage and even grief among the old guard. Letters were written to the board. But by then the moving truck had already come and gone.

It wasn't just the C line; there were crazy musicians all over. Seaton, my babysitter, who like us lived on the A line, joined the Hare Krishnas not long after I started college. He had left the building several years earlier, and I was surprised to hear his voice on the phone one evening while home from vacation, suggesting I ship him my drums so he could play them and chant Krishna. Many years later, he popped up in my life yet again, and he began to write and call. He expressed a love for me that felt unhinged, but I forgave it, because I recalled my own childish love for the older boy he had been, which was also unhinged. At six, I had a screaming, crying fight with my mother after realizing that she'd been paying him to spend time with me. He was my friend, I protested, and he didn't *need* to be paid. For years now he has sent me music, carefully compiled playlists, the technology evolving from things he sent in the mail to links sent via email, but the sentiment unchanged.

His parents sold too soon, before the boom. He lives in Oregon now, with a much older woman, and smokes a lot of pot. His voice, lambent, open, tremulous with mischief and a kind of distanced emotion, has changed not at all. I have learned to take his calls and talk to him with patience. Sometimes I think I am humoring him as one does a person on a ledge threatening to jump, with whom you want to engage in small talk only to reassert the gravity of what is normal; but other times I think that whatever the asymmetry of circumstances, I should take the affection for what it is.

And what about Ezra, my dear old friend on the D line? He has vanished, though I greet his father warmly whenever I see him. His father, a lovely man, is sly, attractive, rich, on the fifth or sixth of a series of wives or girlfriends, all young and slender. One of them was the first naked woman I saw. She was putting her hair up when I walked in, two hands behind her head, small breasts, long legs. She smiled at me and slowly pronounced my name in a Southern accent. I fled.

Ezra, when I last saw him, was fraying in an odd way. He had a law degree and an MBA, he told me, but wasn't working, or was working for his father; it wasn't clear. He looked swollen and heavy.

At twelve, Ezra had loved sitcom theme songs and told me that he ran warm water over his penis in order to masturbate, the implication being that by not using his hands, it was somehow more ethical. Sometimes he wet his bed, though whether there was any connection between these things I do not know. He made every effort to tape-record the theme song of every single sitcom on television. He had his own archive of those jingles—everything from *The Bob Hope Show* to *The Jeffersons* to *Mork and Mindy*, *Lost in Space*, and, from further back in time, *The Dick Van Dyke Show*, a particular favorite of his.

And those female babysitters whom I subjugated, making them listen with a straight face to all those lies I would tell about my adventures in life, my street battles, epic quests, romantic entanglements—they, too, are somehow present with me down in the laundry room.

Gail, one of the earliest babysitters with whom I remember the thrill of telling these fabulous stories, and of her indulging them, drifts into view. She is a bit stocky, wears a black turtleneck, and has short, black, curly hair. Once, she wore a devil mask for me and danced around while I attacked her with a sword. A theater person, Gail once took me to a play that kept me out too late. My dad had just died. I am sure I remember her in part because I was getting old enough to remember things, but also because this was a strangely vivid time. The deck of cards I brought with me to the performance marked the first summer after his death, when I was ten. Each card featured a different fighter jet on the back, the contrails reliably streaking a clear blue sky.

The play was *Spider-Man* and took place at Westbeth, all the way downtown. What I remember now is not the play itself but the long, moiling wait before it started, the dim light, all those kids and grown-ups sprawled on cushions arranged on the floor. We returned late that night to find my mother standing in the foyer with red eyes, tissues balled in her hand. She had called the police. Not the last time this happened, I should add, but the last time it wasn't actually my fault. All those babysitters have come and gone, but I feel their presence in the laundry room.

Winter turns to spring, the weather warms, and in April we return. Elizabeth is very pregnant. She wants to have the baby in New York. I moved into the building when I was two weeks old. My son will come here sooner.

The pianist, his belt still a knot at his waist, drops by the lobby frequently to discuss his case with the doormen. He is sleeping in the park, I'm told. The story he unfurls is well worn now, like those soft, well-handled pages he used to slip under the door. I bump into him on the street, greet him warmly, and in no time he is explaining, emphatically, that his piano teacher's piano teacher's piano teacher's piano teacher was Franz Liszt! It was madness what they did, he said. They took everything out of the apartment and put it in a truck! Files, furniture, even the piano itself! He, of course, has sought redress. I give him my best wishes and peer at the plastic bag dangling from his hand. It doesn't bulge, yet I can't help imagining it contains his toiletries and other possessions. He is optimistic that he will soon be back.

The laundry room, a hot little engine room during the winter, is now a place of coolness and repose. Two white molded chairs against the white wall, the floor painted a sensible basement gray. I take a seat as though in the waiting area of a bus station, collect my thoughts. I close my eyes to clear my head, but even now the building rocks like a ship and the world comes rushing in, echoing through its frame.

Us and Them

1. I stand at the back of the crowded room. Before me, like sunflowers ripened and swaying in the breeze, is a sea of raised hands, each holding a smartphone or camera aimed at the rabbi and the children assembled at her feet. She is telling the story of Hanukkah to a captive audience sitting cross-legged on the floor in clumps, each representing a pre-K class at the Riverside Church Weekday School. Among them is my daughter Evangeline, four years old, but not for long. Tall enough to see over everyone, I stand in the back, not wanting to block anyone's view, but this also affords me distance, across which now and then I allow a flicker of emotion and feeling to leap, from warmth to hostility to mere annoyance, and then back to warmth again.

2. My daughter has taken to drawing a curious form, a kind of sign: It's a U shape at the ends of which are arrows. As iconography it could be read as a smile, or instructions for a U-turn.
"What does it mean?" I ask.
"It means you should get off the computer."

3. Much of my conflicted feeling about Jewishness can be summed up in a single pronoun, and it is not *I* or *thou*. It is *us*. And one cannot focus on the word *us* without thinking of its corollary, almost its doppelgänger: *them*.

I root for Jewishness like I root for the Knicks. In fact, my fealty to the Knicks, inevitably mixed with disgust and contempt, seems expressly Jewish. The whole Patrick Ewing saga, for instance, in which Knicks fans heaped contempt and frustration on Ewing for years until they no longer had him, at which point they more or less fell in love with him, or at least his memory, has always seemed, to me, an explicitly Jewish conundrum, which in turn makes me happy to root for the Knicks.

4. The novelist Vince Passaro—Catholic, if you are keeping score—writes:

> I said "Happy holidays" to a woman in the laundry room yesterday and with pert self-satisfaction and Irish piety (the absolutely most infuriating kind) she shot back, "Merry Christmas to you," and walked out. I wanted to chase her down the hallway shouting "I'm a Jew, OK? I'm a Jew, goddamn it, not everyone has to believe what you fucking believe." I didn't. Wouldn't be fair to the Jews, really.

5. Elizabeth—also not Jewish—recently discovered *Curb Your Enthusiasm* and tore through all one hundred or so episodes over a matter of months. Midway through this *Curb*-a-thon, I remarked that she seemed to have a thing for contentious Jews.

"Only on TV," she said.

6. I come from an aristocracy of Jewish atheism. This may sound like a contradiction, or a euphemism for self-regarding Germans, but it also applies in a way to the members of the kibbutz where my mother grew up—a socialist and explicitly atheist commune dedicated to rebuilding their ancient homeland.

My mother was at the kibbutz because *her* mother had taken her there from Germany when Hitler came to power in 1933. My mother was one year old. My grandmother, who had grown up in Frankfurt, was eighteen years old when she read an article by Martin Buber that made a great impression on her. The same age as the century itself, she had only recently learned she was Jewish.

As my mother recounts the story:

> That summer of 1918, my mother worked as a counselor at a children's summer camp. One fine summer day she was sent with a cart and a donkey and the children's shoes to the cobbler for repair.

On her way she passed a house and saw a plaque saying, "Martin Buber." So she left the cart and the donkey and the children's shoes and went into the house and declared (to Buber): "Here I am!" Her words. And she stayed. She apparently was offered work as a secretary, but my mother was no secretary. She was a gardener—she was being trained at the time as a gardener, which was itself a very serious profession—so she worked as a gardener, first at the Bubers', then later, on his recommendation, at his friends' houses as well.

A decade and a half later, they all found themselves in Israel. Professor Martin Buber, Professor Hugo Bergman, and others, all living next door to one another in Jerusalem and teaching at the Hebrew University. They were all my parents' friends.

7. Here in the Riverside Church Weekday School, the rabbi is telling the story of Hanukkah. I love the Riverside Church Weekday School, and not only because some of my earliest memories are of the playground on the fourth floor when I attended the school, at age four; or because Riverside Church features in the title story of my first book as a romantic, if phallic, prop; or how, when flying over Manhattan, one can see the church standing alone, far from all the other skyscrapers of Midtown, a moral beacon; or even that the church's theater has for decades been host to progressive performances of dance and theater including performances of my mother's dance company way back when, performances I have vivid childhood memories of attending. I love the school because, its name notwithstanding, it has a Hanukkah celebration, not to mention posters in the lobby announcing its support for Occupy Wall Street, and is about as progressive and affirming of liberal values as is possible while situated in an enormous limestone edifice built with Rockefeller money. It is located, satisfyingly, on a street named after Reinhold Niebuhr, who once credited Buber as being "the greatest living Jewish philosopher."

8. The rabbi, wearing a kippah, speaks in an open, sing-song voice, not patronizing, exactly, but not oblivious to the nature of her audience, either. From my place in the back, I remain tuned in, trying to glean facts. I have always been spectacularly obtuse about the facts of Jewish history as they are relayed by religious rituals. For example, at Passover, which I grew up celebrating and still do, we used editions of a Haggadah that my mother had annotated. I was highly attuned to these pencil markings, not least where they rather vehemently crossed out the words "The chosen people." And yet I must have sat through thirty of these ceremonies before one day saying, "Wait a second. Avadim hayinu: We were slaves. Like . . . actual slaves?"

The rabbi has brought a menorah that sits behind her on the windowsill, against the backdrop of that marvelous view from the church's sixth floor. I feel confident in saying there is no preschool anywhere whose classroom can have a view more romantic and glamorous. Standing there with a large picture book in her hands, the rabbi turns the pages as she tells the story of the ransacked temple, and the pressing desire to restore it. She uses the word *clean*, says the temple was "very dirty." This opens, for me, a previously unexplored dimension to the unfailing oil lamp—for this was the light by which the temple was restored. For the first time I have a notion of Hanukkah as a celebration of tidiness, cleanliness, and good housekeeping, something that might be sponsored by Clorox, say, or Purell.

9. The word flies by but I catch it, excited, as though it is a prize I have been waiting for. I should be standing here with an open heart, and I am—I swear! And yet I can't help but litigate, contrary as I am. Let's call it a form of engagement. Hearing this word, I respond like a lepidopterist leaping forth with his net to bring back the prized species. For here it is, the word *us*.

Among the kids present—and, I should add, most assuredly untroubled by the word *us*—is my daughter. I look at her and wonder what side of the word *us* she would even fall on. Surely, her own notion of the word is, for the time being, so encompassing it precludes any corollary of *them*. But sooner or later someone will alert her to these distinctions.

10. "Dear Parents," began the rabbi's email only a few days ago, "the children have brought up questions and statements about the differences they are noticing between each other. Because of this we are encouraging everyone to join us in a discussion about how to talk about similarities, differences, and inclusion in a respectful way that your child will understand."

And so we met, this very morning, ahead of the Hanukkah event, to cautiously circle the topic. It is a pretty diverse classroom, and the meeting had an air of mystery because it had been called on account of an unnamed crime. Eventually, though, it became clear that the matter was not about race, or religion, but rather disability. The child with braces on her feet had become a kind of prize. One boy in particular wanted to play with her, he announced, because "she has things on her legs."

Seeing these foot braces as some extra-cool kind of sneaker, all the kids had come to covet them. Only this made the girl with the foot braces cry. That her race could also be seen to set her apart was a detail that the conversation, sensitive as it was, could not assimilate, so to speak.

There was a short break after which we all reassembled, with parents from other pre-K classes, for the Hanukkah celebration. And now here we were—*us*.

I made a note to discuss this question of mine with the rabbi when she had finished.

11. The holidays are known to be a time of some unease among Jews. Usually, this dynamic is framed as concern for how to relate to the other, dominant holiday—the one upon which a war has been declared, according to at least one cable news outlet. A recent example of this is a column by Katherine Rosman in the *Wall Street Journal* that outlines life outside the New York bubble, in some unnamed exurban small town where everyone is very nice and has Christmas wreaths on their door. Her kids want one, too. Suddenly she cannot take for granted her Jewishness as a norm.

My own anxieties on the subject face in the opposite direction. For two seasons, summer and a fall, during which I have a sabbatical, we have lived on the Upper West Side. The neighborhood is filled with a curious new species, the modern Orthodox. I know their progenitors, literally; I grew up in a building where a famous rabbi and his circle lived; his exquisitely well-mannered wife still lives here, in fact, and asks after my mother and my children. The rabbi and his extended family, these extremely observant neighbors of ours, were always warm and cordial to us. At one point, there was what amounted to a recruitment push, a few dinners, but when I proved unresponsive, there was never any sense of judgment.

My only feeling of antagonism toward this rabbi and his world regards the No Parking sign that went up in front of the synagogue across the street. Though even that is not exactly right: I am in some ways grateful for the spontaneous street theater that springs up every time a car pauses in front of that empty space. Strangers in a strange land, they think they have ended their search and will now be released. You can see the driver squinting at the sign, incredulity melding into resignation upon realizing that no, they have not been released, their irritation easily enough inferred from the manner in which the car pulls away.

Parking is itself a kind of theology in New York—a unifying one—with believers and nonbelievers alike giving thanks for the many days on which alternate side regulations are suspended out of respect to the many religions practiced here.

Anyway, I am in the building's playroom with Evangeline one day when a whole minyan of little kids with yarmulkes comes barreling in. Mayhem ensues. Merriment, too, for the holidays are just around the corner. The one adult who accompanies the kids wears a yarmulke. We have an amicable chat. When I tell him I am a writer of personal essays he absorbs this for a moment and then asks, "Do you ghostwrite?"

"No. Why?"

"It just seems like someone writing personal essays would, I don't know, naturally ghostwrite for other people."

I find this assumption odd and a little depressing and change the subject to inquire about his work; he's a business guy, it turns out, in "the new media space," working on an app for busy parents who need help organizing their photographs. I turn now to the hordes of screaming youth, braced against what exactly I cannot even say.

12. It is during the Riverside Church Weekday School Christmas pageant eight days later that I remember the business card in my wallet.

My holiday ponderings about Judaism, belief, nonbelief, my kid—all of it's been swept up in a whirlwind of topicality connected to the death of Christopher Hitchens, the world's most famous atheist.

The school Christmas pageant is a big production, requiring the big assembly space downstairs. It doubles as the school's farewell event of the semester. My daughter's class is dressed in headgear and robes. I am not sure what they are supposed to be—pilgrims, disciples, wisemen and women? Later, when I ask her what she was dressed as, she thinks about this for a moment before answering, "Savages."

I had used the business card to reach out to the rabbi—who was so nice, so accommodating—to talk through some of my questions. Most of the resulting conversation, however, served only to remind me of how difficult it is to focus on the conceptual aspects of theology. I did perk up, though, when she referred to the list of irreligious, or should I say nonbelieving, Jews who have made such stellar contributions to modern thought and life. The all-star team of Jewish atheists: Freud, Einstein, Marx!

My interest in science extends mainly to its richness as metaphor. Clinical data itself leave me cold. But I do believe in magical realism, by which I mean the magic *of* realism—where you take the empirical and make it into a story, such that it begins to levitate, and in this way you have a kind of mysticism. I don't believe in God, but I do believe in *the* gods, the ones you don't want to anger, for instance, and to whom you must pay respect, if only as a hedge against hubris.

The rabbi did share with me an impressive fact: The Reform movement in America recognizes patrilineal descent! Also, there are more members of the American Reform movement than all the other movements combined. I find these facts heartening. If I wrote them out on a fortune cookie scroll and slid it into my daughter's shoe, perhaps she could pull it out and wave it in the face of the first kid who tells her she is not Jewish.

13. At home, we sing our Hanukkah songs in Hebrew, and I have only the faintest idea about the meaning of the words, which are printed phonetically on sheets of music handed out to guests at our party, copies of copies of copies. My mother sings the words. I hum and the words I sing are abstract to me. I have to ask over and over what they mean. These mimeographed pages with their funny-sounding words in English and accompanying text in Hebrew are homemade and have been touched by every iteration of myself once a year since I was ten. My mother, to whom I have outsourced all my Judaic identity, plays the piano. She had to wake up before dawn, she told me, on the kibbutz where she was a child in order to have time and space to practice. Her connection to Hebrew and knowledge of the Bible are curiously paired with the socialistic commune on which she lived as a child. Her Judaism is unassailable, as is her humanism. She doesn't need to explain this paradox. She embodies it. Perhaps this is one of the reasons I am always so happy to see Evangeline nestled beside her or on her lap. The transmission is not of facts but feelings.

Sometimes I look at my daughter, who is about to turn five, and feel torn between the feeling that she is vulnerable and the feeling that she is invincible. I mention this because I feel like the subject of religion generally, and God in particular, is something she will have to withstand, as if it were a blow. I can almost hear the choir of well-meaning voices arguing that it should be the opposite, that such news of the afterlife, the Bible, God, should be a boon. But that is not how I feel. Because I don't believe in God. And also, I am Jewish and want her to feel connected to her legacy. The question is whether to say it directly or to let the fact seep in by osmosis over the course of however many passing Hanukkahs and Passovers.

I may not be a believer, but she is. As of last year she believed in Santa Claus, for one thing. Even more powerfully felt is the Easter Bunny, whom Elizabeth has imbued with a curious problem-solving authority, so that Evangeline will sometimes say, at an uncertain moment, "Why don't we call the Easter Bunny?"

She says a lot of interesting things. Recently, for instance, she said, "Dad, I have a kooky hypothesis." Her phrases rush by like flowers on a river, and in the time it takes to wade in and grab one, hold it, write it down, whole wreaths and bouquets have rushed by. *Kooky hypothesis* I managed to rescue, but not what she said when I asked her what exactly it was.

The Topographical Soul

I was at the last show of the night in a New Orleans movie theater. The movie—a documentary about Hurricane Katrina and its aftermath—was loud, cacophonous, upsetting, and I stepped out midway to use the bathroom. As I peed, I stared absentmindedly at a tile on the wall in front of me.

There was nothing remarkable about this tile, but I felt an involuntary shiver. I was alone in the bathroom, but it occurred to me that the bathroom itself had once been alone and empty for days, weeks, maybe months after Katrina. It had been frozen in time like the figures in Pompeii captured in midlife, midgesture. What resonated, even tonight, three years after the hurricane and the collapse of the levees, well after the city had ostensibly come back to life, was a stillness that persisted.

Cities are not meant to be emptied, and most of them never are. Even in their quietest hour they course with a rustling sense of communal breath. But I had once spent time in another city that had once been emptied: Phnom Penh, which was evacuated under the Khmer Rouge in the 1970s.

Phnom Penh was, from the moment I saw it in 1994, a place that refused comparison. At first I accepted this. I had come for new experiences and I was happy, if often unnerved, to let new experiences prick me with their unfamiliarity. But then I began to feel a certain resistance in me, an effort to corral all the stimulation and make it adhere to some context with which I was familiar. I was trying, as I always did, to see Phnom Penh through the lens of my hometown of New York.

But there was no Upper West Side in Phnom Penh. No Central Park West. No Soho or West Village. No Empire State Building, or H&H Bagels. There was a river, but unlike the Hudson, the Tonlé Sap fed from a giant lake, and twice a year, as if laboring under some deep ambivalence, it changed direction. The Hudson, I felt, was consoling; the

Tonlé Sap, secretive, not least in relation to its alter ego, the Mekong, which from the promontory of the Foreign Correspondents Club, my preferred view, was hidden behind an island.

If in Phnom Penh I abandoned myself to disorientation, I nevertheless expected it to come into focus, expected that eventually I would begin to see the correlations between the landscape on which I walked and lived and the landscape of New York that I carried within me—the grainy black-and-white asphalt, the gray octagons that ran along the edges of the parks, the facades of the apartment buildings. New York was a dense musical notation I had internalized, every inch, every hill, every pothole. In Phnom Penh, I waited for what my eyes saw to correspond to this inner resource. It never did.

What happened instead was that I drew a new map. It took a while. My first visit was in 1994, then I returned in 1995 and 1996. I rented a scooter and rode it everywhere. The great flaneurs get around on foot; me, I require two wheels to fully imbibe the rhythm of unfolding neighborhoods.

In this, I fit right in, I guess. Phnom Penh was a two-wheeled city. There were cars, but they waded through the throng of motos (as scooters are called), bicycles, and cyclos (which have three wheels and a driver), like irritated oxen shouldering their way through flocks of oblivious birds. I drove with the curious combination of caution and abandon that was characteristic of everyone there. There were, in 1994, two functioning traffic lights. Otherwise the traffic was governed by traffic cops, who were ornamented by the finery of a military uniform and stood on a sort of circus master's platform—a dented cylinder with faded red and yellow paint—making smoothly assured hand gestures with their smart white gloves. We all paused in respect for these commands, before taking flight. Turning left required you to slowly drift into oncoming traffic, inching farther and farther to the opposite curb, so that by the time you reached your intersection you slithered around it. I remember the way certain boulevards, lined with oak trees, would open up. The French style asserted itself like this often, never more so than with Independence Monument, with its echo of the Arc de Triomphe. Careening around that roundabout I always felt a thrill and wanted to laugh out loud. More than once, I think, I did.

Having made the connection between New Orleans and Phnom Penh, I started seeing other correspondences. They are both lush, tropical cities, prone to lashing rain that ends as fast as it starts, the setting for epic puddles. And in the civic culture of both cities there is a hint not only of the misunderstood victim but also of the complicated ego that comes from being on the receiving end of charity. New Orleans, in the aftermath of Katrina, felt profoundly abandoned by the rest of the country. In Phnom Penh, the feeling was more complicated, and considerably darker, but there was also a sense that the attention and concern of the powerful is trained elsewhere.

And yet, if both cities are recovering from post-traumatic stress syndrome, they are similarly endowed with an unabashed sense of public mirth. At least the Phnom Penh I saw in 1994, 1995, and 1996, which was chock full of young children, felt rife with laughter, a lovely, bright kind of melody that counterpoised with the terrible poverty—it wasn't all laughter, obviously—and, more subtly and maybe more ominously, with the fact that there seemed to be so few old people in comparison to the young.

Both strongly influenced by the French, New Orleans and Phnom Penh are similarly nestled beside famous rivers—muddy, meandering bodies of water dutifully carrying freight, tourists, party boats, mythology.

As I said, I went back twice more in successive years, just long enough to pretend it was more than a visit; and there is something similar in my strangely qualified relationship to New Orleans, to which we moved in 2008 but leave each summer (and usually during the winter break, too), just often enough to pretend our entire life in Louisiana is an extended visit.

What does it mean that in traveling to new places we always yearn on some level for the old places? Is it simply nostalgia? Separation anxiety? Maybe it's that we all have an internal map we consult no matter what the terrain, this map corresponding to places but also to emotions, a way of accessing personal history and integrating it with the present.

When I was in Phnom Penh, I thought it was like the moon, a place utterly unfamiliar. What I saw would never translate back to the rest of my life but would rather adorn it, like a souvenir. But in New Orleans, years later, I realized I had held on to more of Phnom Penh than I knew, my point of reference expanding. Now Phnom Penh, once the strangest and most forbidding place I had ever set foot in, somehow came to occupy that same internal map, a touchstone and point of reference, a place you could, in some strange way, even think of as your own.

Negative Space

1.

Maybe it was because it took place on the gorgeous promenade in the middle of Central Park, which during the day feels so stately and European, its huge trees interspersed with a parade of heavy-duty statues of thinking men, the whole thing funneling into the band shell and beyond it the Bethesda Fountain and the lake with its rowboats. Or maybe it was because we were young kids, angry at some insult we could not really name, beyond the endlessly humiliating fact of being fourteen, but the guy who antagonized us that dark, silent summer night would need to be reprimanded, punished, his act accounted for. This was clear.

We came to this agreement, Nick and I, without saying much. Nick was a Stoic. He was in constant touch with the ever-flickering scoreboard of fate and karma from which he alone could see. I tended to shut up around him, the better to let the silence creep in and provide a kind of black velvet pulpit from which he would speak his few, profound words, or I would speak my more copious, less profound ones.

So we circled back in a long arc to the start of the promenade on the East Side, the lights of Fifth Avenue visible through the trees, the two of us poised like drag racers, while the offending party, the enemy, walked alone, his back to us, unsuspecting, a solitary figure held firmly in our sights.

Somehow it was agreed that because the guy was walking right down the middle of the promenade we would both charge on either side, coming from behind. We did not intend to lay actual blows upon him. We were not even going to touch him. Like two fighter planes roaring in formation, we would merely buzz him on either side, for maximum disorientation, and then disappear into the enveloping darkness of the park.

And so we went into action, each mounted on our respective bike, slowly picking up speed, and soon were flying. The target was in our sights. Payback time.

Who was he? What was he doing by himself in the park at night? What were *we* doing in the park? Most importantly, what had he done to piss us off? I have no idea. I just know we had felt antagonized. We were out late, summertime exploring in that sweet spot where the Great Lawn was, and the band shell, and the Bethesda Fountain, and the lake, the spooky brambles not too far off.

Turning to see us coming at him on either side, he charged at Nick, who tried to steer clear, couldn't, and crashed right into a concrete-and-timber bench. He was already braking like crazy so it wasn't a violent crash, just kind of . . . ignoble. I could tell from his body language that the first thing he wanted to do was check to see if his front wheel was damaged but the guy was already up in his face. I came over, I remember, all of this lit like old-time cinema by streetlamps spaced at such dignified intervals, more dignified than the scene unfolding, surely.

"What the *fuck*?" Nick yelled in the strangled voice of someone who is both truly alarmed and also deeply invested in being unphased by everything at all times.

"What do you *mean* what the fuck?" said the guy. "What the fuck were you doing coming up on me like that? That's what the fuck!"

Nick and the guy got into a strange argument about the ethics of the whole thing—Nick, in classic fourteen-year-old logic, arguing that he was not actually going to *do* anything, and was just biking fast, was there a law against biking fast? Et cetera. The guy pointing out, agitated, that two guys coming up on him fast on bikes, two guys whom he just had words with . . . but here it fades to black, a faceless void, the scene illuminated by just one streetlight of memory that extends only as far as the scene itself, not its particulars.

It ended without blows, that much I can say. Surely we went home after. Was this one of the nights our mothers called each other anxiously, asking if the other one knew where we were? The memory vanishes. 1979, I would guess. Or maybe 1980, the summer we were bike messengers. Old New York. Statistically much more dangerous than the New one. And also, somehow, more private. Maybe what we were arguing about, in fact, that dude and us, was the right to have the whole place to ourselves.

2.

If you grow up in New York City, or maybe just Manhattan, as I did, you become a connoisseur of negative space. For hardcore city-philes, I mean the people who allow for the texture and topography of the city to enter their soul, these spaces are refuges, tiny oases, sought after, multipurpose. They are meditative temples. They are moments of rest.

There is so much action in New York one is sometimes perversely excited by those places when you are not part of it. Where nothing is happening. These places, in turn, become little air pockets of possibility. Unidentified, off the grid, these are the staging areas for trysts, seductions, encounters, the places where crimes are committed, of one kind or another. And the most conspicuous, hiding-in-plain-sight negative space in New York is Central Park.

3.

There were four of us, the West Side freaks. Worth and I lived on Riverside Drive. John and Nick lived on Central Park West. We attended a private school in the Riverdale section of the Bronx. Most of the kids in our school were ferried to school from Manhattan on private bus lines that picked everyone up at various points and then rumbled through Harlem, across the 133rd Street bridge, up the Major Deegan, past the Stella D'oro cookie factory, with its useful clock on top and its fleeting whiff of sweetness, and at last into the verdant cloistered world of Riverdale. There were something like seven or eight buses that ran up the various East Side avenues. The West Side had two, one for Central Park West and one for West End.

We were West Side kids. I now look at my whole generation from that school, the rich, the sort of rich, and not so rich kids of private school Manhattan circa the 1970s and early 80s, as a group that had OD'd on affluence, safety, and prosperity. Also, despite a serious crime wave and depletion of city services, we were undoubtedly the last generation of kids who were allowed to roam around the city with relative autonomy. Being on a long leash in the city at the age of ten or eleven was unremarkable.

We were surrounded by the iconography of ruin. The city had just survived a near-death experience. You didn't have to actually see and comprehend the famous *Daily News* headline "Ford to City: Drop Dead!" to sense it in the air.

When you're a kid, pending anarchy is something you root for. It means school is out. All bets are off. That the city was in a state of extreme dishevelment only heightened this manic behavior. I'd like to say it made my peers and me, on some level, feel guilty about our good fortune, but that was not the case. Rather it made everyone into a barbarian, sacking an already crumbling world for fun. We were destroyers.

Three of us, within that West Side Gang, were children of divorce. Of those three, two were living with stepfathers with whom relations were complicated. Nick was the youngest of four kids and the only one living at home with his mother—in his stepfather's apartment. He had a room of his own, where we spent a lot of time, but there was always the atmosphere of the stowaway back there, his mother having been swept into the lair of the stepfather. Worth lived with his older sister and mother and stepfather, an out-of-work actor who was always lounging around in a less than cheerful mood.[1] John's parents had divorced. He lived with his mother and brother, but the father's temperamental presence lingered like the smell of his cigarettes; the shiny purple wallpaper of his apartment's enormous rooms seemed, to me, to be the color of secrets. The one kid who was not a child of divorce was me. But my father was also absent, having died when I was nine, a year or two before we all started to hang out.

The group's tightness lasted into the first year or so of high school. All of us lived on a park. But not all parks are equal. Riverside Park was a splendid place for adventure, an excellent playground resource, a good place to go by yourself to throw a tennis ball against a wall, and the setting for the formative basketball court of my life, on Seventy-Sixth Street. But Riverside Park did not pull you in. It had none of the glamour, the gravitational pull, of Central Park. When you were in an apartment that overlooked Riverside Park, your eye went to the river, the astonishing fact of it, its breadth and flatness. Then you examined the fairly hideous New Jersey coast, though pretty at night, when its lights reflected on the water.

If you were in an apartment that overlooked Central Park, as Nick's did, you stared at the park. You stared at the thing itself and also the weird neatness of its parameters. The way it set itself off so completely from the city into which it had been dropped. Later on I came to understand the grand accomplishment of the park's design, the hugely artificial nature of its terrain. But as a kid staring into it from above, I couldn't help but feel that the park itself was the original terra firma of the city which had somehow been given exterior walls, like a fort, around which the city grew. What was inside the walls was a kind of original sin of nature. To have a view of it was to have access to a strange kingdom. You became entranced by the intricate patterns of its winding paths. By the weather systems that seemed to exist over the park alone.

When I first saw, through an airplane window, the lost kingdom of Angkor Wat, in northern Cambodia, its territory sharply set off in a symmetrical rectangle of stone from the mass of surrounding jungle, my first thought was of the view of Central Park from above, the way it, too, was a world delineated sharply from its surroundings, a kingdom of its own.

Nick's place was on Eighty-Ninth Street and provided an opportunity for close examination of the Reservoir in particular, with its strange, faintly kidney-like shape, the shushing patterns of light, the ripples pulling across the surface in one direction and then another, to reveal an otherwise invisible, inaudible wind. The little scampering bodies jogging around its perimeter. Central Park was mystical. Across its expanse rose the Upper East Side, a formidable foe kept well at bay. We gazed at the park, we felt its pull, and we entered into it. It was a kind of no-man's-land, a place of possibility. The ultimate negative space.

4.

We were into skateboards. It amazes me to think of this—my membership in early skateboard culture. When it came roaring back, whenever that was, the early nineties, and became like surfing, a permanent annex to the world of cool, I was impatient for it to come and go. I didn't dislike it. I just thought, we did that already. I never could have guessed how enduring it would be, I didn't count on the fact that twelve-year-olds through eternity would be thrilled by the feel of rolling.

That had been me at the time, with my West Side Gang. I discussed different kinds of trucks and boards. I partook in the great wheel debates about Road Runner, soft and candy-like, versus the more subdued Kryptonite. I preferred the latter. I had opinions about trucks. My board was FibreFlex.

As a group, we would spend weekend afternoons skateboarding the hill next to John's apartment. It was a long, curving hill that started around Sixty-Eighth Street, near the Great Lawn, and swung down past Seventy-Second Street, leaving you at the bottom of another hill at the top of which was the Bethesda Fountain and the band shell, the physical and spiritual center of all youthful parkie dereliction.

The spot's biggest draw, however, had to have been the horse-drawn carriages. We would start at the top and slalom down amid the crowds of people and the piles of horseshit. The carriage route was counterclockwise through the park, which is to say, back up the hill we had just come down.

At the bottom we would loiter until a carriage went by. There were massive bongo drum circles nearby, a barrage of bongo beats and cowbells, guys standing with a jug of Bacardi at the end of an outstretched arm, bandana around their neck or head, whooping it up. It was like skateboarding down into some mad party. We'd let it pour over us until a carriage passed, which, on nice weekend days, was never more than a few minutes. Then we would skate up behind it, crouch down, and grab hold of the rear axle, or whatever was down there to grab. Staying crouched low was important. You had to be able to see and avoid the piles of horseshit, both old and newly fresh, that dotted the road. Some of the drivers, knowing we were there, would flip their whip back over the carriage, though by some fateful miracle these whips always snapped just above our heads. But they snapped with malice. They weren't warnings.

I sometimes wondered how the driver explained this gesture to his passengers. Because of the wrath of the driver, and his whip, one person per carriage was ideal. Two people OK, and three was pushing it. Either way, we lived in giddy fear of the whip as we rode back up the hill.

In winter, our forays were less frequent but more dramatic. Snow days were surreal dreams, the snow day itself being pure negative space.

The cancellation of school. The plunge into the whiteness with sleds. The eventual retreat to Nick's or John's place for hot chocolate.

The Blizzard of '78 was an epic of staggering through an endlessly white landscape, the place mostly empty. None of us ever said it, but I think the fantasy was that we were the last people alive on earth. Why was Central Park mostly empty in the middle of a blizzard? Because it was a blizzard. But was it really empty? Did we go hours without seeing anyone except an occasional cross-country skier? All those arrival tracks zigzagging this way and that would have suggested otherwise. But such is the glory of Central Park and its many nooks and crannies that at any given moment it holds thousands of people who feel like they are alone.

5.

The difference between the Upper East Side and the Upper West Side used to be substantial. Now it is a question of subtle gradations. This lack of delineation is one of the weirdest changes to the psychic landscape of New York in the last twenty-five or so years. Today a visitor might wander through the park from one side to another and feel it was a kind of oasis in the midst of a continuous fabric, but not so very long ago it also served as a kind of moat, a Maginot Line separating two worlds and worldviews.

And if the park was a kind of DMZ in which one could wander, it was also a means to cross the border efficiently from one side to the other. No one asked for your passport, it was merely an interval of stopped time: The Central Park Transverse.

6.

Halfway through Central Park and the bus is careening. It is the rush-hour crush, the after-school press. One hand holds the bar above his head. The other hangs there by his side, oblivious. The bus has a momentum of its own, as though it's a pinball, hitting the curves at speed. The passengers are packed together, swaying together, knees loose, surfing the transverse.

A sharp curve delivers an ass cheek into his open palm. His body understands this before his mind can find words to match the fact.

A woman's ass has fallen into his open, blameless hand. Its shape matches the curve of his palm. The fabric of the dress is light, a tiny filament separating his hand from the thing itself. Then the bus swerves. Back. What gravity gave it now takes away.

He is twelve. He stands there. She stands there. A lot of other people stand there, but the world had narrowed to his hand, her body. The bus rolls as it takes a curve through the tunnel.

Those mysterious tunnels. Some have ceilings lined with elegant brick. Others look as if a giant had bitten a mouthful of rock, chewed, and built a tunnel out of the boulders he spat out.

The bus shoots into a tunnel. The many faces that were in light are suddenly thrown into darkness. It lasts a blink. It mimics, for a second, the effect of the flickering lights of a subway car.

The bus shoots out of the tunnel, speeding, though not fast enough for the impatient tight line of yellow LTDs and Impalas—the New York City taxis of the day—behind it.

It takes another curve and the ass cheek is back.

The passengers tilt like a field of wheat blown by a gust of wind. The coming and going of the anonymous passenger's ass is as blameless a gesture as the soft slap of wake on pier after a boat has long since passed. He stares straight ahead. What is she staring at?

Through the window he sees only the blocky stones of the transverse. They are in a subterranean world. The negative space of the transverse.

A tiny sidewalk lines the road. Anytime he sees someone walking on it, he feels pity for them, these souls who have so clearly taken a wrong turn. A mistake, he thinks; anyone on that sidewalk has made a terrible mistake.

He stands there frantically trying to imagine what the woman behind him is thinking. He slowly turns his head and glimpses a young lady with curly hair down around her shoulders peering into a magazine. All he can see is a slender neck tilted down in concentration, unperturbed. Has she not even noticed his touch? Or is she standing there in a state of burning indignation, prevented from turning and accusing him only by the fact that the bus is now careening a little recklessly through the transverse curves? Is she contemplating the difficulty and embarrassment of making a scene?

Then there is the delectable possibility that she had felt the initial pat, the subsequent flip of the fingers, lifting the cheek up to shudder down, and then the final, gravity-aided pat, almost a light slap, in ways that defied the like/dislike axis spectrum and existed on another spectrum entirely—one of arousal, guilt, anger, fear. Which is to say, maybe she felt exactly as he did! Wasn't this the necessary atmosphere for the actual combustion of sex? He didn't know.

He goes into the fat boy swoon, an exaggerated version of that fantasy common to young boys, in which their friend's hot older sister, a freshman or sophomore in high school, anoints them worthy and delivers a kind of communion of sex: Kneel and receive! The woman in this fantasy descends like an angel. Sex is not conquest so much as an act of beneficence, a kind of sensual philanthropy.

On the other hand, he thinks, maybe she is pissed as hell and he should bolt as soon as the doors open, before she has a chance to call the police.

He stands there in a state of terrified arousal.

The bus arrives at Broadway with a cranky, gasping grunt. He emerges onto the street, the enormous green Converse All-Star book bag on his back. Broadway smells of William's roast chicken. He never saw her face.

7.

I had my first encounters with the park at night when I was a kid, usually with Nick or some combination of the West Side Gang. There is one stretch of time that now emerges from the mist: For a week I was left alone at age fifteen. Alone in the apartment, but not to be trusted with a lump sum of money.

An arrangement was made. I would commute every other evening to my grandfather's place on the East Side to collect an envelope of cash left with the night doorman. I did this at night and so never actually saw him or my grandmother. This doorman was old, with watery blue eyes, and I suppose he had seen me grow up. He wore the formal gray uniform of that building, and white gloves, and had a rim of white hair around his shiny bald head. I still remember the way he peeled off those gloves a couple of years later to shake my hand the night my grandfather died. How watery his blue eyes became as he offered me and my mother condolences. For that week on my own, he was the most friendly face I saw. After he handed me the envelope, he saw me off with a big wave.

I would take the envelope to the steps of the brightly lit Metropolitan Museum to examine its contents. Then I would head home. On the way east, in eagerness, I took the transverse. But going home I went through the park itself, tempting fate with my envelope of cash.

There was one spot on the north end of the Great Lawn where I would pause to look at the skyline. Regarding the city from that vantage point, I felt small, like a stowaway, and kind of huge and powerful, too. The spangled lights, the huge towers, the movements of planes in the sky—it all created a vivid perimeter of brightness that accentuated the darkness of the park.

It was like staring at a partly cloudy sky at night, when after a while the patches of clouds and sky become confused, and you don't know which area is the hole in the clouds and which area is the cloud itself. Which parts are far away but relatively near, and which parts are as far away as far can be—the bottomless black universe? This is a variation on the dream/reality problem. You know when you are awake and yet, especially when you are young, there is something about dreams, their vividness, that creates a doubt. Which is the real and which is the imagined? Where is the division between positive and negative space?

I felt this way about Central Park at night. When I was outside its borders, it was a strange, mysterious territory. But once inside, I nestled within it, felt cosseted, protected. Everything beyond its boundaries was what seemed dangerous. I was inside a reality that protected me from reality. I loved the view from that spot at night. From inside the darkness, I filled up on the power of negative space.

Note

1. It was a shock when, a couple of decades later, an old gangster film made in the sixties, *The Plot Against Harry*, which had the unusual twist of having a sharp-dressing and very Jewish protagonist at its center, finally had its debut in 1990 at Film Forum and there on the screen, in the title role, was Worth's stepfather, Martin Priest.

The Purple Krama

I was pushing my bike up the hill and out of the park at Eighty-Third Street and Riverside Drive. It was a bright autumn morning on the Upper West Side. I had just passed the playground I played in as a kid, and where my children now played. I was moving through the landscape of my childhood, but I was not a child. My mother's apartment building was up ahead. My family and I were living there for the fall semester before returning to New Orleans. The building emitted family history with a force sufficient to be nearly visible, like heat waves. I had just dropped Evangeline at school and was on the phone with my mother, even though I was on my way over to her apartment.

And then I had another in the long line of intermittent encounters with slightly crazy guys who get my attention by insulting me, in this case by calling me a faggot.

Maybe it was because I was wearing a purple krama wrapped around my neck. A krama is a colorful piece of all-purpose cloth used in Cambodia in all sorts of inventive ways—mostly as a scarf, but also as a sarong, a hammock for children, a towel, and a whole variety of things by every strata of Khmer society. I got it on a trip to Cambodia from which I had recently returned. Cambodia, where the men sometimes hold hands. My previous visits to Cambodia, in the mid-nineties, had been unsettling, literally unbalancing. We are not such limber moral beings that once our sense of reality gets stretched out of shape it immediately bounces back to its previous form. The Cambodia I had just returned from had been, relative to the one I had known, a more stable place, at least on the surface of things. I, too, was in a more stable place than I had been when I first visited Cambodia, at least on the surface of things.

It had been parents' night at the Riverside Church Weekday School the previous evening, and Evangeline, four years old, had brought me and Elizabeth to all the projects she and her class had been working on. I enjoyed making a show of being impressed and surprised. She showed me the way she could spell her name. She took me to the numbers caterpillar and counted all twenty-four little green circles, and then put her finger where the twenty-fifth circle would be later that day and looked up at me with mischievous pride.

The next morning I biked her up to school and then went home. The air was cool but the sun was warm. I had dressed casually, in the black cloth shorts favored by rice farmers in Southeast Asia, high-top sneakers, a black waffle shirt, and over that a light blue button-down shirt made in Germany that I had bought many years ago. It once had a fancy sort of sheen to it. Now it had ripped, unbuttoned sleeves that flapped around my forearms. I also wore aviator shades, and the purple krama, wrapped scrofulously around my neck.

The guy who insulted me was sitting on a bench at the entrance to the park. He seemed to be in a state of repose, taking in the nice weather. He was very big, brown, heavier than me but not taller, middle aged, and wore gray sweatpants, patent leather high tops, worn but still shiny, a green trench coat, and a cap. The cap lent him a dapper air, faintly English. Thinking about us from a distance of time, I can say that we both looked like men with confident if somewhat confused ideas about personal style. I had called my mother, even though I was about to see her, as we were living in her apartment for the semester. Sometimes it was easier, quicker, to talk to her on the phone without all the emanations of tenderness and history and love that register in her eyes when we are face to face. Pushing my bike with one hand and holding the phone to my ear with the other, I still had one foot in the parent bubble. Within this bubble one simultaneously roots for the world to be friendly and kind, and is therefore more likely to nod hello to strangers, and also keeps a vigilant eye out for any sign of threat. You become wildly garrulous or very paranoid. I lean, as a rule, to the former. When I made eye contact with the guy on the bench, who was looking at me, I nodded hello.

He responded with a deadpan glower, and, after a couple of beats, he muttered, "Faggot."

On the phone, my mother was in the middle of telling me about her trip to the doctor. I felt a shiver of pleasure and adrenaline, cutting her off to tell her I would be upstairs in just a minute. As I got off the phone, I thought of how unaware she was of what these next seconds might hold for me. Phone in my pocket, I turned around and pushed the bike back toward the guy on the bench. Before I could even get a word out he said it again, right to my face. "Faggot."

I received it like a slap, the clear contempt of it was shocking. But it also organized my thoughts, and in a way it organized my schedule, at least for the next few minutes.

I leaned my elbow on the seat of my bike in front of him and said, "Hey!" like I had a bright idea I wanted to share. "Fuck you!" Then I stared at him. He stared at me. It was an oddly decorous interval, like we were two gentlemen who had just slapped each other with white gloves.

Then he reached down into the pocket of his sweatpants. I wondered if he would remove a gun. Beside him sat a brown bag within which sweated a bottle of Mountain Dew. Out of his sweatpants pocket now came a beat-up black phone. He was getting a call.

"Yeah?" he said into the phone.

I started walking back up the block. But I had only gone about ten steps when he called after me again. "Faggot."

I stopped. The wind was whipping, the clouds raced across a gorgeous blue sky. Dry leaves rustled in a whirlwind on the ground, a counterpoint to the rustling trees above. These moments of rushing brilliance are exalting but also provocative. I turned and walked back toward him.

Was I standing up for faggots against this rudeness and presumption, or did my reaction mean I shared his assumption that the word *faggot* was the ultimate insult? The complexity of the situation reminded me of an incident involving Joakim Noah, a star NBA player for the Chicago Bulls.

Joakim Noah grew up in downtown Manhattan. His father was a French pop star and before that a tennis star, his mother a former Swedish model with Bohemian leanings. His mother's best friend, the dancer Robert Tracy, was Nureyev's lover. Such was Tracy's presence in his life that Noah has remarked, "We used to call him 'Mom.'"

Noah offered this autobiographical fact in response to an incident where he was caught on camera emphatically saying "faggot" to a heckling fan. His mother, he said, was shocked. The NBA fined him fifty thousand dollars.

The word *faggot* can be generically hostile, or it can be a personal attack against someone's sexuality. I was not angry at being confused for a gay man, but I was angry at the presumption in the word that I would do nothing in response. If he had called out "asshole" (let's not get too interpretive here), it would have been laughable. *Asshole*, *bitch*, and *loser* are hostile, but *faggot* is also a directive. It says, I know how you are going to react, you are going to do nothing. So I did something to show I could, even if that something involved standing in front of a man on a bench while he chatted pleasantly on the phone. Was I engaging with an insane person? I waved my hand hello a few times. He gave me a "just give me a second" sort of look while I turned my hand around and slowly gave him the finger. He looked elsewhere and saw none of it.

I walked away. He called after me again: "Faggot." I walked back again.

"I can say whatever I want," he said.

"You say whatever you want. I'm not going to stop you," I said. "And I can sit wherever I want." I sat on his bench, not right next to him but on the other half of it, a metal divider between us.

To my utter delight he stood up and started walking away.

I followed him and now, at last, found the courage to perform the aria of invective I had learned thirty years earlier from a scalper outside of Madison Square Garden. I had been in the midst of trying to scalp Knicks tickets when some sort of kerfuffle erupted nearby and I turned my head in time to see, and hear, a little man bellow the words, "I'm going to reach down your mother-fucking throat and rip your fucking lungs out!"

It was said with such ferocity. It really impressed me.

Now my harasser walked down the street while I followed him, swearing clumsily. The wind swept my words off toward the river but they felt very good as they left me. Then, in a bit of a non sequitur, I said, "There are kids around here!"

What in the world did I mean by that?

Was I saying he shouldn't call people a faggot because there are kids around? A park is many things, but in the morning on a sunny autumn day, with a playground in sight, it's a kid zone. Was I saying that you can't be a surly fuck in a kid zone because you will set a bad example? Or maybe I meant that if you transgress against the kid zone, the seemingly mild-mannered adults pushing strollers, all of whom contain these outrageous libidinal monsters which they are obliged, being parents, to keep in check for the sake of setting an example, will have an excuse to unleash on you.

If you fight under the righteous banner of protecting the children, can you be as barbaric and murderous as you want?

We kept barking at each other, from fifteen feet away. I glimpsed the doorman in the building across the street from mine talking to someone behind his glass door. I thought, "If I can see him, he can see me." This doorman, who greets me warmly on the street, is in close contact, via a kind of doorman Morse code, with the doormen of my building. Word could get around. "Beller, with the little children, living with his mother, is getting into it with huge crazy guys in the park. He's out of his mind and going to get shot."

Nevertheless, I trash-talked while the guy backpedaled to another bench. "You didn't see the size?" I called after him. "What? If I was five feet tall you'd be in my face?" A ridiculous comment. I am very tall, but not all that imposing. What I was really alluding to was the size of my craziness. Why was I acting crazy? I had thought I was in a good mood.

For a second I made as if to sit beside him again. But I walked past. He said "faggot" again.

I let it go. I entered the zone of my life. It was like walking through a membrane. The same clear, bracing wind on my face. The same purple krama around my neck, acquired in the town of Kep, on the coast, where the big villas were built on a hill overlooking the sea and then blown up by the Khmer Rouge.

I crossed the street without looking back. Beneath my feet, a rough gray stubble of asphalt. Up ahead, at the intersection, the stoplight swayed high above Riverside Drive like some lantern on a ship. And rising above the opposite sidewalk, a giant slab of brown and orange brick whose color is a melody I have known my whole life.

The lobby, the doorman, then the elevator, which, as it rises, makes the sound of an album on a turntable before the song starts. I enter the apartment and its familiar smell and see that Elizabeth is about to commence with the peas for Alexander. He has just started what are euphemistically called "solids." He has a diaper on and nothing else.

He is big for five months. The morning light falls on his pale skin. When he sees me, his whole body jerks in recognition—arms shoot straight out, legs jerk, eyes widen. A body-wide twitch of pleasure. The smile registers pure delight.

I think, as I do often: Do not get yourself killed. Do not be stupid. This kid needs you. They all need you. As I needed my father, who escaped Vienna in 1938, surviving on a bag of apples on the train, then running through woods at night until he fell in a freezing river and was pulled out by the Swiss. He was cautious in life, at least the part I saw, and died early of cancer anyway.

The Rights

Loose Teeth

We wind our way up and over the bridge, leaving downtown New Orleans behind us. The Mississippi River appears below us, in all its torturously winding, self-reversing glory. The sky is gorgeous in the late afternoon. We're heading to our favorite Vietnamese place.

Up on the span of the bridge I ask Evangeline, age five, about the day. Nine times out of ten I get no response to questions like this, and feel both astonished at the insolence and comforted that we are part of the cycle of life: After all, I can recall being her age and returning from school to the question, "How was your day?" The only possible answer was a single nonword (*good*, *fine*, *OK*) or, more honestly yet, silence. In spite of this, I often feel hurt by the way she crosses her arms, furrows her eyebrows in exasperation, as though I have again said something stupid, and refuses to give me even one word.

Now, before her refusal can gather momentum, I remember that there was an unusual event that day.

"Wait, the dentist!" I say. "How was the trip to the dentist?"

"I have two loose teeth!" Evangeline responds without hesitation.

"What?"

"My bottom two teeth are loose!" She is genuinely excited.

"No way." I look at Elizabeth. "Is it true?"

"Wiggle them!" she says.

"But she's five!"

"I have two loose teeth!" Evangeline yells again. It is unclear whether it is their looseness that elates her, or my distress, or both.

"How old are people when they lose their baby teeth?" I say. "I thought that was, I don't know, like seven."

"I guess it varies," says Elizabeth. "And they're just loose, anyway. They're not out. Yet. One can't keep baby teeth in one's head, accumulator."

The moment passes. We eat with our friends and their kids; it's a regular thing, the two families joining one another at this Vietnamese place on the West Bank, Phở Tàu Bay. I enjoy the food and atmosphere but also the enormous and mostly empty parking lot, the random businesses that populate it. The biggest structure is a giant pink building, once a bowling alley, now abandoned. It's their boy's first birthday. He's one month younger than Alexander. There is a cake. Afterward, standing in the bereft parking lot that I find so strangely thrilling, with the Nail Supply 2000 sign, and Barry's Fashions, the kids run around laughing while the parents talk.

The boy is on my hip.

"Be careful!" yells Elizabeth.

"Carmen! Don't run in the parking lot!"

"Evangeline!"

I just stare. My parental willpower wobbles in the face of these long New Orleans late summer dusks. They bleed so slowly into night. Bedtime for the kids, by which I mean Evangeline because Alexander is too little to have much say, requires a hardness of will. But the air is so soft, the light so gentle, and the news of her wobbly teeth makes me want to savor the moment. When we get home, it's still light. Elizabeth takes Alexander inside, and Evangeline and I have an adventure in Audubon Park, just the two of us.

We take some bread for the ducks. Evangeline throws crumbs at them, gets excited about duck chicks, and then negotiates with the geese, who can be aggressive, while I sit on a bench. After a while she comes over, points to another bench nearby that also faces the water. "I think the geese over there are less aggressive," she says.

I need a beat to process that she just said "aggressive."

"I'm going to take you to the monkey rock," I say.

"Why is it called the monkey rock?"

"Because it looks like a monkey," I say. "Or because *you'll* look like a monkey climbing it."

The golf course is empty in the fading light. We walk until we see the strange jutting rock erupting from the flat green surface. She starts to run. I start to run. We race over the manicured green grass. I point to a few bumps and try to sell it as looking like a monkey. She is not buying. However she does start to climb up the rock. Halfway up she needs a push before making it to the top.

It looks like it is made of volcanic lava. But if ever there was a landscape that was not volcanic, it is New Orleans. I later discovered that I conflated two local myths. This one is "the meteor," rumored to be an asteroid. It has nothing to do with "Monkey Hill," which urban legend claimed the WPA built to show the children of New Orleans what a hill looks like.

She surveys the view from the top of the rock and, even as I yell, "Don't jump!" she does so.

We head now to the playground to swing. Against a nearly dark sky, again and again, she rises and falls. The playground is mostly empty now. Like last call for kids.

On the way home I offer her a ride on my shoulders. We used to have huge fights because she would begin every expedition by shouting, "Shoulders!" It's been a while since she did that, and now I have to offer her a ride. She accepts.

At home I hustle her through the brushing of teeth. Then Elizabeth asks if Evangeline has taken her vitamins, which are gummies. So I get them for her followed by another brushing of the teeth. (All that chalky sugar.) There is much slowing down and procrastinating. She insists she is not sleepy.

"Don't start," I say.

"But Daddy!" she wails. "The night is so long!"

"Don't start," I say, loudly, loudly enough, almost, to make a scene. The good feelings cannot survive bedtime, I think. It's infuriating. But then she is in bed and I read her *Little Quack* while she attends to her little animals. She is licking her palm and then petting her favorite animal with her wet palm.

"Don't do that," I say. "Why are you doing that?"

"Leopard needs his bath."

I go back to reading the book. Then, toward the end, she looks up from my shoulder and says, "Daddy, could you start over? I wasn't exactly listening."

"No, honey, you have to listen. I'm not starting over."

"But Daddy..." Tears. Hysteria. "Daddy, *please*! I wasn't paying attention!"

"I'm going to keep reading, all right? Next time pay attention."

A terrible feeling comes over me; I am a hypocrite. All those moments of her babyhood and toddlerhood when I wasn't paying attention, looking at my phone while I pushed her on the swing, things like that. There is no going back for me—why not afford her this little luxury of starting the book over?

Strangers are constantly telling me, when I am walking around with Alexander on my hip, "Enjoy that baby!" They don't need to tell me. When you have seen it go by so fast with your first kid, it chastens you.

And yet I move right on to the next page. She weeps copiously. "But Daddy, it's so close to the end!"

This chokes me up for some reason. It is true. There are just a couple of pages left. I waver for a moment, then steel myself. You are the adult, I remind myself. You cannot cave every time. It's after 9 p.m.

I decide to keep going. Then, just before I get to the last page, I turn to her and say, "Open your mouth."

She opens, and I reach over and wiggle her two bottom teeth.

"They don't *feel* loose," I say.

Her voice gets very low and mysterious, almost somber. "Only the dentist knows," she tells me.

Degas at the Gas Station

She comes marching out in her black leotard. Blonde hair up, skin shocking in its clarity. Behind her the next ballet class has begun, Degas ballerinas struggling with the fifth position. She is still wearing her tap shoes. Her face, impassive and blank in a way it rarely is at home, makes a curious, tiny twist when she sees me. Her mother usually picks her up from dance class.

We march down the stairs. Outside the enclosure of the dance studio the world is summery, sunstruck, even at 5:30 in the afternoon. We stand there a moment, squinting in the dappled warmth and light.

"Daddy, I'm thirsty. Do you have any water?"

"No," I say, "but I'll get you some."

The dance school is located in a strange no-man's-land between River Road and a gas station. Beyond River Road is the levee, and beyond that, unseen, the Mississippi River. In the other direction is where Carrollton and St. Charles Avenues meet, each with their enormous live oaks. But these calming trees feel distant in the short stretch of sidewalk on the way to the gas station, which is hectic with cars. I hold her hand.

"Daddy," she says, "sometimes I get to see the older girls do hip-hop. I'm jealous of their moves."

"Really," I say, "you're jealous?"

"Yeah. They're really good."

I walk beside her, enrobed in the idiot silence of fatherhood, stumped as to how to respond to this. You are never entirely past a potential freeze when talking to a pretty girl, even if that girl is your six-year-old daughter.

She is still wearing her tap shoes. Their clicks are like a metronome counting the beats until I can formulate a response.

"Wait here," I say, when we step inside the gas station store. Her shoes click loudly on the hard tile. I peruse the enormous offerings behind glass, searching for water, hoping to get out of there before she starts whining for a Sprite, or a Coke, or some other sugary thing I am not going to give her. Suddenly, even as I frantically scan the windows packed with beverages, the place erupts with a shockingly loud noise, as though an entire case of marbles has crashed down across the floor. I wheel around to see Evangeline doing an impromptu tap dance session, with just enough skill to make it charming and not obnoxious, I hope, though it's a fine line. I turn around, find the water, and head to the cashier, who, thank God, is smiling.

"OK! OK! Enough," I yell.

By some miracle this causes her to stop. I pay for the water and we head for the door.

"I want to sit down," she says when we get to the doorway.

There are boxes of soda stacked in the window. She plops down, turning them into an improvised café. Once seated and comfortable, she hands me, her trusted assistant, the bottle. I stand there like a butler, twist the top off, and hand it back. No words exchanged.

Sitting there on those cartons of Diet Coke and Coke Zero, sipping from her bottle of water in a manner both poised and carelessly slouched, she looks like something Degas might paint if he went on a field trip to the Stop & Shop. But as Elizabeth, a former ballerina, often points out, Degas painted those young dancers with contempt, making their faces somehow piggish and smudged. Whereas Evangeline in the window is so beautiful and vivid. So present in herself. She lifts the bottle and tilts her head up and takes a few gulps. Then she sits leisurely with her drink. I try not to stare. Sunshine everywhere, the mellow gold color of late afternoon, a faint aura of playing hooky, the two of us in the gas station.

While she sits, I watch the expressions on people's faces as they pull into the gas station. The corner of Carrollton and St. Charles is busy, everyone either fighting their way into the heart of New Orleans or fighting their way out of it. A man pulls in very fast, navigating between two cars and stopping abruptly at a spot rather presumptuously near the front door; he is young, tough-looking, this agitated guy with his seat way back. The car is a ratty blue Neo. Or a Neon. I can't quite read the name from here. I wonder when it last broke down. When it will break down next. I wonder what his problems are. Who he is mad at. What his job is. What kind of physicality it requires.

Earlier today I was moving bricks in our backyard. It was intensely physical work, yet I couldn't find a way to make it feel like a workout as opposed to just work. Handling little children is similar; the body refuses to let it contribute in any way to your vanity. Harder than any workout and yet it somehow produces no muscle tone or sense of energy.

Suddenly I remember the pieces of the nice cheese I had taken from a reception that afternoon and carried with me folded in a napkin. I reach into my pocket, unfold the napkin, and hold it out to her. She peers at the selection, chooses one, and nibbles noncommittally. I keep my hand out, near but not too near, like someone feeding a beloved but possibly dangerous animal in the zoo.

Her gaze drifts to the boxes on which she is sitting. "Coke Zero," she says matter-of-factly. And then, as though it were a puppy, she strokes a box a few times and says, "Ah, lovely Coke Zero."

A bizarre moment. She sometimes surprises me with her goofy sophistication, this six-year-old with a homing instinct for gentle irony.

A moment later she declares that this last piece of cheese, pecorino, is not to her liking, and disgorges a half-chewed wad of it into the napkin still in my hand.

I take a few steps to throw it out and when I turn back around, I see that Evangeline has stood up and walked, with the impeccable timing of a kid who always gets in the way, right into the surly-looking dude in the crappy blue car.

There he is, nearly tripping over her as he walks to the door, his burly body suddenly inflected at the waist as he reaches for the door handle. Tattoos running up his arms and neck. There is a delicacy to the way he avoids stepping on her. Something about the way he twists his body around and over hers is incongruous with my earlier impression. Balletic, almost, the exertion of someone wishing to be discreet. He smiles. There is a softness to it.

"Excuse us!" I exclaim loudly, like a bull bellowing its way across a meadow.

"No problem," he says, almost laughing. Looks me in the eye. Such sweetness to the moment. It shocks me. But he is through the door before I can express my gratitude or my guilt, the moment done.

"You all finished?" I ask.

She nods abstractly.

"Knock back one more sip," I say. When in doubt, encourage hydration.

She dutifully raises the bottle up high and, like a sailor draining a bottle of beer, knocks back a solid gulp.

I take her hand, and we march out of the gas station. I see another parent come in with their leotarded little girl and note she's got sneakers on below the pink tutu. Evangeline is in a black leotard and tap shoes. I should have changed Evangeline out of the tap shoes, I think to myself. Bad for them to be out scraping on pavement. But the sound of their clicks is just so lovely. Surely she'll outgrow these shoes before the taps wear down. For now, it's worth it to hear the clip-clop of her feet as we walk to the car. A mysterious thrill runs through me with the sound of each click.

Thanksgiving Panic

There is a room in New York City with which I am very familiar. It is a room where my mother sits and works, surrounded by piles of papers. I have known this room all my life. It was once my father's study. It has since changed a bit. He died, for one thing. But much hasn't changed—the dark French Desk is still there. The bookshelves, and the books, that were there when it was my father's study—they are all still there, though the books and papers accumulated in the course of my mother's documentary films are new additions. She never remarried. She made movies.

Also unchanged are the framed drawings crowding the walls. Some are tiny Rembrandt etchings that are interesting when you take the time to bring your face close, which I rarely think to do. This is the room I glimpsed through the doorway as a little kid as I walked, half asleep, to the bathroom. What made that glimpse of the room, and my father in it, so memorable, I think, was that it was one of the first times it occurred to me there was a whole other world of activity in that apartment after I fell asleep. Besides my father, the other notable absence is his Olivetti typewriter with the gleaming black keys. After he died it moved under the piano, where it sat in its maroon case in dignified silence for the next few decades.

Then I hired a professional organizer to spend some time with my mother in an attempt to simplify and discard, but the few sessions they had were mostly futile, and nothing much changed. The one tiny revolution, the one thing that my mother had agreed to discard, was my father's old typewriter. I could see a giant wave of remorse come over her when she reported this fact.

"You threw out the typewriter?" I said.

"Why would I have done that?" she said, and brought her hands together as though to grieve.

I assured her it was fine, but I felt bad for her—the instinct to hold on to things had proven wise, seemed to be the lesson—and for a moment I was upset with myself for bringing in the organizer. I assuaged whatever sense of grief I felt with the idea that the gesture seemed rich with symbolism—of all the things to discard, the beautiful Olivetti! Maybe she unconsciously resented all the time he spent with it?

"It's crazy, but it's fine," I said. "It's probably better to have this anecdote than it is to have the typewriter."

There is another version of this room with which I am familiar, the same in every respect as the one described above, except it exists on a screen. For a number of years after Evangeline was born, my mother would sit in her chair accompanied by an array of toys and funny stuffed animals, who are like recurring characters on a show. Here is Monkey, and Duckie, and Flamingo! She keeps these on hand for the benefit of Evangeline and Alexander, both of whom enjoy her puppet shows. Whenever she appears on this screen, the animals and instruments come trotting into view one at a time, to their delight.

Our video conferences with my mother used to take place Sunday morning. Now they occur scattered throughout the week, sometimes for the benefit of the kids, and sometimes for the benefit of my mother herself.

On my mother's end it is a still shot—the camera on her iMac remains where it is. But on our end, existing on a laptop, she is portable and she sees many tableaux. I recall one instance when we left Evangeline in a room with the laptop featuring my mother and these puppets, and Evangeline was still talking to them, and they to her, when we returned ninety minutes later.

Who knows what Evangeline was doing with the laptop in that time. When I came back the laptop was on the floor and she was lying stomach down, chin in her hands, feet in the air, watching the puppet show. Had she spent the whole time in that position? My mother's stamina in these video conferences leaves me in a kind of awe. A virtual babysitter, almost, she dazzled with her endless inventiveness. All these characters!

If there is one shortcoming to all this, it is her limited mastery of the computer. A documentary filmmaker, she is doing pretty good with technology for her generation. And you would think, given her generosity as a virtual babysitter, that I might reciprocate with my time to provide some measure of grace when providing tech support. But it is not so.

What is it about coaching parents through their adventures in technology that brings out the worst in people? By "people," I really mean, "their children," or more specifically, me. I recently had an epiphany that I was being a jerk about tech support, and vowed to be patient. The vow lasted as long as a birthday candle. More usefully, I discovered a tool that allows me to access my mother's computer and control it remotely. No more did I have to carefully describe the paper clip icon she needs to click on her email when she has forgotten how to attach a document. Now I can access her computer and do it myself. Likewise, this tool has made it easier to set up a video chat. But the tool has produced a strange, unexpected bit of cinema, or opportunity for espionage: It is now possible to access her computer and see the room without her.

There is something very strange about seeing streaming footage of a still room. The chairs are at odd angles. The absent presence is felt but not seen. For a period of time, I would log in and just . . . stare. There was a strange pleasure in just taking in the empty room, the light at different times of day. A few times I have called out, "Mom! Mom are you *there*?" and in this way circumvented a phone that was off the hook, say, and so forth.

This past Friday she wasn't there. I called on Saturday morning. She wasn't there. I sent an email. I called that afternoon. She wasn't there. That night, we had guests. It crossed my mind to call my mother again, but I was swept up in the preparations. Then the evening came and went. It was pleasant.

Toward the end of dinner, one woman told a story: Her father died when she was twelve; her mother met another man quickly. They took a vacation alone, just the two of them, in the Caribbean. Her mother called her to check in. The woman telling the story was drinking, her mouth purple from wine. Her eyes narrow. There she was at twelve, her mother on a faraway island. . . . The story faded, trailed off. Something about the way she held her head suggested she was seeing footage from this memory but could no longer assimilate it, or no longer wanted to share it. It wasn't clear what the point of the story was. Maybe just the feeling of intense loneliness—being twelve, her father dead, her mother far away. The feeling of being abandoned.

Then, something clicked, and she started talking again. Her tone changed. She tried to redeem the story. "My mom came home tan. She seemed happy. She had a great experience."

I found this coda depressing, a whitewash. *Just say it was awful!* I wanted to say. *You don't have to blame her. But don't try and make it sunny. Trying to make it all OK makes it even more sad.* Of course, I did not say this.

Instead, I had the horrifying thought that something had happened to my mother. A terrible image now entered my thoughts, my mother lying on the floor. I let it go. I was being silly. The woman's story had just hit me the wrong way, in a vulnerable moment. Which is how Houdini died.

Sunday morning, I called. I got the machine. Is there anything more chilling than a voice on an answering machine belonging to someone about whom you are worried? That naive, innocent voice that could not know, when it was speaking these recorded words, about all that has since transpired?

The relevant detail I have omitted, somehow, is that a year earlier my mother had a fall. Broke her hip badly. The feeling of visiting one's mother in the hospital, or one's parent, is very particular. Seeing her asleep. Nearly beatific. The confusing sensation of vertigo—the thing you have dreaded now having happened at last. You are in a hospital, there are machines hooked up to your mother, making beeping noises.

These images came back to me that Sunday morning while the answering machine asked me to leave a brief message. I did not leave a message. Instead, I hurriedly accessed her computer. There was that familiar room. The still-photograph-like livestream of her study. A lovely morning light came in. The chairs were askance, in conversation with one another. Papers piled on the desk. The ambiguous sense that life had been here a moment earlier. Or that death had. I was in full melodrama mode now. *I should have called last night!* I thought.

I called the neighbors, then the doorman. A full-on panic attack. The neighbors were out. "I'll go up and check," the doorman said. "But someone just left with their dog. I have to wait till they come back."

"Who? Which dog?" I wanted to ask. "Who gives a shit about the dog walker!" I wanted to yell, "Get upstairs!"

I needn't spell out the sort of scene I pictured, having crossed the line of panic. Your mother is a thousand miles away. You are streaming footage of sunshine falling beautifully into her study. Its layered topography is a complex map of past and present. It is, in a way, a map of her mind, and only her mind can navigate its meaning. Surely, she is just out of the frame, lying on the floor.

"Give me a few minutes," said the doorman. I got off the phone. I gave him a few minutes. I pictured a dog squatting. I rooted for the dog to hurry up. I didn't even know which dog. Was it the lab that belongs to David, on 4? Or was it Judy's geriatric dachshund, Willow?

I called back.

"I rang the doorbell," he said. "No one was there."

That's because my mother is lying dead on the floor! I refrained from shouting.

I was starting to panic. It was a feeling I sometimes had in the years just after my father died. The feeling that my mother could be anywhere that exists alongside a certainty that I am being silly. The dialogue between the two ideas: "Horror horror horror!" says one, and the other says, "Oh for goodness sakes, take it easy." The part of the apartment that most frightened me when I returned to find it dark and empty was the space under the piano. I thought there might be a monster of some kind down there. This is where, for many years, the Olivetti had lived.

The doorman went on with what he was saying. "I just saw that there were a few newspapers on her front door."

Newspapers piled at the door generally means only one thing: The resident in question is taking a trip. To the country, to the moon, to Long Island. Somewhere. And it hit me: A week earlier I had been in that room. I sat at that computer and helped my mother buy train tickets to Boston.

A joy rose within me. I thanked Andrew the doorman. I got off the phone. I paced in circles. What an idiot I had been. I nearly cried with relief. Then another thought entered. She had recently had shoulder surgery. Arm in a sling. Not a good time to travel to New Orleans for Thanksgiving, we had decided.

I went into the kitchen where Elizabeth and the children sat.

"I'm an idiot!" I yelled joyously, and then I told the whole story.

"If she can take a train to Boston," Elizabeth said, "why can't she fly to New Orleans?"

"That's a good point!" I grabbed Alexander, eighteen months, and shot a brief and rather castigating video which I emailed my mother posing just this question.

She got home late Sunday afternoon and called. We laughed about it. But then I said, "Seriously, you should come down here and visit us!"

What I meant, though, as I think she knew, was, *I thought you died! I need to see you!*

We agreed to mull it over. Monday morning I called and pressed the point. She was coming around to the idea. I looked into airfares. JetBlue, no fools, will kill you for flying on the Wednesday before Thanksgiving. And so we bought the cheapest available flight. Tuesday at dawn. I handled the tech, making all the arrangements. That night she packed. The next day she would arrive.

While she traveled I imagined our Thanksgiving Day. I would gather my whole family—wife, kids, mother—and log on to her computer to start a video chat. There on the screen would be the moving picture of that still room. We would all watch the stillness of her study, and the light, together. And give thanks.

The Pink Comma

Friday night home game. It starts at seven. We don't leave the house until 7:15. The drive is about two minutes through the fascinating darkness of New Orleans—fascinating because it is so very, very dark, in spite of the streetlamps. I find a parking place a couple of blocks away from the school.

"What are you doing!" Evangeline practically screams.

"I'm parking, sweetie."

"We're so far away! You cannot park here!"

"It's not like we can just drive right up to the entrance and park," I say.

"Why not?"

"Because you can't just drive up to a football game and park in front of it," I say.

"But Daddy! Don't park here, we are so far away!"

The childish force with which she expresses her wishes offends me on terms I recognize as childish. I don't want to be told what to do, and especially not by a very bossy six-year-old. But this is exactly how kids feel all the time, I think. So I collect the scattered indignations that are flying around my head and pull out of the parking space where I just parked. A life of parking in Manhattan has made me very reluctant to give up a good spot in the hopes of finding a better one. I drive for half a block, see another spot, pull in.

"Daddy! Why are you parking so far away!" she says. "We are going to miss the whole game!"

I jump out of the car, nearly rip the back door off the hinge in opening it, and confront the little tyrant strapped into her pink booster seat, wearing her pink pants, and her white shirt, and blonde hair, my furious little lollipop of a daughter. "Listen," I say. "Listen. You can hear the announcer from the game. You can hear him. That is how close we are. What is your problem?"

She unstraps herself and steps out into the dark street, ignoring my outstretched hand.

"Just because we can hear it doesn't mean we are close!"

We start walking. She refuses to hold my hand, which is reasonable since it's the sidewalk and the rule is she only has to hold hands crossing the street, but I insist, harshly, a bellicose, furious dad insulted that his magnanimous act of taking his six-year-old to a high school football game is going unappreciated. It faintly crosses my mind that there might be someone sitting in silence on their darkened porch hearing this harsh father-daughter music.

"Can we run?" she asks.

"No."

"Can we speed walk?"

We speed walk past about twenty free parking spaces, including several that are within a block of the game. I hate it when she is having a fit and making sense at the same time. She says nothing.

When we arrive, I stop at the gate to pay the eight dollars for my ticket. Kids get in free. She runs ahead, into the enormous circle of light.

"Hey!" I yell. "Hey!"

I catch up with her at the edge of the field; she is suddenly bashful and gnawing on a finger.

"What's the score, Daddy? Who's winning?"

"It's on the sign over there," I say, pointing to the scoreboard at the far corner of the field. "You read it."

"22–0," she says. "But who is winning?"

"We're winning."

She is elated. From where does all this come?

Evangeline had asked to go to a game two weeks ago, and I took them. I kept Alexander on my hip and let her roam around. The next two weeks the team had away games. I was not about to travel all over New Orleans to attend high school football games for the school at which she is a first grader.

Now I looked over to the metal bleachers, full of parents and kids I had never seen. This was the world of high school.

By the standards of serious high school football the crowd was small. The field itself was the same rectangle of brightly lit green as in any game, and we were all very close to it, and it was this proximity, I was sure, that was part of the attraction. You could stand at the end of the track that surrounded the field. Masses of cheerleaders stood on the track and faced the stands.

"I want to go to the football game!" Alexander had said earlier, following us to the door. He said it in his semi-intelligible, two-year-old way, his voice lamenting the exclusion. I tell him he needs his rest, which is a ridiculous thing to say to a two-year-old, but I felt the need to say something. I felt bad for him. But it was exciting to be off on an adventure with my daughter.

We are not a football family. We had been part of the drama of 2010, watching the Conference Championships and then Superbowl on a borrowed TV. When the Saints won we cheered like we were long-time fans and ran out into the street. There was a bar on the corner of our otherwise quiet Uptown neighborhood, and we rushed over there, me, Elizabeth, and Evangeline, who was two years old. I count the scene outside the bar on the corner of State and Magazine as one of my foundational New Orleans experiences, the crowd on the sidewalk delirious. It was a cold night, and I put Evangeline inside my coat and zipped it up, just her head sticking out. I did this for purposes of warmth but also because it was a rowdy scene and this was my way of protecting her, putting her in this papoose. In the first moments after the game ended, a city bus came down Magazine Street, a box of bright light on an otherwise dark street. It came to a stop on the corner. The driver emerged, the bus still running, and rushed over to shake everyone's hand, as though we had all had a baby together. Then he got back into that box of light and rolled down Magazine Street. For all I knew there were such gatherings all along his route and he stopped to shake the hand of every celebrant.

I saved the newspaper the next day, but I am as detached from the Sunday afternoon football ritual as I am from the Sunday morning ones commemorated by church bells all over town. In New Orleans the streets go silent on Sundays when the Saints play. But we have never really gotten on board.

But who knows, maybe the night the Saints won it all was a formative experience. Now, almost four years later, she is interested in football games. But then surely football itself is the least of it. Her school is pretty good, but it's not a cult-of-football sort of school, and the stands are filled with a couple hundred people, parents and kids. Off to the side is a little table with refreshments. There is some grass where kids run around. And a track that circles the field. And then the lights, the cheerleaders. There is hip-hop and the playing and sound of the announcer echoing across the field and the very bright lights on the grass, reflecting off the helmets. The players are abstract, even at this close proximity, but you can hear the beating-hooves sound of them all running at once, followed by the crumpling sound of a tackle. The cheerleaders come out.

Evangeline is so keen to be independent. She wants to enter all this and pretend she is a part of it, not just a little kid. We find a place on the crowded little bleachers and she says, "I don't want to sit next to you."

"Too bad," I said. But then I couldn't help but add, "Why not?"

She shrugged. But I knew. All these kids. Older kids. A kind of public forum. I remembered the adrenalin such night events gave me as a little kid. The wish to be able to see and experience it on my own, untethered. I made some rules to which she agreed—she could never leave my sight without asking for my permission. She agreed and for the whole night she abided by it. But she kept expanding her parameters. At one point she wanted to go visit the opposite side of the field. We walked over. I talked to a lady standing and cheering.

"That's my boy out there, number 35!"

"Congratulations!" I said. A minute later I watched as number 35 was run over by a stampede. She seemed unfazed.

When we got back to the home bleachers, Evangeline sat a few rows ahead of me. Now and then she looked back. Our interactions were curiously formal, as though both of us were a bit self-conscious. I barked commands at her now and then but mostly let her have her desired five feet of space. At the same time, she was unusually compliant, as though the chaos of it all reminded her why it might be useful to have a father around.

Then she asked if she could walk to the other side on her own. I agreed. She set off along the curve of the track. She was wearing pink shorts, so it was easy to keep my eyes on her. By the time she got halfway to the other side she was a very small little dot of pink. I watched her arrive on the far side of the field, walk around, ogle the cheerleaders. I kept my eyes on her the whole time. It was an enclosed space, fenced in. Very limited downside. But it felt strange.

When I think of it now I can't get over how I was aware of her most acutely when I let her move away from me. When all my attention and focus was on that pink dot getting smaller and smaller and then getting bigger and bigger as she returned.

By the end of the night she had made several of these expeditions, each time coming back to sit near me but not next to me. She had done very well, all in all, except one time when she was blatantly staring at an older girl as she was preparing to eat a hamburger. I summoned her to my side, a few rows up in the bleachers.

"Do not stare at someone when they are eating their food," I said forcefully. "It's rude. And it's not a good look."

She nodded gravely, signaling that she had absorbed this profound lesson, and went back to her spot. I sat there thinking, "Not a good look? Who says this to a six-year-old?"

During one of her solo expeditions I snapped a picture and sent it to my mother with a note, "Find your granddaughter."

The next morning she wrote me back:

> But of course. My favorite girl is the pink dot running at the far side of the field (it looks like a fence. Is it?). The energy, and the exuberance. Everybody else there is stationary, standing, or sitting.
>
> Most recognizable.
>
> Very alive picture. Beautiful with lighted area and people framed with the night's darkness. It makes me think of "The Bad Bears" movie. (Nostalgic). Someone's red jacket is perfect, reminds me of a van Gogh painting with one red flower in an open field. (It's a Football game, judging from the helmets?)
>
> Thanks for this unusual beautiful picture (with the running pink dot).

Needless to say, my mother is not a sports person. What struck me about her note was the idea of the pink dot. It also evoked a comment by Reiner Kunze, a German poet who was persecuted and thrown in jail by the East German government for a subversive poem. The poem that was deemed subversive is about the author seeing his wife return home in the afternoon to the rather drab row of houses where they live. She is wearing a blue raincoat. He sees her from a distance and notes that the blue raincoat, and the person in it, is what gives the whole picture meaning.

The poem in its entirety:

TO YOU IN THE BLUE COAT

I read again from the beginning

the row of houses

searching for you

the blue comma,

the one that lends meaning.

The East German government felt threatened by this assertion that an individual is what gives meaning, and put him in jail. Kunze tells this story in *The Burning Wall*, my mother's film that starts with the idealists in East Germany who hoped to build a better country from the ashes of the Nazi era and World War II which then evolves into the East German police state. When my mother mentioned the pink dot, I immediately thought of the blue comma. Evangeline on the track, running, was a pink comma, the punctuation that gave the whole scene meaning.

How I Found My iPhone in New Orleans

I was smiling as my iPhone was being robbed. They were kids. A group of eight or maybe ten little boys on bicycles, some of them riding handlebars or standing on rear axles. To call them "black males," as the police later did, is a bit absurd, though factually correct.

I was standing in a suit and a tie on the Tulane campus, having my picture taken to go along with an article in the *Wall Street Journal* on my tech habits, of all things, when I noticed this little gang of youth ride through the quad on bicycles, pause for a moment in front of a bench, and then continue on. I was, at that moment, preoccupied with the exhausting argument I always have with myself when getting my picture taken about whether or not to smile. I would rather not. But the photographers always want you to. When I was younger, I fought them off, but I have grown weak-willed in recent years and, to the detriment of certain pictures, have started to oblige.

When I got back to the bench I saw my wallet and keys, but my iPhone 4s was gone, so I raced back to my apartment, with the photographer in tow. He snapped pictures while I checked the find-my-phone app on my computer to see if it would turn up. But the phone wasn't online.

"Could they possibly know how to disable it?" I said. "They were like nine years old! Maybe they just threw it in the lake in Audubon Park."

I used Elizabeth's phone to call AT&T and file an insurance claim. Alexander, age one, came over to the computer and banged on the keyboard in a concentrating-gorilla sort of way that I assume he has learned from me. I sat there, disconsolate, trying to enjoy my child's playing, and entered the philosophical mode of the robbed: Everyone is all right, I told myself. It's just a thing.

Going through voicemail prompts of AT&T's phone interface was almost as bad as having a phone stolen. I was being subjected to a form of gratuitous torture that had been engineered, no doubt, because some consultant calculated that if you make it sufficiently unpleasant,

X percent of people will be dissuaded from even filing a claim. I was not one of X percent and filed my claim. The deductible was 199 dollars.

Then I glanced at the computer and saw the phone icon drifting along pleasantly on the map. "There it is!" I yelled. "Moving at about the speed of a bicycle."

I went after the phone. But first I changed out of my suit and into khakis, high-tops, and a Knicks T-shirt while Elizabeth implored me to be careful.

"Call the police," she said. "Don't do anything crazy."

The photographer agreed and said I should let the police handle it.

"OK," I said on my way out. "But why?"

"You don't want to put yourself in a bad position," he said.

"What do you mean by 'a bad position'?"

"You just want an official third-party witness in case something weird happens," he said.

I sped down St. Charles Avenue on my Vespa, Elizabeth's iPhone in hand, feeling elated at the prospect of getting my own phone back. I pulled over a couple of times to make sure the little phone icon was still on the map. It was.

It was joyous. To be free of the deadening experience of filing an insurance claim. To be back in the real world of action, people, crime, redemption. To be in pursuit.

I really did not want the police to be involved. These kids were very young. Nine-year-old delinquents I could manage on my own. I had left my wallet, keys, and a phone out on a bench in broad daylight, after all; if the ten-year-old version of me had biked by with some friends, I may well have snatched one or all of these things, too. My ten-year-old crimes, it should be said, had mostly involved shoplifting junk food—the Suzy Q being a preferred item, along with Yodels—but the sentiment behind a theft like this, as much as it is explicitly about some material gain, is also the deep wish of all kids to not be bored, to have some caper, some project, some agency of revenge against the world.

I zigzagged past the familiar stretch of Oak Street, its cafés and shops, and back into a more derelict but still perfectly nice area, drawing closer to the phone icon displayed on the map. The phone icon stopped moving. The thieves had returned to their den.

I arrived at an empty corner lot. There was a guy across the street on the phone—I peered at it to see if it was mine, but it was a clamshell. Other than that, I was alone. A grid of piers sat in the grass, little white platforms forming a curious grid on which a house had once stood. I used the satellite feature on the find-my-phone app. It was remarkably precise. My phone was located in the rear left corner of this grid, next to a white house that, to judge from the overstuffed mailbox, was empty. There was a mop leaning outside near the front door. All the blinds had been pulled shut.

I spent a fair amount of time searching in the grass, calling my phone. I looked under the white house, which was raised, and listened for the sound of ringing. It was by now a sweltering New Orleans noon, and the neighborhood was silent. Even the man on the phone had gone away.

Then I was startled by the sound of the phone in my hand ringing—Elizabeth calling her own phone to check up on me. "It's either in this field," I reported, "or under this house, or in the house. I am thinking of knocking on the door."

"Do *not* knock on the door!" she yelled. "Oh my God, you're going to get yourself shot."

"I am not going to get shot," I said.

"Promise me you won't knock on the door."

I promised.

She told me she had updated the police on the location, which she had been monitoring on the computer. I got off the phone and consulted the map again. The phone icon had shifted a little. It was at the back row of the grid. I walked around staring at grass. I called the phone. There was a derelict fence, on the other side of which was a very run-down house, apparently abandoned. A perfect place for young kids to make into a clubhouse. Or a crack house. Could go either way. I called the phone again. I paced back and forth along the fence. I yearned to hear that familiar sound and yet, as hard as I listened, it would not materialize.

Then I heard it. Very faint, but unmistakable. There is nothing else in an abandoned lot that sounds like a ringing iPhone (ringtone: Marimba).

I had to call a few more times before I found it, carefully hidden within a little pile of bricks.

I called Elizabeth to tell her. The phone in my other hand began to ring. She had called me using Skype, I realized, as we no longer had a landline. Standing there in the silent alley between an abandoned house and a field filled with vestigial piers, a phone in either hand, I was elated.

I savored the triumph for a moment. Then it occurred to me to replace the phone I'd just retrieved with a copy of *Huckleberry Finn*. You could see the levee of the Mississippi River from that corner. And there was something about the pile of bricks that was redolent of that book. *Huckleberry Finn* is the book those kids should read, I thought. I knew of a used bookstore on Oak Street. I rushed off on my Vespa.

A block away, crouched in another vacant lot, I saw the band of thieves. They appeared to be in conference. One of them was rushing off somewhere in an agitated state. Ah, I thought, excitement about the bounty. What to do with it. How to divide the spoils. My Huck Finn errand was not entirely philanthropic—I liked the idea of them coming upon their treasure transmogrified into a book, their momentary distress and disgust transmogrified into lasting wonder. But I also thought it might stave off any intragroup recriminations—suspicions that one of the gang had made an unauthorized withdrawal—if I replaced the phone with something else.

The good news was that Blue Cypress Books had several copies of *Huckleberry Finn*. The bad news was that I had no money to pay for it. The much worse news, from my point of view, was the realization that I had been carrying several hundred dollars in cash in my wallet, and that had been stolen, too. Now in a state of shock and real distress, I nevertheless persisted in my Huck Finn errand, though I had to explain everything to the woman behind the counter because I needed her to give me the book on credit. I suppose I was a bit frantic, which did not help her in grasping the finer points of the situation.

"Why don't you just have the brats arrested?" she said.

I looked at her exasperated and said, "Because these kids need *Huckleberry Finn!*"

I finally persuaded her to part with the $2.50 used paperback by letting her hold every piece of ID I had, though I held on to my driver's license. At the last moment, I borrowed a pen and inscribed the book to the thieves.

I raced back to the vacant lot. They were gone. I walked around, kicking at the weeds and grass. There was a decrepit shack at the rear of the lot and some broken-up bricks next to it. I commenced a small-scale archaeological dig in full view of a bunch of folks sitting on a stoop across the street and various passersby. I was hoping the kids had stashed the cash in the same manner and spirit that they stashed the phone. But there were many broken bricks. You can't have GPS for cash, I thought to myself. Still, I persisted for some time, unwilling to accept that my initial loss and recovery had been only a prelude to the real loss of all that cash. Finally I picked up a brick that revealed a horde of ants teeming beneath.

I went to the alley where the phone had been, found the bricks, and slid in my copy of *Huckleberry Finn*. Then I remade the stack. And that should have been the end of it.

But then I bumped into a police cruiser a block away and flagged it down. There was a young guy with wraparound shades at the wheel, and next to him an older guy, a seasoned, doughnut-eating sort of guy. The two officers were responding to Elizabeth's call, it turns out.

They listened expressionlessly to the story before responding. Shades did the talking. Doughnuts said nothing. I took them to the alley. Then we drove around for a while looking for the gang, me in front, a big white guy in a Knicks T-shirt on a black Vespa followed by a squad car. I was ready to give up, but they said a detective was on his way.

"I feel like I'm wasting resources here," I said. "If it was a phone, you never know. But trying to find cash out here is just a lost cause."

"I don't think you know where you are," said Doughnuts, his first words to me. "People get shot back here."

I took this in. They took a complaint. I gave them my driver's license.

The detective arrived. Young, in a polo shirt, driving a gray unmarked Mercury with a squawk box on the dash. He got out and talked at length to the officers while I loitered on the corner, at first in the sun, then the shade. The vacant lot where the kids had been crouched was a block away. A yellow house was across the street. A pretty color. A sign said Car Wash out front. I didn't see any cars.

Then it occurred to me to look into what was happening with the cops. I found them standing in the alley next to the vacant clubhouse, arranged like a trio of angels, with the detective in the middle, holding *Huckleberry Finn* in his hand and reading from it. Not Mark Twain's words, but mine, the ones I had inscribed in the kids' edition. The two uniformed officers looked down at the book while he spoke the words, "I forgive you."

He didn't read the next line, which was, "Now read this book."

In fairness to them all, he did not read this with facetiousness or mockery. He didn't have to. My presence noted at that moment, I was aware of experiencing a humiliation of such intensity it was almost cathartic. "Sir," the detective said, "could you please step away and wait for us to come talk to you."

I waited on the corner. A few minutes later the detective arrived, and I went over the story again. For some reason it was hard for the detective to grasp the concept that I had left my possessions on a bench on the Tulane quad and a bunch of kids on bikes rode by, swiped it, and then hid the phone in another neighborhood, which I then found using GPS, and replaced with a very famous Mark Twain novel—all totally reasonable and plausible to my ears. It was as though I had been speaking Esperanto to the bookstore lady, the cops, and now this detective.

"The thing is," the detective said, "there are some unspoken boundaries about where people in this part of town go and don't go. They're usually observed, not always, but usually. And Tulane is pretty far away."

"Not that far if you're on a bike," I said.

"Here's the thing," the detective said. "If there was anything you were doing, or buying, or trying to buy out here that I should know about, now would be a good time to tell me."

I blinked at him, absorbing this twist.

"I can assure you," I said, "that the dynamic you are suggesting plays no role whatsoever in this situation, and I can bring forth all sorts of evidence to back that up."

He looked at me, cocked his head a little. "It's my experience that the longer and more convoluted someone's answer is, the less likely I am to believe them. And that was pretty convoluted."

I looked off in the distance, sighed, and said, "Then how about: no."

"Tulane has just about everything on that campus on video. And if what you are telling me does not match up with the video . . ."

"Well, then, you know where to find me."

Elizabeth called while he conferred with the other cops. "There's been a complication," I told her.

"What kind of complication?" she said.

"It seems I might be a suspect."

I borrowed three dollars from Charlie, the piano player at the Oak Street Café, and got my stuff out of hock from the bookstore, though not before one last session of kicking bricks around in the empty lot, hoping to find my cash. This was interrupted by the squad car, passenger window down, Doughnuts smiling broadly at me.

"Hey, you forgot one thing," he said, and held out my driver's license.

I went back to the alley where I found my phone the following morning, just after dawn. The neighborhood, I had learned, was called Pigeon Town. I wanted to know what became of my copy of *Huckleberry Finn*. I found it lying in the grass. The cops had dropped it where they stood. I dusted it off, carefully rebuilt the stack of bricks, and slid it into place, covering it up.

Later that morning, at breakfast, Evangeline pulled up the short movie I had shot with Elizabeth's phone in the first moments after I found my phone under the bricks. I had forgotten about it, and froze, not sure what to do or say now, while the phone panned from the pile of bricks to the abandoned house and back as I babbled elatedly about finding the phone. Evangeline was at first absorbed, and gradually became quite pleased. Then she asked, "Daddy, did some kids hide your phone?"

The Two-Thousand-Dollar Popsicle

The guy who owned the house on Calhoun Street that we had sublet had been out of town while we were there, tending to his triplets, and our correspondence had the comradely tone of people dealing with little children and the general chaos of life. But then, two weeks after we left, he popped up with a new tone. There was a problem. It involved the long, white couch in the living room. Apparently, the cleaners had found an exploded Popsicle underneath the cushion. "Still in the wrapper, with the stick in it," he wrote to Elizabeth.

He sent pictures. The Popsicle was red.

Replacing the slipcover cost two thousand dollars. Could we please send a check?

I somersaulted into a state of grief. If you have little children and find yourself subletting a place that has a long, white, linen-covered couch, you should throw sheets on it. This is obvious. And yet we did not take these precautions. Why not?

I lamented this oversight for about one second before moving on to the real issue, which was much darker—it was my fault. I have a weakness, indulged only occasionally, for sugar-free Popsicles. I like them in combination with NBA basketball. I had watched the playoffs during that month in his house, and once—*once!*—had bought a box of these Popsicles. I must have let one slide down between the cushions. Then, at some impossible-to-determine point, an hour or a week later, while we were innocently going about our lives, a silent bomb exploded and incinerated two thousand dollars.

Our life in the sublet had been mostly happy. The house was located on a prim, pretty street in New Orleans right next to Audubon Park. Sometimes, in the morning, I would stroll out into the heat shirtless, my baby boy on my hip wearing a diaper and nothing more. In the park, with its birds, water, and sweating joggers, we fit right in. I rejoiced in the feel of his skin on mine, in the smiles his baby fat elicited. But now, hearing of the Popsicle, this indiscreet shirtlessness felt like a rationalization for being a slob.

Part of the horror of the two-thousand-dollar Popsicle was, naturally, the money itself. But another part was the fact that, in my marriage, Elizabeth is the neat, fastidious one worried about germs, while I am the easygoing one who doesn't mind a little dirt. She finds this tiring. And now this.

"I try and keep this family organized and in one piece," she said, despairing.

"Let me handle this," I said. I had made a mess, I would clean it up. I wrote the guy an email asking him to call me.

He called Elizabeth instead.

We were in a kids' shoe store when his name came up on her ringing phone.

It was a hot afternoon in New York. I stepped out onto Broadway. Elizabeth had dropped her phone a week earlier and the glass had badly cracked. She was now keeping it in a Ziploc bag.

"I'd like to discuss a way of setting things straight with your couch that doesn't involve two thousand dollars," I said, pressing the sandwich bag to the side of my face.

His voice was terse, clipped, annoyed. We had "treated the marble countertops like a chopping block," he said. (I recalled Elizabeth saying, "You can't use a knife on marble," to which I responded, "It's stone! What can a knife do?") "But I don't want to deal with that," he continued. "All I want is the couch the way it was. It was brand new."

"Two thousand dollars is a lot for a slipcover," I said.

"There's actually a one-day sale today at Restoration Hardware: 10 percent off. So it's eighteen hundred."

"Can it be cleaned?"

"It's a red Popsicle stain," the guy reminded me. "Look, you can just not pay this. I suppose you could just, like, walk away and . . ." It was hard to hear him through the bag. "It's up to you," he concluded.

"Let's be clear," I said, adopting as majestic a tone as is possible while talking into a sandwich bag. "I'm not going to say, 'To hell with you, I'm gone, you can keep my deposit but there's nothing else you can get out of me, and if you want to sue me, be my guest.'

"I'm not going to do that. I just want to explore what the options are. Two thousand dollars is a lot of money."

Even as I said this, though, I thought of the white linen chairs, which had also suffered. He did not bring these up.

I told him I would send him a check.

Inside the store, Elizabeth had picked out the shoes. Alexander, a size five just six weeks earlier, was now a size seven. Several sales ladies cooed at him, to which he offered only a long, cold stare. Then he walked away, pausing only to look back over his shoulder and blow them all a kiss. It elicited an uproar of swoons.

Evangeline, meanwhile, presented me with her choice: a pair of pink cowboy boots studded with rhinestones.

"No," I said reflexively.

"But Daddy!"

New summer shoes. One pair for each kid. The Popsicle, I calculated, could have bought them twenty pairs each.

Afterward we stood on Broadway, at a loss, literally. Evangeline held the pink balloon she had been given, to her delight, and asked me to tie it to the stroller so it wouldn't fly away. I did this, making it extra tight. One had to hold on to whatever assets remained.

We walked to Central Park, and on the way stopped at a grocery to buy a bottle of lemonade and some sliced melon. Ten dollars, almost. I did the Popsicle math.

I had a rubber ball in my pocket. I'd bought it with Evangeline the day before. (The Popsicle, I calculated, would buy sixteen hundred of them.) I bounced the ball as I walked with Alexander on my hip. He made one of his little squeaking noises, some kind of bird sound that connotes interest, and held out his hand. I gave him the ball. He bounced it on the sidewalk. He didn't merely drop it. He threw it! It bounced hard on the ground and high in the air. I caught it. This was a delightful development. Teaching my children to play catch had been extremely high on my parental agenda.

We took turns throwing. It was heaven. Except, (1) every second or third time I gave him the ball to throw he would bring the filthy rubber thing directly to his mouth, and (2) the boy's father had just incinerated two thousand dollars in an act of sloth and stupidity. This ball, these shoes, they would have to last.

The two-thousand-dollar Popsicle made a mockery of nearly every financial consideration of the summer: How much summer camp could we afford? Would we able to rent a place in the country for a week? Or a weekend? What about Whole Foods? Two thousand dollars was exactly the sort of sum I was protecting. And now it had flown out into the ether with my blessing, because I was being honorable to some stranger upset about his sofa's slipcover. I wondered if taking the high road and agreeing to pay for the stained slipcover was as much a form of sloth as the original offense itself, a cowardly shrinking away from a conflict at the expense of my family.

The air and light were lovely as we walked along Central Park West, munching on melon slices. At Columbus Avenue Elizabeth and I had a conference, mostly in glances, about the pink balloon. Evangeline loved balloons. Alexander did, too, which was a problem—he tried to eat them. Her face explained to me that it was a safety issue. Mine replied that the children love balloons. The girl and the boy ate melon abstractedly while their pleasure was weighed against their safety. The decision was easy. Elizabeth untied the knot I had made and let the balloon go.

"It's so hot it can barely go up," she remarked.

We watched it slowly rise as the children focused on their melon.

I struggled to remove the phone from my pocket. By now the balloon had gained altitude and was on the verge of drifting out of sight. I was frantic to take a picture of the departing balloon. This felt like the nadir of the Popsicle afternoon and for this reason I wanted to document it. I held the phone above my head and pointed to the sky, but instead of a blue sky with pink balloon, the screen was filled with images of my anguished, distraught face squinting upward. The camera had been set to reverse. My face looked Fellini-esque—that of someone from another time trapped in the modern world where no one can understand him, filled with personality to the point of being grotesque. I didn't take the picture.

My mother was home when we got back, and I told her about the Popsicle.

"A terrible waste," she said, and looked away, stricken, shaking her head. She has given us occasional gifts—for child care, things like that. The Popsicle mocked her magnanimity.

Elizabeth bathed Evangeline, and my mother played with Alexander while I got Restoration Hardware on the phone and on the computer. Between the two, I deduced that the entire nine-foot couch could be had for a thousand dollars more than the slipcover I had agreed to replace. For one second I was excited.

I pondered how Restoration Hardware had managed to insinuate the innocent-seeming sofa into an increasingly tricky business model by which the thing itself is cheap, but the parts you need for it are extremely pricey. This happens with printers and toner, with razors and razor blade cartridges. Now they'd found a way to do it with furniture—very reasonably priced, but if you stain the slipcover . . . look out.

Meanwhile, Evangeline had been very upset while getting a bath; she had wanted a big communal bath with Alexander like the one we took the other day. But she was too dirty, Elizabeth said, and her howls of despair floated down the hall, echoing how I felt. When we all sat down to dinner she was still teary eyed. I put a colander on my head and pretended to be a robot. Amazingly, this worked. She stopped crying, and soon she was laughing.

The storm had cleared, as far as Evangeline was concerned. Or so I thought. A few minutes later, as Elizabeth bounced Alexander on her knee and fed him tiny bits of broccoli, Evangeline looked at her fourteen-month-old brother and said, with crushing matter-of-factness, "I wish I had your life."

A flurry of distressed noises rose from me and Elizabeth. In short order the girl was sitting in her mother's lap and I had Alexander.

But after dinner, my mother said, "Thank God she said that."

"What do you mean?" I asked.

"Just that. Thank God she was finally able to say it. She's been feeling it for so long and acting up, and then finally she was able to find the words to express how she felt."

"You think that's a positive thing?"

"Yes. It was wonderful."

My daughter's words had felt like a dagger in my heart when I first heard them. Now my mother was reframing it as a gift. The depression about the Popsicle lifted a little. I glanced into the living room. There sat a lovely white couch, dignified, faintly nineteenth-century in its bearing, like much of my mother's furniture and, for that matter, like my mother herself. I redoubled my resolve to never let any food enter her living room.

On Finding a Spot

Parking in New York—it sends you to ecstasy or rips your heart out. Which is to say, it's a natural continuation of family life. I try to convince myself it is joyous because some of my happiest moments have come in connection with finding a good parking space. But it can also be hellacious. For this reason, parking the car is always an occasion of great suspense.

Take one recent summer evening, a Wednesday: We arrived in our neighborhood after an ambitious expedition to the Bronx, the kids' bedtime schedule by now in shambles. Alexander, age one, was already asleep, while Evangeline, age five, was experiencing the familiar (to me) elation of breaking past the usual boundary of bedtime. Coming down the Henry Hudson Parkway, we witnessed an awe-inspiring sunset, but our pleasure was dampened by the fact that Alexander would soon need to be woken and bathed. The only question was if Evangeline might still get to bed at a somewhat reasonable hour.

This would be determined by the parking.

As we approached our block a tremor of hope that a miracle would occur moved through us. I asked Elizabeth the usual question, like the riddle of the Sphinx: "Do you want to get out with the kids, or do you want to drive around with me looking for a spot?"

She is always conflicted about this. I don't blame her. In this sense I have it easy—I will park the car. It is a necessity. She is an excellent, if emotive, driver, but somehow this parking duty feels fatherly, hunter-gatherer, stoic—a task to be suffered alone. And so she must choose between herding the youth upstairs, to bathe them, dealing with this drama alone, or sitting on the banks of Hades watching corpses float by, which is what it feels like on the occasions that the parking expedition devolves into endless awfulness and you cannot find a spot. You start thinking that Sartre titles like *No Exit*, *Nausea*, and "What Is Literature?" are descriptive of your life, and why didn't Camus write a book called *The Parking*, which would sit well beside *The Plague*, *The Stranger*, et cetera?

On this night Elizabeth tried to split the difference, going around a few times with me in search of a miracle. And miracles do occur. You sometimes find a spot, and you sometimes find a great spot, and you even at times find a magnificent spot. But this was not one of those times. And so, after a few times around the block, she decided to get out and take the baby upstairs.

Evangeline stayed with me. She loves to look for parking with me. She tries to help, which is a bit tiresome, because she always sees lots of spots that are not, in fact, spots. It is left to me to introduce her to the cold realities of New York City parking. The dialogue sounds like this:

"Ooh! I see a spot."

"It's a hydrant."

"Ooh! I see a great spot right there!"

"Bus stop."

"I see a really good spot!"

"That's a crosswalk, sweetie. You can't park in a crosswalk."

"Ooh! Daddy! Right over there!"

"Hydrant."

And so it goes.

If I can't find a spot right away, I'll call the building and confer with whichever doorman is on duty. The doormen usually drive and have this magic ability to find spots, spots that are sometimes on "the good side," i.e., you don't have to move the car the next morning. Teddy had a good spot, he told me now, but he didn't get off until 11:30. Christian, a parking maestro, had already left: His shift ended at 7:30. There had been a moment, on our wandering on Arthur Avenue, when we considered sprinting to the car and trying to make it back in time for Christian to get off his shift. But this would have involved calling to see if he had a spot on the good side or the bad side, and if he had promised it to someone else. We were briefly embroiled in the question: Do you park to live? Or do you live to park?

In the end, I found a spot at a metered space, where I would leave it for a couple of hours before returning to do the Teddy switch at 11:30. But we didn't get out of the car. Not just yet.

Evangeline and I have a ritual once we have parked: She gets out of her booster seat and crawls into the front seat and we play rock, paper, scissors. Sometimes people walk by and look at us funny, sitting there doing things with our hands. It is, for some reason, a delicious thing. We're in our spot. The car is private, pleasant, ours. And then there is the game itself. For a long time it was the normal, familiar version. But recently we have moved on to a wild style variation.

"Rock, paper, scissors and . . ." we chant. Then, instead of the usual hand shapes representing each object, we throw shapes representing . . . anything.

"What's that?" she always asks first.

"A shark," I say. "What's that?"

"Mine is a gun! I win."

"But a gun can't fire underwater," I reply. "*I* win."

Hers are often quite creative.

"Rock, paper, scissors and . . ." we chant.

"What's that?" she says.

"A germ," I say. "What's that?"

"An antibody," she says. "I win."

In this way even the difficult, Hades-like expeditions to find parking can have a sweet closure.

My car has Louisiana plates, but when I am back in New York during the summer, visiting at my mother's, I drive like a New Yorker. I know the lights. The good avenues. I enter the topographical flow. Sometimes I consider the fact that there is, at any given moment, a precise number of cars with Louisiana plates moving through the streets of New York. I have no idea if the number is ten, or a hundred, or a thousand, but of all of them, I must be the driver most at home on these streets.

This extends to the logistics of parking, which take two fundamentally different forms: Sometimes you have actually gone somewhere, and it's time to park the car. Other times, you haven't gone anywhere, but have to abide by alternate side of the street parking rules, its own kind of journey.

Once I saw Mr. W, our downstairs neighbor, in the elevator. It was 9:28 a.m. We were both going down.

"Going to move your car?" I asked.

"Yes," he said glumly.

"I think it's a form of civilization," I said.

"Why?"

"It's a comforting ritual."

"That's one way of looking at it," he said, one eyebrow arched slightly.

On another occasion when we were in that same elevator for the same purpose, I announced to Mr. W that I kind of enjoyed the ritual of sitting in the car.

"Why?" he said.

"It's a kind of religion, alternate side of the street parking," I said.

"I'm an atheist," he replied.

Because my mother and I were, for a span of decades, in a kind of cold war with Mr. and Mrs. W, exchanges like these counted as warm encounters, the arched eyebrow tantamount to a bear hug. I have known Mr. W for almost my entire life, but I have only witnessed him in the confines of the elevator, the building lobby, or out in the wilds of our block, moving his car. I have seen him get out of his car to measure the distance from the curb, then get back in and wait, then a minute later before the appointed time get back out again looking up and down the block with his hands on his hips, wondering, even though he has done this twice a week for half a century, if it would be OK to leave a minute early. The traffic officers with their ticket pads, now scanners with little printers attached, do not just appear like fireflies beside you; they can be seen at a distance with their white hats, walking on pavement like any other mortal, and if no one can be seen, why not look up and down the block and go away now, with one minute to go? A minute is a valuable thing!

I know he has these thoughts partly because they are written on his face, and partly because I also have these thoughts.

Alternate side of the street parking has a circadian rhythm that enters the marrow of your soul. To have a good spot becomes a source of well-being, inducing feelings of rootedness. It's also a total waste of time, which is why sometimes I ask my mother to come sit in the car for me. I get the car situated, wait till the street sweeper has come and gone, and then call upstairs.

"Mom, I'm ready for you."

Whereupon she'll emerge from the lobby in a hat, a scarf, sunglasses, sometimes a coat, generally carrying a book or a newspaper.

"Mom," I'll say, "it's warm, you don't need all that."

"Just in case," she responds.

I open the car door to let her in. She is doing me a favor, after all, sitting here for an hour while I rush off on whatever errands. She sits in the driver's seat, key in the ignition, even though she doesn't really drive. It's a legality—if you want to avoid a ticket, you can't be just near your car or even in just the passenger seat.

Invariably, once I get her installed in the driver's seat, and am finally free to go, I instead go sit in the passenger seat. We talk there, in that curiously private space of a parked car. Sometimes we talk all the way until the no-parking window is closed and we are free to go. Sometimes well beyond. With a wife, and a kid, and now a baby, I don't really get this kind of sustained private time with my mom inside the apartment. It's an odd fact of our life: From the distance of New Orleans we have long phone conversations, exchange emails that bear a strong resemblance, in length and style of greeting, to letters. In the old life, where I lived in my own apartment in the same city, we would go a few weeks at a time without talking and then convene for a very long lunch.

During our summer visits, when I'm living in her apartment, our conversations are fleeting, and we tend to wave as though passing on the street; even at dinner, which we all have together most nights, we communicate mostly through glances.

At some point we will be back in New Orleans, where parking also elicits strong emotions, if for a very different reason: Everywhere you go, you can find parking. If you go to a restaurant, you drive your car and park. Sometimes right in front! Maybe you have to park a block away. On the other hand, people in New Orleans get very jumpy if you encroach on, or even just crowd, their driveway space. I respect this neurosis, because parking engenders a kind of insanity, as do cars in general.

I think this is because we have been encouraged to confuse a car with a home. We finance cars as we do our homes, and in some cases spend more waking hours in them. Cars represent a similar source of pride, too, which may be why, whenever circumstances allow, they tend to get bigger. Unlike a home, however, a car is just an agent of transition. Within a car's promise of exploration is also the fear (or pleasure) of being lost. Which is why I so enjoy parking in New York. However hard-won, what you get in the end is that wonderful feeling of having arrived.

Saying Goodbye to Now

1.

One recent day in New Orleans, as the sun began to hide behind clouds and the wind picked up in a way that reminded you, in spite of the warm temperature, that this was November and not the middle of summer, I walked with my family the two blocks to the Latter Library, an old converted mansion on St. Charles Avenue, the broad lawn of which cascades down to the cracked and undulating sidewalks at its perimeter.

The children, Evangeline, five years old, and Alexander, eighteen months, ambled onto the lawn. A streetcar rumbled by and Alexander turned to wave. Evangeline, having finished giving me the complicated instructions to her new game, ran to the top of the sloping lawn.

When she was little, I would throw her into the air, swing her around, and roughhouse with her. She is no longer little, yet her appetite for athletic playing has only increased. And so, without having understood a word of what she said, I knew that I had been cast as the strongman in the day's circus. I braced myself.

My daughter was now airborne, a flying monkey coming right at me, headfirst: straw-yellow hair, a blue skirt, blue spaghetti-strap shirt, apple cheeks, and lips garishly smudged with pink lip gloss within which is the whiteness of her bared teeth—

Stop! Right here, let's freeze the frame. Here is an image that I will never see again, save in my memory. A girl in midflight, waves of green behind her, her face all bright with the colors—blue, pink, yellow, white—of joy and delight, and behind her, as though it were a place she had just fled, the old, dignified mansion.

Right then, as she was airborne, my hand twitched and slapped my pocket in the dim hope that I could locate my camera, pull it out, and shoot while the moment still held. But there was no camera in the pocket, and anyway there was no time.

I will never forget this image, though I may already be embellishing it. And you will never see it. You may picture it, but the picture itself was not taken. I had to fight off a sadness about this, because the moment, after all, was happening, and it was beautiful, and anything that detracted from my perception of that was a shame.

2.

While on the phone with Apple tech support recently, I was told, "You are not a normal iPhoto user."

"I'm not?" I responded.

"No, you have many more photographs than the average user."

It was conspicuous, this comment, breaking as it did from the Zen-like calm with which the Apple customer-service representative goes about ascertaining a problem and then working to help fix it. Do I take more pictures than other people? I wondered. How could that be? More than other people with children?

I have always taken photos, but the volume increased when I got my first digital camera, in 2004. Then, a few years later, when Evangeline was born, it increased exponentially, and exponentially again when I got my first iPhone. When something notable or beautiful or just atmospheric unfolds in my family, I often reach for the phone and start tapping the camera icon, accumulating images.

I like action shots. I don't use a flash. A little blur is OK, so long as the flavor and mood of the light is there. I don't ask for poses; in fact, I actively discourage them. I still remember when my daughter, at the age of three or four, first displayed her fake camera smile. It was awful.

3.

The photojournalist Tim Page wrote a memoir, *Derailed in Uncle Ho's Victory Garden: Return to Vietnam and Cambodia*, that made a huge impression on me when I read it in Phnom Penh in 1996, a year after it was published. Page writes in a lighthearted, vaguely inebriated mode about working as a journalist in the region, stumbling with a kind of fated grace through all sorts of perils. It was the specificity of the scenes and the vividness with which he wrote about covering the Vietnam War that initially drew me in and kept me reading, but what has stayed with me is my recollection of a casual aside he made in an interview about how he wrote the book. The memoir's almost cinematic specificity was achieved, he said, by starting every writing session with an examination of his contact sheets from the era. He would peer at them through a loupe, and the images would serve as a prompt to his memory.

There was a simple logic to this that held huge appeal to me. Being a professional photojournalist, Page had taken Christopher Isherwood's famous opening gambit in *The Berlin Stories*—"I am a camera"—and made it literal. Having contact sheets for all sorts of episodes in your life seemed to me both intriguing and desirable. So much of my own history is beclouded by time, but a few sharp rays, in the form of pictures, falling upon a given day, may resuscitate whole contexts. And from this archipelago of moments, scenes, episodes, if you are lucky, you can see the larger tectonic movements of your life forming and reforming to be reminded of who you are. Or at least of who you *were*.

In 1996, this condition was the luxury of professional photographers, with their rolls of film and endless contact sheets. We are now all Tim Page. Or, at least, we have contact sheets. At least, all of us who snap streams of images as though they were jelly beans being scooped into one's hand. But a jelly bean in the hand makes sense, at least so long as you eat it. What would you say about a person who collected jelly beans simply to collect them?

4.

It has occurred to me that this picture taking might in some ways be an excuse to touch and pet and hold the iPhone itself, which has a weirdly calming effect on people, as though it were an amulet. I am guilty of all the smartphone sins, which come down to the same original smartphone sin: staring at the phone when you should be staring at life. It's possible that the act of taking a picture has such appeal because it manages to do several opposing things at once—to pet the phone, to let the phone flatter me with its news, to let the phone mediate reality for me, to bear witness to any given moment in my children's lives, even if I am technically seeing it on-screen. To mitigate this, I often shoot blind, looking past the phone, or just quickly, like a glance.

Am I deceiving myself? Because if you are taking a picture of your children, which is to say if you are holding a camera (in the form of a phone) and snapping a picture, then are you, in that moment, looking at them? Or are you simply anticipating a moment in the future—ten seconds or ten years—when you will be looking at this very moment?

Sorting through the glut of images, I notice that the ones that seem valuable change with time. What seems like the best shot of the group a day later is often different from what seems most beautiful, or moving, a year or more later. Perusing these images you become a detective looking for patterns that you did not even know to look for at the time.

5.

As we walk back from the library, I think of another moment, from a few months earlier, that lives in my memory with no assistance from iPhoto.

We were at the beach. They had opened the cut between the bay and the ocean. A strong tide rushed out to meet the incoming waves. A group of kids and parents stood on a sandbar, balancing in the current rushing past their calves, knees, or, in the case of the smaller kids like Evangeline, thighs. She stood a few feet ahead of me, facing the horizon, looking for big waves, screaming and jumping up as they passed, stealing glances at the older kids around her, playing it cool while I stood behind her and regarded the horizon with panic.

Nothing to be afraid of, I told myself. Shallow little waves. Many other kids. It was scary but safe. And yet, at her own insistence, she was on her own—if within arm's reach—jumping, shouting, even getting tumbled underneath once or twice. Little silvery minnows went by at our feet. There was the feeling of hugeness. The blue-green of the water. Crashing-wave sounds. A few steps to the left, the sandbar gave way and the water was darker. When I stepped there, it was icy cold and up to my waist.

The baby, Alexander, and Elizabeth were up on the beach where the waves thinned to a hiss and receded—I would turn now and then to see Elizabeth holding him as he looked down to watch the white froth run over his feet. Evangeline was hopping from foot to foot like a boxer, waiting for the next wave. The silver minnows in their tight formation darting around our knees seemed to me like some pious team of nuns, or saints, doing last rites. Of course, I had no phone, I was in the ocean. And later, on the beach, in our towels at last, I discovered that the batteries of our phones had died.

All of this exists in my memory and nowhere else. The clarity of each silvery minnow in the ocean, or the boy's head outlined against the bright blue sky as he brings a chip to his mouth beneath the umbrella. About them all I must ask: Are they any more vivid to me because there are no photographs? Conversely, would photographing have taken me away and made it all less sharp in my mind?

It's an era of detoxification, controlled deprivations, of fasts and cleanses. Perhaps everyone should make a weekly ritual of twenty-four hours of undocumented life. Periods of time in which memory must do all the heavy lifting—or none of it, as it chooses, the consequences being what they may be. No phone, no eclipse glasses to mitigate the intensity of what lies before you. The only options are appetite, experience, memory, and later, should one be so inclined, writing it down.

My wish for visual souvenirs slaps against the clarity of those memories for which I don't have pictures and yet remember, because I have to, in the way that two currents of water slap against each other in the ocean.

Such crosscurrents, I am told, are a sign of a riptide, which is what I had most feared while standing with Evangeline in the ocean—that she would be swept off by a cold current to a place I couldn't reach. That she would be taken away. She seemed to recognize this potential, too, and wanted me near, just not too near. It was important that I be behind her as well, not in front or even beside her, so her view of the horizon could remain unimpeded. We were practicing for something, some kind of independence from each other.

Remembrance of Snows Past

1.

With one exception, my memories of snow all start around the age of thirteen and the great blizzard of '78. I went sledding before then, but just can't remember it. The one exception took place during the brief span of years when my mother and father and I had a country house, behind which was a steep hill. One winter night a heavy snow fell. The next morning was sunny. A thin crust of ice formed atop the powder. I went sledding down this hill, and at the bottom the ice broke. I lay splayed out like an angel, embalmed within the snow. I remember the feeling of lying there for a long time looking at the sky, not so much unable to move as unwilling to try.

What I remember about heavy snow as a child is sitting up in bed at night, after the lights were out, and opening the window to discover a tiny drift of pristine white snow on the window ledge. I would take a scoop in my hand and eat it. A delicacy that encompassed not just a soft texture, and cold, but a sense that I was engaging in the nightlife of the city, just by sticking my hand outside the window.

Still, what about sledding? Where are the sledding memories?

I asked my mother what she could tell me. She responded by email. "Snow—" she begins.

What comes to mind immediately is the snowstorm in N.Y. many years ago. I think we still lived on Eighty-First Street opposite the Hayden Planetarium—a small house next to the sprawling Beresford. 11 W. 81st St. The Hayden House, eighth floor. I remember climbing over huge, well-packed snow mounds. I remember the first time I was incredulous—and grateful—noticing the generosity of New Yorkers in times of adversity. Everyone was friendly, involved, helpful. People talking to one another, exchanging information, joking. It was with Papa that you did most of the snow surfing in the park. I remember your red nose and hair in disarray coming up the snowy slope. You loved the snow and gliding down over it, unperturbed by the cold. I can't recall any special event connected with the snow. The few times I glided with you I remember your exhilaration, which was infectious, that helped me to overcome the freezing cold.

I went sledding with my father? In Riverside Park? I don't recall. Why not! Why is so much of childhood lost to us? What evolutionary purpose does this vanishing serve? Would there be something about these early childhood memories that would confuse or inconvenience us as we molted into adolescents and adults? Is sexual feeling such a fascist state that all that came before it must be totally eradicated?

2.

When I was a kid, the possibility of nuclear war or nuclear meltdown was part of the psychic landscape. Sometimes, sitting in Ms. Ryan's geometry class, I would find myself wishing for one or the other. I distinctly recall lying in bed one night and staring out at the orangish sky, the clouds low and threatening; snow was called for but had not yet arrived. I was hoping for a torrent of snow, and the ensuing snow day. If not that, I remember thinking, maybe the orange sky meant there had been some kind of nuclear attack. Such were my priorities at the age of fourteen.

To this day, I like an impending snowstorm.

3.

The Flexible Flyer sled was ubiquitous in my childhood. The body was wood. The frame was metal, painted red except for the front, which retained its cool metal, like the fender of a car. Centered on the wooden slats was its logo, an eagle or some kind of warlike bird. You saw it between your legs if you rode sitting up, steering with your feet or a rope. If you lay down on your stomach, which is what I mostly did, your heart beat directly over that fierce bird. The lettering itself was ornate, faintly Victorian, but it was not a pastoral that was evoked; this was a festive contraption, the parts moving just so, built for speed.

I know this not so much from memories of sledding on a Flexible Flyer, and not from pictures either, belonging, as I do, to those generations for whom photographs were, if not scarce, then intermittent. My image of this childhood sled derives from an encounter of not too many years ago, when I found one in my mother's closet. It was shortly after Evangeline was born. We were excavating the closet in my old bedroom so that my little family would have room to visit for extended stays. My mother's closets were so stuffed with things that each one was like a miniature attic, crowded to the point that it was impossible to insert an arm, let alone one's own body. Sometimes this was oppressive. More often it was magical. It was as though each of my mother's closets were one of those circus Volkswagens out of which clowns would continuously pour.

I had mixed feelings about bringing all the ancient mysteries into the light. But, if I wanted us to visit New York and to see Evangeline playing with my mother, I was going to have to drag them out of the closet, and ultimately the apartment. So out came the mysteries. Clothes, shoes, boxes of papers, vases, old set designs from my mother's dance company, various costumes from the same. And then, ridiculously, an entire sled. A Flexible Flyer. Bearing a sturdiness, a heft, that immediately identified it as coming from another time. The colors, the logo, the metal bumper at the top, were so familiar, it was a shock.

I noticed a name scrawled in block letters on the handle: Billie E. I felt a chill. Billie was my childhood friend Worth's older sister. I must have borrowed his sled, which turned out to be his sister's sled, and held on to it for a span of decades.

For a few years, between ages ten and fourteen or so, I saw a lot of Worth and, by extension, Billie. Like many older siblings, she lived in another world. Clogs, reddish long hair, blue eyes lined with black eyeliner. I recall the night when, sleeping over at Worth's house, Billie, who shared a room with him, had been sequestered elsewhere in the apartment because, as his mother put it to Worth in front of me, "Your friends are getting to be too old to spend a night in the room with Billie."

Whether this was weighted toward the friends, i.e., me, or toward Billie herself, I didn't know. Worth had told me outrageous stories of his sister's sexual adventures, but I was not inclined to believe them. At the time, my thoughts about Billie, unquestionably full of longing, were fairly innocent. Her mother was just ahead of the game though, for at some point in the next year they became something else entirely.

The older siblings of your friends! I don't know how this worked with girls, but with boys the dynamic could be fraught. I can still see Billie as she stood in the doorway one morning when I had come over to play—my eyes met her pale blue eyes, then dropped down to her bare feet, and then moved up over her pale, smooth, chunky legs, panties just hidden by the length of T-shirt, breasts, much closer to me than the rest of her, mouth, again her eyes. We stared at each other. Her expression seemed to register mild disappointment. We spoke rarely and mostly about diet strategies, both of us heavy, though I would say she fell more into the voluptuous category. That moment at the front door probably lasted all of two seconds but it felt like an hour, and I would have been happy if it had gone on all day. The exertion of not staring at her breasts was so complete, it was a miracle I didn't fall to my knees. I finally managed to croak, "Hello," as she stood aside and I passed into the apartment and headed toward Worth's room.

Now I stared at this antique that had emerged from my mother's closet, intact and ready to go, and it occurred to me that I could use the occasion to write Worth, or Billie, and have a reunion of sorts. Or was that a little melodramatic? Worth and I had drifted apart, after all, as high school went on; he was very smart, but somehow he always seemed apart from everyone, and I had my own problems. Once, as we completed a pot deal—he was always well connected—he nodded at the typewriter in his room with a piece of paper in the carriage and said, "This is an A paper in progress."

I had no doubt it was an A paper. Worth was one of the brightest kids I knew. But there was something off in the declaration, at once too boastful and hollow, somehow, as though he had read instructions on how to brag. That's not how you do it, I wanted to tell him. But I was in no position to lecture.

So the sled was swept off into storage along with all the other stuff that neither I nor my mother was ready to throw out. Elizabeth rolled her eyes at this. I knew she had a point. I had recently read that Proust kept all his parents' furniture, no matter how beat up, near him through his life. This was consoling.

Worth and I were part of a tight little group of four that functioned as something of a unit from around the ages of ten to fourteen. He and I were the Riverside Drive contingent; the other two were on Central Park West. We were West-Siders at a school mostly populated by East-Siders. After the blizzard of '78 we traversed Central Park. That was the apotheosis of snow-day bliss, three days in a row. But Worth and I must have had more low-key sledding adventures in Riverside Park, too. Where had I been sledding the day I took his sister's Flexible Flyer and didn't bring it back?

4.

These memories would have been merely quaint if not for the fact that, a couple of years after that Flexible Flyer surfaced, I inquired after Worth and discovered that earlier in life he had killed himself. He had kids. Was a Libertarian. Involved with computers. The facts were paltry and absurd. But I had lost touch completely, and this is what happens in such situations—you get twenty years compressed into all the stark dispassion of a forensics report.

I wrote to a friend from that time to confirm. "Yes, Worth did a very bad thing," this old friend wrote back. The guy had little kids. I wondered if this childish phrasing was the result of being with children, as so many of us were now, or if he was just speaking from our point of view from the days when we all hung out—young kids prone to getting in trouble.

I wrote Billie a long letter about her brother. She wrote back gratefully, though clearly in great distress. I didn't mention the Flexible Flyer. By then it had moved to a storage closet somewhere else in town. Part of it was I didn't want to go dig it out. And part of it was the unbearable thought of presenting it to her, this object of our youth, almost a corpse in its own right. It just seemed ridiculous—"Here, on the occasion of losing your brother, I want you to have your old sled back."

5.

Now I have a daughter who gets excited at the mention of snow and loves to sled. We've got a slick piece of colorful plastic; it's an efficiency not just of production—no moving parts—but also of gravity: just a thin sheath between you and the snow.

A couple of years ago, the last huge storm we were here for, I took Evangeline to that steep hill on Eighty-Ninth Street in Riverside Park next to the Soldiers and Sailors Monument. We rode down a few times laughing like crazy until she fell off and her pants got pulled down, at which point I realized she was wearing (a) pajama pants, thin as a T-shirt, and (b) no underwear. I couldn't believe it. "Oh my God!" I started shouting. "Pull up your pants!" I was amazed at how she tolerated the cold.

But Evangeline is a polar bear. She just kept laughing her head off. I went nuts and insisted we rush home. I carried her most of the way, feeling guilty that I had not dressed her properly.

Part of me likes the idea of fishing out that old Flexible Flyer and riding with her on it. But Billie's name is on there. . . . It might feel too weird. Now it's in a dark storage room, like an archaeological relic of little value. I can picture it though, and still hear the hissing sound of its blades cutting through the packed white snow, still feel the thrillingly small distance between my body and the ground rushing beneath me.

6.

When I was barely old enough to walk I started having playdates with Mel, my upstairs neighbor of the same age, and we stayed close until I was about eleven or twelve years old. As soon as I write this, I realize that maybe my father's illness had something to do with my being around him so much in the last years of our friendship. My father's dying was a long process—for about six months he was in and out of the hospital—but living with the diagnosis, the ongoing worry, that went on for years. It wasn't my worry, though. I didn't know about it until the very end, the last year or even less than that, when he actually got sick. At that point I started spending a lot of time with our friends upstairs.

Toward the end, when my father was in the hospital, they took me to their country house. On the way back to the city, the three kids, Mel, his younger brother Joe, and me, all fell asleep. At some point, the sun was setting low enough over the Hudson that it streamed into the car, filling it with a deep orange glow. That woke me. Joe, a few years younger, had slid down in the back seat and lay half on the floor of the car. I was bleary eyed, still half asleep, and so was he. He looked up at me. I looked down at him. His dreamy brown eyes were fixed on mine, I remember, and a very strong sense of worry about my father came over me, the first time I had thought of it that weekend. For some reason, it felt to me that Joe understood this, that he somehow knew what I was feeling.

A faint play of freckles across the bridge of his nose, I remember. He was a very beautiful boy. None of us would have thought about it that way at the time, but in hindsight I can see it. He was touched by something, an aura of fate. You could feel it even then, when he was just seven. What kind of fate, though, that was unclear.

Joe was adopted. "His mother was an eighteen-year-old junkie," Mel, also adopted, informed me matter-of-factly on a number of occasions. That his mother was discussed at all was owing to the fact that one day when they were home alone the intercom rang and the doorman said someone was there who wanted to see Joe. He went downstairs, had an impromptu meeting with his deranged birth mother in the lobby, then came back upstairs.

Now he was just a glazed, sleep-addled seven-year-old. But I remember that look, and the fiery sunset over the Hudson as we came down the Henry Hudson Parkway. And it turns out my father had died that weekend.

Joe drove me and Mel completely crazy because at a certain point, as we messed around with our GI Joe's or whatever else, Joe would call out with a plaintive cry whose every sonic dimension I can still inwardly hear: "Mo-om! Mel and Thomas aren't letting me play!"

And the refrain, from another room, stern and in no uncertain terms from their mother: "Mel! Play with your brother!"

Mel and Joe and I must have gone sledding together in Riverside Park a hundred times. Most of the sledding in my neighborhood took place on that hill at around Eighty-Second Street behind the playground, in Riverside Park. It is just steep enough for some drama, and levels off into the field where in summer we would play softball, where you could glide for a long time.

There was one time, though, that even today remains maybe my most vivid sledding memory, and it took place in the weird, sharply sloping hill just beside the entrance to Riverside Park at Eighty-Fourth Street, where Mel, Joe, and I had decided to sled. That there might have been a reason it wasn't widely used for sledding did not occur to us. In summertime, this was a dense and spooky bramble. At the age of seven, against the rules, I was exploring back there with a friend when we encountered a man with dark, slicked-back hair carrying a plastic bag, with whom we had a brief conversation that had somehow led, in that strangely dreamy way of youth logic, to his big, pale penis hanging out from his fly, and his encouraging us to touch it. I declined on the grounds it might have germs. But my friend and I had to discuss it. For this reason, the hill may have seemed a tiny bit loaded and dangerous. But now it was winter, and a fresh snow had fallen, thick and deep with a perfect crust of ice. The sky had cleared to reveal a bright, blinding blue. We ambled into the park with our sleds, no longer tykes, exactly, but still packed up like Michelin Men. I had a Flexible Flyer. (This is part of the mystery of Billie's sled. I had one of my own. How had I ended up with hers? Had there been an accidental switch?)

It only took a few tries down the hill to figure out why this was not a popular spot. You didn't have much room, for one thing, though it was steep enough to get some good speed going. But at the bottom of the hill were the park benches on the Riverside Park promenade. With proper steering, you could navigate between the two. But proper steering could not be counted on. Anyway, we hardly had time to get tired of smashing into the concrete supports of the benches before the incident with the dogs.

There were two of them and they seemed to be playing. It was Joe, of course, who they jumped on, these lithe, brown Doberman pinschers. Their clipped ears were covered in white bandages which did nothing to soften the terror of their prominent snouts and ferocious teeth. I don't know how long it took to grasp that the playful dogs jumping around Joe, who had just smashed into one of the benches, were not being playful at all. Or at least that Joe did not see it that way. Such brightness, such glare on the snow, and Joe with his hands up near his face, ducking his head down and then thrashing suddenly upward, so that you could see his tears. The dog's owner got them under control soon enough. But Joe cried for a long time after that. This is what happens to younger brothers, I thought. They never catch a break. We went home and I don't recall ever sledding there again.

Years later Joe killed himself. There is a story. Drugs, among other things. I won't defame him by summarizing it, as if that were even possible. By the time it happened, they had moved out of the building. "We lost Joe" is what his mother told my mother, who in turn told me.

I had seen him around on the street, big hat and army jacket, his virtuoso piano playing long since folded into the Doors. He had been into psychedelics. His mother, I had heard, had gone to Central Park once, at dawn, and found him on the rocks in the Great Lawn. There had been some time at Phoenix House. One day he went to a gun shop with bullets in his pocket, one of those shops behind the police building in what is now the edge of Chinatown, though then it was Little Italy. Why did he have bullets and no gun? I don't know. Pretending to shop for a handgun, he took the gun, put a bullet in the chamber, and did it right there.

I went sledding with many people who did not kill themselves. Why do these memories force their way to such prominence? Maybe the juxtaposition of that celestial feeling of snow everywhere, the cessation of all the rituals, most importantly school itself. Maybe it's the incredible passivity of having just toppled off a sled into the snow—nature's very own Posturepedic mattress, where you are plastered into immobility and there is nothing to do but lie there. Or make angels. Which is to say that even if you are not lying there moving your arms and legs, you feel on such snowy days, as a kid, like you are in heaven. This sounds nice until you really focus on the sentiment, as seen from a kid's point of view—it means life is over, the suspense of what is going to happen has been relieved. All the corrupting messiness of experience has been avoided, cheated. You, and the snow, will stay pristine forever.

Repeat, Memory

Summer in New York, and Evangeline was enrolled in theater camp, on Twenty-Eighth Street between Broadway and Fifth Avenue. I ferried her downtown on the back of my bicycle. At six, she wore sneakers that were too big for the foot slots of the baby seat, but it was too long a trip for her to do on her own bike, which still had its training wheels, and the weather was so gorgeous that I couldn't stand the idea of the subway.

The first half of the ride, that long stretch along the Hudson River, was like a dream in its beauty and weightless speed, though complicated, as so many dreams are, by other people. Speedsters in spandex on fancy bikes whipped past us, while we ourselves overtook the slowpokes. At Twenty-Eighth Street, we left the river and its bike path and cut into Midtown. The initial blocks were long, empty, industrial. At Eighth Avenue things got complicated. I had promised Elizabeth that I would stay on the sidewalk. But the sidewalk was crowded with folks using it for its appointed purpose.

The real difficulty began at Seventh Avenue. Twenty-Eighth Street is the flower district, and at that hour the sidewalks are lined with wholesale flowers. At the corner of Twenty-Eighth Street and Seventh Avenue, on the north side, was an especially dense thicket of plants that we dubbed "the Jungle."

"Just like New Orleans!" I said as I threaded the bike in the narrow space between clumps of green foliage. But I knew even as I said this that I was confusing the issue. We were in New York for the summer. We had been here three weeks already. Where was home?

The next morning, as I was crossing Seventh Avenue on the south side of the intersection, Evangeline pointed across the street and said, "Daddy, the Jungle!" This was not a remark, or even a request. It was an instruction. (I'm told that six-year-old girls are notoriously bossy. Evangeline, I can say with confidence, was in the prime of her sixness.)

I crossed over and bumped up onto the sidewalk. A moment later we were in our own green world.

For the rest of the week it was a rule that we went through the Jungle. She would reach out and grab a frond, or try. A bit farther down the block there was a stack of green grass on shelves, and as we passed it I would run my hand along the soft little blades and she would, too. Our movements quickly became ritual. On the first day the Jungle was a discovery. The second day it was a requirement, an orienting point in time and space. Thereafter, it was simply ours.

Childhood is paradoxical in its relationship to change—a time of flexibility and openness, but also of rigidity and resistance. In the course of one day Evangeline had taken this unfamiliar landscape and found a way to make it her own, creating a private grid of property, sensation, and memory she used to protect herself against the city's fluctuating external facts. Which is to say, over the course of a single morning she became a city girl.

When Vladimir Nabokov was four years old, he walked hand-in-hand with both his parents down a garden path and had the sudden realization that he was three, and that they were twenty-seven and thirty-three, respectively. Essentially, he discovered that they were separate entities. This, he would later write, in *Speak, Memory*, was his first conscious memory. The image is reprised at the very end of the book, when Nabokov and his wife walk on either side of their young son, holding his hands, toward the shoreline in France where at any moment he'll see the huge boat that will take them to America.

Nabokov was consoled by patterns in time and space, which for him had a nearly religious aura. Another of his earliest memories was of meeting his father's friend, an army general who, to entertain the youth, lined up matches on a divan, end to end. "'This is the sea in calm weather.' Then he tipped each pair so as to turn a straight line into a zig-zag—and that was 'a stormy sea.'" Fifteen years later, he had a chance encounter with this same general on a bridge—Nabokov's father, now in flight from Bolshevik-held St. Petersburg, was "accosted while crossing a bridge, by an old man who looked like a gray-bearded peasant in a sheepskin coat. He asked my father for a light." It was the general, in "rustic disguise."[1] Nabokov in the book hopes that the general evades Soviet imprisonment, but the significance of the moment is tied to that serendipitous request for a light.

That week of theater camp I found myself thinking of this pair of recurring images—a boy's first memory, age three, holding hands with both his parents. It has a wonderful sense of wholeness. The pair of memories about the matches, on the other hand, conveys something else—that at any moment we are on one side of a partition, and we cannot fathom what is on the other side until history and fate take us there. And suddenly we are in another world, disguised and sneaking over the border. Once, there was a line of matches placed end to end on a divan. Now, the sea becomes stormy.

That weekend I took the training wheels off Evangeline's bike and I ran beside her as she wobbled along on the promenade, unsteady but fast. I was panic-stricken, and soon panting like a dog. At the same time, I realized what a delightful moment this was—not only to me, but to others, too: Even the dog walkers with frail old dogs seemed not in the least put out by this mortal threat careening toward them.

A woman called out "great job" as Evangeline pedaled by, knees pumping. People seemed to recognize this as a significant moment.

The next day we went out for another practice ride. In the hopes of not having to run so much, I tried to persuade Evangeline to practice up and down on the sidewalk in front of the building. This held no interest for her.

"It's a great spot to learn," I protested. "It's where I learned when I was your age!"

"Daddy, you have your childhood and I have mine."

She biked for a long time that morning, with more assurance than before. I ran and ran beside her until I couldn't possibly keep up. In the end, she just kept going down the promenade and left me behind, a pink dot on wheels. I saw her head pivot quickly to the side to see if I was there. She turned once, twice. Then she looked ahead, and it was a long time before she stopped.

Note
1. Vladimir Nabokov, *Speak, Memory* (G. P. Putman and Sons, 1966), 27.

The Perils of Precocity

Something strange is going on with my six-year-old daughter's reading habits. Until a few days ago, Evangeline had no reading habits. Now she suddenly has her face stuck in all sorts of books that are not age appropriate.

This book engagement is especially striking because Evangeline has always been drawn to the screen. Her appetite for movies—watched not on a television set but on a laptop, at close range—has always exceeded what one would normally expect from a little kid. At some point, when she was three or four, before her younger brother was born, I turned to Elizabeth as we departed for a night out and remarked that she no longer cried when we left.

"She knows she's getting movies," Elizabeth said.

"Is that a good thing?"

"Her not crying hysterically when we leave—that is a good thing."

"Yes, but when we are gone, shouldn't we ask the babysitter to actually play with her? I mean, once we are out the door, won't she come around to just playing with someone, and not watching a movie? We are paying her, after all."

No response. I let it drop.

The unstated thought was that we were often afraid of our daughter's temper, and it seemed—how to put this?—unbrave to ask a young woman to take on a task that we ourselves approached with trepidation. And what if she didn't stop crying? Our night out would be ruined.

We did set limits. We used movies both as a form of reward and as a means of punishment. The first words that Evangeline ever wrote came the summer after Alexander was born—not a high point of good behavior—when we banned any kind of screen time for a whole month. The results were fairly good, only, one day, I walked into a room to discover her carefully writing out a phrase with marker on a piece of cardboard: "I WANT MOVIES."

A terrible image formed in my mind of her standing by a road, displaying the sign to passing cars: my daughter as a media panhandler.

All this emphasis on the screen made me root for the advent of her reading. She progressed in fits and starts, neither lagging nor dazzling. I figured that she'd read the way I did: that when she found a book that interested her, she'd dive in and read it nonstop. After which she might go through an uninterested period, until that next engaging book came along. Or so I thought.

Things changed when I acquired a Kindle—the paper-white model. I had never owned one. At night, in bed, I sometimes used a little clamp-on light to read—like a tiny streetlamp—but that was never comfortable. With the Kindle, I could read in bed when the lights were out. Not a cutting-edge observation, I know, but one has technological epiphanies when one has them. I decided to inaugurate this device with a book that I had long put off reading, knowing what a narcotic treat it would be: the first installment of Robert Caro's multivolume biography of Lyndon Johnson, *The Path to Power*.

One night, as I happily read in the dark, Evangeline migrated to our room, as she often does, saying she couldn't sleep. She got in bed beside me. I kept reading. She stared at the screen for a while.

"Wait, I'm not done," she said, when I reached up to turn the (figurative) page.

"You're reading along?"

"Sort of."

She watched the screen, observing the pages turn for a while, and then, sometime later, drifted off to sleep.

The next night, she was back, lying in the dark beside me, her face illuminated by the screen's dim glow as she stared up at the backlit words. She tried to adjust the font size. She asked to try out my reading glasses.

"Stop stalling," I said harshly, "or you have to go back to your room."

Still, as I turned the next page, she said, "Wait. I'm not done."

"OK," I said as an experiment, "tell me when."

A minute passed. "OK," she said. "Turn the page."

She could turn the pages herself, I said, when she was ready. Thereafter, I would read a page, then lie there for a while, wondering if Evangeline was playing with me, which seemed likely, or was actually trying to read the words. There were some anxious moments over Lady Bird Johnson's childhood: "Aside from Negro playmates," wrote Caro, "her mother was her only companion."[1] I didn't want to have to answer questions about that.

No questions came. This is a pantomime of reading, I thought, as her hand periodically reached up and tapped the surface of the screen to turn the page, just another way to keep from going to sleep.

It happened again the next night, when I was in the middle of a passage concerning Lyndon Johnson's courtship of and marriage to Lady Bird Johnson. Evangeline is interested in such things. Also concerned. If there is anything about dating or kissing in a movie we are watching, she puts her hands over my eyes, or looks at me with an outrageous expression of embarrassment, as though I were the one who should not be exposed to these adult facts of life.

On this night, she asked me now and then how to say a word. She got through a few pages—including a tidbit about Johnson cajoling and browbeating his shy fiancée, Lady Bird, to agree to an instant wedding. In the middle of the ceremony, his best man "dashed across the street to a Sears, Roebuck store and brought back a tray of inexpensive wedding bands—the one she chose cost $2.50—to complete the ceremony."[2]

When I started to turn that page, she said, "Wait! I'm not done."

I lay there, wondering what in the world she might make of "Sears, Roebuck." Or what, for that matter, she would make of the improbable name Lady Bird. And what about this abrupt, hectoring way of getting married?

Caro's biography itself casts in a new light the carousel of pride and anxiety that parents experience while assessing the progress of their kids. On one hand, you have to admire a poor country boy who pulls himself up on the strength of his own work and ingenuity to become first congressman, then senator, and ultimately president. But that is the picture only when seen from a distance. Up close, at a granular level, the level at which Caro's narrative proceeds, Johnson is mostly despicable. How many times, reading this, did I find myself vowing to be less focused on accomplishment? Fortunately, day-to-day life also proceeds at the granular level, though without the luxury of being able to put the narrative down. Just the other day, Evangeline shocked me by picking up Louis Menand's collection of essays *American Studies* and peering at its pages.

I was sure that this was some sort of pose, a lark. It was impossible to imagine that she could actually have been reading it. But having picked it up, she then took the book outside and, as we put her brother in the car, stood with it, open, in her hands, looking perfectly engrossed. She kept reading it in the car, too, until finally she put it down with a sigh.

"What were you reading?" Elizabeth and I asked, more or less in unison.

After a long pause, she said, "Something about construction."

"Yes!" I shouted, all of a sudden totally ecstatic. "Yes! That's right!"

I was beside myself. The introduction to that book is a riff on how change happens in society—the strange, incremental nature of it, both slow and fast. Menand writes about the experience of driving by a work crew on a highway: "You see five guys sipping coffee and watching one man with a pick while he hacks halfheartedly at some gravel.... Six months later, there is a new road."[3] Then he makes a similar analogy about the demolition and reconstruction of a building. Nothing happens, and then, all of a sudden, it already has. The change has occurred.

What Menand doesn't say, but what seemed obvious at that moment, was that the metaphor extends to children and to their development. With the sheer, intractable force of their childishness they harass, entertain, and exhaust you; they have temper tantrums, during which one fights the desire to say, "Why can't you just be rational?," with the obvious retort being that they are two years old. Or three. Or six, or sixteen. And then, all of a sudden, there is a person. Maybe not a fully formed one, but when is any of us "fully formed"? And by extension, when does this sense of surprise at the development of your children end?

Never, I hope.

This morning, I woke up early and, for some reason, pulled down *The Second Common Reader*, by Virginia Woolf, where I found this evocative line: "Reading is a longer and more complicated process than seeing."[4]

As someone who now goes to sleep reading a Kindle, yet who can't seem to leave the house without at least three pounds of books stuffed into his bag, I felt provoked in ways that the author of the line could never have imagined. I've heard the Kindle described as "the same coffee, without the cup." Is this the world at your fingertips, or a task that never ends? A book, the singular object, has the virtue of tethering the reader's experience of closure with the actual ending of pages and words. But then, some authors—Proust, Musil, Salinger, maybe Caro, too—seem to be working on books that never end, only evolve from one volume to the next.

At some point, Evangeline wandered in and attacked me with a ferocious session of whiny pleading to see a movie, even though it was a school morning. I told her to go outside and look for worms, something she'd enjoyed doing over the weekend. She curled up in a ball of lamentation. I decided to scan the shelves for an inappropriate book to give her.

I paused over Sylvia Plath's poems and let out an unexpectedly demonic cackle.

"Why did you laugh like that?" came the little voice. No comment.

A moment later, I tossed her Rilke's *Letters to a Young Poet*. I walked out of the room to make breakfast, and glanced back to see her examining the cover.

When I returned, she was outside, looking for worms, wearing a shirt of mine to keep warm. I watched as she bent down to inspect the earth. Then she stood up to remove the shirt and, with the impeccable logic of childhood, gently spread it over the moist, muddy ground and stood on it to keep her feet dry.

Notes
1. Robert Caro, *The Path to Power: The Years of Lyndon Johnson* (1981; Vintage, 1990), 295.
2. Caro, *Path to Power*, 302.
3. Louis Menand, *American Studies* (Farrar, Straus and Giroux, 2002), ix.
4. Virginia Woolf, *The Second Common Reader* (1932; Harcourt, 1986), 259.

Drain You

A few days before the start of Christmas vacation, my family was in a post-dinner slump. The mere contemplation of the upcoming holidays—the traveling, the festivities—left us exhausted. Then Evangeline had the idea of playing loud music. I wasn't in the mood, but relented.

I played a kid classic I played from years gone by, called "It's Peanut Butter Jelly Time!!!" As soon as the song started, Evangeline began to jump around and to demand that I do so, too, while Alexander pulled the cushions off the couch so that he could stage dive onto them. "Peanut Butter Jelly Time" had been a big hit in our family about three years before this, when our family comprised only three people. Was this part of Evangeline's excitement about the song—that it reminded her of when she'd been an only child?

Then Elizabeth, who had stepped out of the room for a moment, came bounding back in, dancing like a maniac. Something snapped in all of us at the sight of her jumping around like that. It was the "Peanut Butter Jelly Time" version of the Harlem shake. Everyone went crazy.

Now we put up the Christmas lights. We didn't have a Christmas tree, since we were about to leave town. We did have a wreath, though, and I strung the lights around this little evergreen contortion. It looked beautiful but paltry. Elizabeth and Evangeline had left the room by then. Alexander, fully ambulatory at age two, if a bit unsteady on two legs, was hanging around—the basic urge to witness construction. To make the wreath seem less paltry, I turned out all the other lights. Now the room was lit by a spooky, multicolored glow.

The computer, in shuffle mode, started playing a Nirvana song called "Drain You." I had not heard it in years, or, at least, hadn't listened to it closely in years.

I turned it up. I started bouncing, and soon I was jumping up and down again. Alexander joined in. Wondering if the song was too dark and angry for a two-year-old, I stopped jumping for a moment and listened. Alexander stopped jumping and listened with me.

I remembered Dave Grohl's bare back, his shoulder blades, the lean exhaustion of his body at the Nirvana show I went to in September 1991, in Trenton, New Jersey, four days after *Nevermind* dropped. Grohl hit the drums so hard, and I remembered how spent he seemed when he walked, shirtless, through the crowd after the set.

Backstage before the show (the guy who made Nirvana's T-shirts, Jeff Ross, made T-shirts for the band I was in, which may have been our biggest distinction), I'd stood there in the dressing room chatting with people and glancing over at Kurt Cobain, who sat quietly for a long time, applying eyeliner. Then, just before he took the stage, he squirted half a bottle of Chloraseptic down his throat, pressing the plunger on the bottle over and over. After *Nevermind* came out, a revolution took place: Nirvana sounded like nothing on the radio, and then, all of a sudden, everything on the radio sounded like Nirvana. Kurt and Courtney Love were on the cover of *Sassy*, there was another record, and, three years later, it was all over.

Listening to the song now, I noticed an abandon that was childlike in its total commitment. You heard it in the force with which Grohl hits the drums, in Krist Novoselic's playing, and, most of all, in the release in Cobain's voice, somewhere between a wail of despair and delighted squandering of the moment.

Everything was going along fine in our living room until the song got to the break—the low, murky part—at which point Alexander called out to me, "Daddy! It's scary!"

Nirvana's music, in its anguish and energy, *is* scary. *Nevermind* is scary. But the break in "Drain You" is especially scary. I either had to turn it off now or find a way to make this work. And I didn't want to turn it off. So instead, turning it down slightly, I did my best to address my son's concerns.

"Alexander," I said, bending over to talk near his face. "This is the part where they are in the swamp, see? The water's dark and murky, and the trees are low. Can you picture that? They're walking through the wet mud in the dark underbrush of the swamp."

He looked at me with wide eyes, the colored lights adding to the mood of discotheque-meets-haunted-house. I worried that he would have nightmares, and that I would rue the night I played "Drain You." People would shake their heads and say, "What were you thinking?"

"Right now, it's very dark, but they are trying to find their way out of the swamp," I gamely continued.

The song was still in its thumping darkness, but Grohl's drum beats were starting to gather force.

"And now they see a ray of light in the distance. They see the light at the end of the swamp. Do you hear it in the music? They see the light and they are going in its direction! Do you see the light, Alexander? Do you hear it?" I sounded like some revivalist preacher. Alexander's face was alert, awake to the idea that there might be a light to see, but he wasn't sure he saw it.

In my years of teaching creative writing, I have encountered quite a few scenes about fathers' sentimental moments with their favorite music. One woman wrote about her father lying on the floor of the den and blasting Bruce Springsteen. At the time, I thought it was a bit cringe-inducing. But now, having entered their ranks, I am inclined to forgive the dads and their music enthusiasms. I have always been an enthusiast, and sort of foolish about the music I love. And for a period of time, I was very into Nirvana. It seemed that they were saving the world of music from itself, and the culture at large from itself.

So much of the catharsis of Nirvana, and the indie efflorescence that came in its wake, was a negativity that was refreshing. As Stephen Malkmus put it in a recent interview, commenting on the years that saw the emergence of Nirvana, and then of his own band, Pavement, "It's a time that seems romantic to people now, whereas, at the time, it seemed like a cynical era. There were all these worries about selling out and the Man and corporate rock and irony and sincerity. But, in retrospect, being cynical just meant that you cared. There was something at stake."[1]

It was important to me that Alexander knew that a happy moment was approaching. The song was now gathering itself for a release. The song was rushing toward the light. The drums were a tribal force. "Drain You" is a bummer, and it is also ecstatic. The essence of Kurt Cobain's style—depressed ecstasy.

"We're going to make it, Alexander! It's going to be all right!" I shouted, as Dave Grohl unleashed a fierce drum roll on the snare. When the guitars came back in, I began leaping around. Then I heard Alexander's voice calling out to me.

"Daddy!" he yelled. "Daddy? Are they all the way out of the swamp?"

I'd forgotten, I realized, to narrate that part. I had left him hanging.

"Yes!" I said. "Yes! They're totally out of the swamp! They are running in a meadow! They are surrounded by sunshine and running out into the open meadow!"

I was leaping around. He started leaping around, too, though there was clearly still some fear to shake off, his eyes shining with excitement at having escaped the murky swamp.

"Drain You," Nirvana itself, that whole era—it had been a dormant chapter until this moment, my life then as unfathomable to me now as my life now would have been to me then, yet, in this moment and this song, it had all briefly come together. The music was propulsive, driving us at once into the future and the past. We were, in some way, traveling to both places together.

Note

1. Rob Sheffield, "Stephen Malkmus on Why Everyone Wants to Be a Nineties Kid," *Rolling Stone*, January 3, 2014.

Her Party

Evangeline's birthday party was held on a Saturday afternoon, a few days after the birthday itself, on which she had been given a skateboard. The morning after she got it, I was roused from sleep to accompany her, in the chill of dawn, to the library parking lot up the street. There, she set about practicing on the skateboard, heedless, fearless, clueless, waving off any attempts at guidance or advice. At least she was in a helmet and elbow pads, I thought, and stood there remembering the many beautiful, fun places I had taken her over the years—places that had had no effect on her at all, save to make her wail about being bored. And now this cracked patch of asphalt behind the Latter Library: paradise.

The party came a few days later. We spent the morning decorating according to its theme, devised by Evangeline: "Disco Dance Party!" Silvery tinsel was hung over the tall living-room windows; light machines that swirled colorful dots in patterns on the ceiling were positioned at either end of the room; the furniture was pushed against the wall to clear the dance floor. Then the smoke machine arrived. Another dad was lending it to me. You had to be careful, he said. His daughter's disco party earlier that year had devolved into a fog through which tiny bodies ran and screamed and the parents looked nervous. "Just don't let anyone touch it, either," he cautioned. "It can get hot."

I filled the machine with the liquid, pushed the various tubes into place, and put it on a pedestal in the back, near the stereo, planning to use it sparingly.

Soon the guests began arriving, as the fading afternoon light filtered through the silver tinsel. I started the playlist of songs that Evangeline had picked out. First up: Kesha's "Animal."

To say that dancing commenced immediately would be accurate, to a point. But . . . was it dancing? To my eye, it was unstructured chaos. Each section of the couch had as many kids as could fit jumping up and down on it, demonstrating an early version of that primal need to get on top of the speakers at nightclubs. Evangeline seemed joyous.

What the hell?, I thought, and pressed the smoke machine's button. From its dragon nostril came a terrifying spew of gray mist. It scared me more than anyone. A few kids fled; a few parents looked worried. But then a familiar fogginess settled in, and the merriment resumed. The kids flowed like water into the room, jumped madly for a while, only to flow out to another room, the kitchen maybe. I stayed in the back, advancing the playlist, and watching the colors saturate the smoke and become darker and darker as the sun went down.

Then Evangeline got sad. I knew she would. Elizabeth noticed it first. She was curled in a ball on a chair at the far end of the living room. Both of us were upon her a moment later, coaxing her hands away from her face to reveal wet cheeks. I thought, at first, that it may have been because all the mayhem of the party no longer cohered; it was her house being trashed, after all, and when the party stopped seeming so great, she had nowhere to go.

I used to feel heartbroken at my own birthday parties. Maybe because the ones I remember most vividly happened after my dad died, and so it was my mother who planned it all out. I remember moments of crushing sadness, even if eventually I would have a good time. The most acute hosting collapse happened when I was fourteen or so and my mother gave over the apartment to me so I could throw a party. No particular occasion other than that is what kids my age were starting to do. At some point that night, I saw my friend Peter, who a couple of years later would rescue me after the Kinks concert, sitting against the hallway wall, in conversation with a girl, with his feet propped up on the opposite wall. It upset me to see his sneakers on the paint. A moment later, already upset, I came upon Jimmy and Rick throwing the little pine cones at one another.

These little pine cones were just one of the many oddities that populated my home when I was growing up. My mother must have gathered them from the country house we had when my dad was alive. We kept it for two years after he died, until it was no longer tenable—the renters had left without paying—and had to be sold. The assembled antiques from the country were imported to the city apartment so that our urbane standing lamp in the living room now had a silent doppelgänger, considerably more rustic, just beside it, like an understudy or a second at a duel. Old teacups, little tables, candlesticks, chairs whose wicker had given way—the house was filled with objects whose virtue was not utility but character, atmosphere, warmth. Among them, a little basket of baby pine cones, soft to the touch and fragrant, nestled in a small basket. They were perfect for pelting, no doubt—quick out of the hand but not so hard that they would break anything. I grasped all of this as soon as I entered the study and encountered this mini–pine cone war.

I managed to quell it without much resistance. I remember wishing in that moment that I had never had the party. I went around picking up the squashed pine cones, feeling a mixture of grief and shame at the thought that my mother collected the little pine cones and put them in a basket just so they could be thrown around a room. And yet wasn't her small, irrational gesture of collecting little pine cones in a basket emblematic of all the irrational fantasies we construct in anticipation of our own parties? It's the hope, really, that makes you so vulnerable.

It's one of the more basic human impulses, crying at your own party, as the famous song attests. But that didn't make it any less pointed when Evangeline said to me and Elizabeth, even as we were petting her and hovering over her tearful face and trying to determine what was wrong, "This isn't at *all* what I was expecting!"

I considered the philosophical implications of this for a second before she added, "I wanted to play all these games! You know? Like that game where you hide the chocolate and everyone looks for it!"

"You should have told us that," I said, my own grief at her grief seeping out in spite of my desperate wish to hide it.

"I *did*!" she said. "I told Mommy."

"You just told me an hour ago," Elizabeth said. She looked at me with a vulnerable face, as though she had done something wrong, fallen short.

Evangeline eventually cheered up, and by the end of the party she was having fun again. We later discovered that her mood had turned sour when a couple of girls started to hide from her. Her friends. Her mood rallied when another girlfriend of hers invited her to sleep over that night. Evangeline navigated the jungle of kid social life well, she wasn't easily bruised, yet this was all it took to send her mood plunging and then to revive it. Does our fragility ever end?

Once, when Evangeline was a tiny baby and we were living downtown, I sat in the Eleventh Street Café and watched as a family came in to say hi to another family. Everyone seemed so happy to see each other. The grown-ups talked to each other, and two little girls, each of whom was six or seven years old, talked to each other. It was the kid conversation that I tuned in to. The girl who had walked in started talking about her toys and what she had done that day. She discussed her new skateboard, her friends, what a great time she just had. It was one endless monologue on the general greatness of her own life. Not once did she ask a question of the other girl, or even let her speak. After five minutes, everyone said goodbye as cheerfully as they'd said hello.

As they exited, I heard the parents say to their little girl, who had not said a word, "Wasn't that great?" The little girl who had not spoken continued her silence. She just nodded. She had started the exchange with the other girl with an alert, excited expression on her face that began to fade as soon as she realized that her only role was to be that of audience. Now, in the aftermath, she looked a bit dazed. Her parents moved on. But the little girl, I saw, was traumatized. The emotional mauling by the other girl that had just spoken at her was compounded by the fact that there was no chance that she could make her parents understand what had just happened. She could barely understand it for herself.

A cosmic unfairness had taken place before my very eyes, and, watching it unfold, I had the slightly sickening feeling that sometime in the next hour, or day, this little girl would weep, or would act out in some way, and her parents would be utterly mystified. There was nothing I could do to prevent this, nothing to be done.

The moment seemed profound to me at the time; how often, I wondered, are we victimized in subtle ways that we cannot even perceive? And while my own daughter was then only four months old, she would one day be around this age, somewhere around six or seven. I held my breath at the thought of the emotional challenges ahead.

And now comes her seventh birthday, and her tears. And the fact that the big birthday gift we gave her, much requested, was a skateboard. I had gotten one, too, long ago, after much lobbying, though not at the age of seven. What I remember about it was that the skateboard belonged to a special category of toy that went beyond mere fun. It was an entry pass into a club of sorts, a world to which you could now belong.

Not long after the party, Evangeline took the skateboard with her to a sleepover, along with the helmet. And the next day, when she returned, refreshed from her vacation from her family and her party, we went to the small side street next to our house so that she could practice some more. She went back and forth while her little brother scampered on a neighbor's front lawn that was bordered by hedges.

The neighbor is very old, and hardly ever seen. A nurse is with her at all times. Still, as I stood in the middle of the street watching for cars and calling to Evangeline not to exceed the agreed-upon parameters (a neighbor's driveway at one end and a pickup truck halfway down the block at the other), I watched Alexander running around noisily on the lawn and wondered if we would be chastised for this intrusion. Then the old lady appeared in a wheelchair on a screened-in porch. She smiled and waved at us. I alone waved back, grateful that she didn't mind Alexander scampering on the lawn, and, beyond that, for her orienting presence, with its sense of cascading generations, each seeing the same scene through a profoundly different lens. Alexander ran back and forth while Evangeline, now with a tiny bit of competence as a skateboarder, rolled to the very edge of the agreed-upon boundary, and then ever so slightly beyond it.

"Evangeline!" I bellowed, elongating the word so that its pitch rose in threat and exasperation.

"What?" she said, all innocence.

For a moment I became furious, but then I softened and embraced the moment's gift.

"Come back!"

Napoleon on the Back Stairs

Every apartment in Manhattan has a Napoleon complex. No matter the size or the neighborhood, they are all imbued, at least a little bit, with an aura of indignation. This is due, in part, to the ridiculously high cost of real estate in Manhattan; the most modest apartment can be the source of an almost dynastic pride, while the most immodest palace exists in a state of inevitable eclipse by one that is yet more grand, of which it may have a view.

Apartments share certain qualities with stage sets—each room, even a bathroom, is a scenario into which people exit and enter. The sense of performance and audience—and, by extension, voyeurism—is built into the landscape. To glance at the facade of an apartment building, especially at night, when the windows are a crossword puzzle of light and dark boxes, is to be reminded that there may be someone looking back at you. This tension—between the apartment as a place of privacy and also a place where privacy is relentlessly invaded—is further amplified by the fact that apartment buildings are filled with spaces that are public and yet, in some ways, especially private, because you never expect to see someone there: places like the laundry room, the storage room, the bike room, or the back stairs.

I step out of the elevator and stand next to the front door of our place, listening. The apartment is silent. Not a peep can be heard above the hum of the air conditioning. But I know that my mother, my wife, my children—they are all in there, even if they are not, at this moment, making a sound. Our children, ages seven and three, are not a silent bunch. We have rambunctious children. I realize this is like saying, "We have green houseplants." But there are different shades of green.

Instead of going inside, I turn and push through the two fire doors that lead to the service hallway and the back stairs. I take a seat on the stairs just outside the kitchen door. I am, in a sense, even closer to my family now than before, but I am also farther away. No one ever comes in or out through the back door; it only opens when the garbage gets put out.

Feeling truant, cozily alone, I set up shop with my laptop, but not before regarding the view. This hallway is virtually unchanged from when I was a kid, aside from the two plastic recycling bins next to the basic trash can. I used to come back here to play basketball and baseball, or the improvised versions of these activities that could be done alone in a service hallway.

It's nice back here, I think to myself. It reminds me of being a kid. Each back door, each hallway, is generic, but I know from experience—trick or treating, or general rambling through the building as a kid with my friends—that each floor nevertheless has its own particular mood and character.

There was once a fitness nut who lived on an upper floor of the building. She was known for avoiding the elevator in favor of walking up the back stairs. Her refusal to partake in the egalitarian ordeal of the elevator gave her a regal air. She entered the lobby through its front, like everyone else, but exited it at the back, rising up the stairs with ghostly ethereality while the rest of us stood like commuters, waiting for the elevator. How pleasant it must have been to walk past everyone's back door, on the other side of which is the kitchen. The smell alone can tell you a lot. The sounds within. The state of the garbage can.

The older generation used to leave its back doors open a lot more, such that you could actually catch a glimpse of your neighbors' lives. They used to keep their windows open, too. The world, really, used to be more porous. Now we live in the era of cordon sanitaire. The woman who once lived across the back hall, Mrs. Bloom, used to have her back door open when I was in that hallway with my ball and bat; she puttered around her kitchen in a house dress, unbothered by me as I took my swings, whacking the ball, the bat itself sometimes smacking the wall. Was she tolerant or just deaf? Unclear. But the walls of that hallway were for years riven with dents. Eventually they got filled in, painted over, though if you look closely you can see still the spots where they were plastered.

Once I used the hallway to make noise and be alone, I reflect; now I have come here to be quiet and alone. I am just savoring this irony when I hear the sound of footsteps rising on the stairway, from just one floor below.

A moment later, Mrs. W appears, stooped, purposeful, and as she comes into view, I have the uncomfortable sensation of watching someone who does not know she is being watched. She looks a bit frazzled, harassed even, perhaps by the very nature of her errand. In one hand she holds an envelope.

I have the advantage of an extra moment to prepare for what I sense is coming. Then again, I am in a compromised position. For if she had no reason to deliver the letter in her hand, whose contents, I immediately infer, pertain to my noisy children, then . . . why am I on the back stairs?

I sit calmly and prepare for a scene that otherwise would have taken place in the front doorway, with my mother or Elizabeth or the kids behind me, looking on with curiosity (in the case of the children) or annoyance (Elizabeth) or smoldering exasperation (my mother), and try to celebrate the fact that it will now unfold in private.

Rising within me, at the same slow but undaunted rate as Mrs. W herself, is the excited indignation of someone who is about to engage in battle, and has the necessary weapon at hand—has in fact been carrying this weapon, honing it, polishing it, and practicing with it, for years now. Seeing my feet on the stairs beside her, Mrs. W lifts her blue eyes. Understandably, she is surprised to see me sitting there.

An apartment can be thunderous without even making a sound. My presence on these stairs, for example, can be attributed, in part, to the tiny blue alarm clock that Alexander recently discovered in the kitchen. It is meant to be a key chain, but the thin silver tail leads to a little ring on which there are no keys, so it's just a tiny alarm clock. He found it in a small wooden box that hangs on the kitchen wall. This little box, on the antique side of the junk/antique divide, has a small drawer. The drawer is mysterious, even alluring, but I never see it. That wooden box exists, for me, entirely as the vessel for the plastic laundry cards.

A more orderly household would have one card that would be drawn down and then rejuvenated in the machine that inhales digital cash and puts credit onto the card. But, at my mother's house, there are usually at least two cards, each with its own mysterious balance, and when I do the laundry, I am always in a state of suspense over which has ample funds and which just a few maddening pennies. Upon my return, I rush to the box on the wall and put the cards back in the little cup inside the box, before they disappear.

I know there are other things in that box—they are comforting, extraneous and maybe even interesting, but I refuse to really see them. They are just the things in the box that are *not the laundry card*.

This is why I did not go directly into the apartment—I needed to escape the distraction of the tiny blue alarm clock key chain, and the many, many other obscure but resonant objects that fill the apartment. This little clock came complete with two little bells on top. It's such a provocative object! It embodies keys and time (access and the finite), and, if that isn't provocative enough, the clock has stopped (which means we will never die, or we have already done so, depending on your mood). It's this sort of associative provocation that tramples concentration, precisely what I had been hoping to avoid by sitting on the back stairs.

None of which I can clearly explain to Mrs. W, who stands a few steps below me, on what I suppose is technically her floor, while I sit a few steps above, on my own floor. The stairs double back at a platform in the middle of every flight. We are now eye to eye, but with the railing as a partition.

"Oh," she says. "I was just coming to see you."

"With a letter."

"I'd like you to read it."

"OK."

She hands me the letter. I open the envelope.

My heart beats with excitement at the thought of using, at last, my secret weapon, even if the fact that I am sitting on the back steps undermines the very ground from which I would launch this weapon. I push the thought from my mind.

The letter is brief, cordial. The message is familiar: We were making too much noise.

"Well," I begin. "I do appreciate the tone."

"Yes, but what about the content? What about the problem? Because it has to stop."

"The thing is, I am not sure if there is a problem here. Or, rather, to be honest, I think the problem may not be located in our apartment."

"I don't know where else the problem could be located," Mrs. W says.

"It could be located in your apartment."

"No one in my apartment is making an unreasonable amount of noise."

"True, but maybe you might be making an unreasonable amount of silence."

"I don't think it's right that you should evade responsibility for what you are doing with some kind of clever nonsense."

"Thank you for calling my nonsense clever."

"This might be funny to you, but it's a source of agony for us. We have every right to have peace and quiet."

"I think you have a right to peace. But quiet is relative. We are in an apartment building in New York City."

"I don't know how you are raising your children or why you cannot control them, but there are consequences for this behavior on your part and their part, and I am bearing the brunt of these consequences."

The insult that she's just inflicted on me—that I am a barbarian unable to raise civilized children—is one that stretched back decades, really, to the insult that she once inflicted on my mother: an insult implying that my mother was a bad mother, a bad parent whose bad decisions were creating a bad child, one who expressed this badness with an ingenious capacity for noise and disruptiveness in any number of charmless forms. And now this creature has regenerated this same depraved cycle in his own children!

In the past, with my mother, this criticism was implicit, perhaps out of some deference to the death of my father and my mother's having to raise me on her own. But now, here on the back stairs, the remark about how I am bringing up my children represents a taking-off-the-gloves moment, as Mrs. W must know and intend. I don't know why she said it. But then, I suppose you can only keep powerfully felt feelings to yourself for so long before they find expression.

Wounded, I reach for the secret weapon.

"Mrs. W," I say, "if you want to complain to the building's super, or the board, as you have so often in the past, be my guest. But I feel your complaints have lost all validity after your complaint about the upstairs neighbors." Without taking my eyes off hers I lift my chin upward, alluding to the people one floor above. "I am sure you know what I am referring to," I add.

"Of course I know, but I don't see why that should undermine my complaint," she says. "They were very noisy kids."

"That is true," I say. "Exactly my point. They were very noisy kids, as I am in a position to know, because we live directly below them. And you know what? Even when it was annoying, we tolerated it!" A slight exaggeration, as I had once or twice stood on a chair to bang on the ceiling with my fist. But I was not going to get into that now. We had never called upstairs, nor called the doorman to complain, nor gone upstairs to deliver letters or to ring the doorbell. Certainly we had never written the building's board to issue a formal complaint. Once, in a chance elevator encounter, Elizabeth discussed things with the mother upstairs, broaching the idea that before 7 a.m. should be a quiet time. No recriminations, however. The upstairs mom was understanding and nice. It did get a bit better, too. Then they moved.

"This is what one must do in an apartment building," I continue. "You cannot expect to live in pristine silence in an apartment building in New York City!"

"I am not expecting pristine silence! But there is such a thing as peace of mind."

"Yes, well, I am not responsible for your mind."

"But you *are* for your children!"

"But not for the children one flight above me! Which is why the news that you had complained about them was, I have to say, such a relief. It was one of the truly great days! Think about how it sounds that you complained about kids *two floors* above you. It's not about if you can *hear* them; it's about what you are able to tolerate. And at some point what is really not acceptable is intolerance, or oversensitivity, or the idea that you are entitled to live in a shrine of silence and anyone who violates it must be attacked! Look, I will try to keep my kids quiet, as I always do, by the way. We are not oblivious to your presence, believe me. The sound of my kids jumping off a bed . . ."—a tactical mistake to admit this, but . . . too late—"sends an actual spasm of pain through me."

"It should send a pain through them!"

"We discourage such behavior, believe me! But if you want to make an issue out of this, I will really enjoy bringing up your complaint about the kids two stories up, which in my opinion changed everything."

Though I had trembled with adrenalin at the start of this aria, I ended pretty cleanly, without much splash, as they say in diving competitions, which I never cared much about, really, and always watched in a state of mild boredom, wishing that one of the better Olympic events would come on. The one image that has always stayed with me from the diving competitions was when Greg Louganis did a triple reverse something or other and smacked the back of his head against the diving board, an image that the TV network played over and over in slow motion. I seem to recall that he rallied nevertheless and won.

We end on as civilized a note as is possible, and Mrs. W descends back whence she came. I wait a moment and then reread the letter. A pang of remorse goes through me; its tone is unusually conciliatory. The W's had kids around my age, girls, who for reasons of family enmity or scheduling or mutual shyness I almost never talked to, or even saw, during our childhood, even though I hung out with many other kids in the building. Over the years I've become aware of a whole world of affinities and interests between the two of us, between the W's and the B's, as it were. These are cultured, smart people. We should be friends sitting together over tea, ruing the destruction of the world's great libraries. Of all the barbarities with which our culture is afflicted, surely we are the least of each other's problems.

I think bashfully of my presumption to speak of this apartment as my own when the truth is that it is my mother's place. But Mrs. W would understand this perfectly well. She is an antagonist who has known me, or at least known the distant rumblings of my noise, my entire life.

My contrition grows until I remember the effect this exchange would have had on my family's state of mind if it had taken place at the front door, or the drama that would have ensued from the moment of that ominously rung doorbell, which, I know from experience, the children would learn to listen for. The way the poison of the complaint would have to work its way through our family dynamic for days, at least. Filled with pride—not to mention relief—at having intercepted Mrs. W and her letter, I rise to my feet, resolved to mention the exchange to no one.

But neither will I throw out the letter, nor put it in a safe and specific place—a file, perhaps, labeled "Fraught Exchanges with Disgruntled Neighbors." Instead, I will stuff it in some random nook among the pleasant, warm chaos of the apartment, which is filled with tiny blue alarm clocks in many forms. Before I do any of that, though, I have to enter the apartment. I stand up next to the back door, walk down a few steps, push through the fire doors into the elevator landing, and then push through the front door, which makes a sound like a bag of change that has been shaken. The door has barely closed behind me when I hear the sound of stampeding little footsteps accompanied by cries of joy and complaint.

The Egg Cream in Mid-Manhattan, 1982

1.

The egg cream scheme commenced one day in the spring of 1982 at the Mid-Manhattan Library, on Fortieth Street and Fifth Avenue, where I had gone to research a term paper. I was, at the time, winding my way through a series of disciplinary hearings connected to an unauthorized student newspaper I helped start, and, unbeknownst to me, about to be expelled from high school. They did not throw me out in the middle of my junior year, but, in the superficially genteel manner characteristic of the place, informed me that I would not be "invited back" for senior year, as though school were some sort of private party. For years I had been a total catastrophe at that school, but after pulling myself together the previous year, I had gotten in trouble again that fall. The crimes were multiple and I won't go into detail, not out of shame, but because I no longer feel like bragging about it.

On that fateful Sunday morning at the library, I had pulled a few books and stacked them in a pile on one of the long communal tables on the fourth floor. I probably had a stack of blank index cards with me. I don't recall the topic. But I do have a vivid recollection of seeing a few sections of the *New York Times* lying a bit farther down the table in a ruffled pile. I half stood out of my chair, stretched as far as I could, got a finger on the paper, and reeled it in. I could have just stood up to get it, but it was important that it be within my reach, which implied that fate had meant me to take a break and read the paper.

I immediately fell into a perusal of my favorite section—business. At the end, like dessert, were the classified ads. They were broken into categories. The category I found most interesting, and always scrutinized, was "Business Opportunities," and its subsection, "Miscellaneous." In missives as brief as haiku, visions of happiness and prosperity would be sketched out by someone who was clearly experiencing a dearth of either or both. One ad caught my eye: the New York Egg Cream Company was for sale. Asking price: one million.

I walked to the pay phones on the fourth floor, which were near the bathrooms, and left a message expressing interest in buying the company. I had made these calls, pranks essentially, several times before. I usually called on a Sunday, left a message expressing interest in whatever company was for sale, and never called back. But I called the New York Egg Cream Company back on Monday; I don't know why. It may have had something to do with the fact that I had recently tasted an egg cream made at one of those very carts. And I had liked it. Also, they gave you a free pretzel stick to go with your egg cream, and there is no limit to the positive feelings people associate with getting something for free, especially something as happy-making as a good pretzel stick.

2.

My one previous experience on the fourth floor of the Mid-Manhattan Library had taken place two years earlier and involved an assignment for Dr. S, my ninth-grade geology teacher. Dr. S was in the habit of throwing rocks at us. I mean, he would now and then call on someone and throw a rock at them, so they had to catch the question and the rock at the same time. I always thought this was a brilliant idea, not because someone might get hit in the head with a rock if they were not paying attention, but because of the vote of confidence conveyed in this gesture, his faith in our abilities to catch something, to improvise.

Dr. S wore pink or blue shirts that had white collars and white French cuffs that he folded up to expose his forearms. His hair was cut short at the sides and longish up front, like a European film star. It was a hue of blond that to my admittedly untrained ninth-grade eyes seemed suspiciously unnatural, though I could not formulate what this might mean. He smoked before and after class, which only contributed to his generally raffish appeal. There was something about the lines on his face and especially the shape of his mouth, sensuous and a bit bitter, that reminded me of my relatives from Vienna—my aunt and uncle, and even my father, who was by then about four years dead.

Dr. S had assigned me to write a report on a dinosaur of my choosing. And in the course of my research at a long table on the fourth floor of the Mid-Manhattan Library, I ended up choosing the *Tyrannosaurus rex*.

The Mid-Manhattan (now renamed the Stavros) was hiding in plain sight on Fifth Avenue, catty-corner from the grand museum-like structure of the New York Public Library itself, the grand staircase flanked by lions. The Mid-Manhattan, though blandly elegant, had been made gritty from practical use—unlike the main branch across the street, it was a library where you could borrow books. The Port Authority of libraries. A lending library. Only now, thinking about the transgressions that took place there, does the word *lending* seem conspicuous, the middle gesture in *beg, borrow, and steal*.

What happened with Dr. S was that I found a copy of *National Geographic* with a lengthy article on the *Tyrannosaurus rex* on which I dutifully took notes on index cards. I numbered the cards, as Dr. S had taught us to do. Later, using my friend's father's IBM Selectric—a magnificent machine that pounded each letter into the page with such force it made writing feel like a military exercise—I typed the index cards up in sequence.

When he returned these papers, my copy had no grade, just a terse remark: "See me."

He pointed out that my paper read a great deal like the article in *National Geographic*. In fact, it was an exact replica. He wanted to know how it happened. I told him. It was an innocent mistake, and though I would never have had the resources to articulate it at the time, I think the problem was that I was being asked to follow a procedure—the procedures of research and citation—that foreclosed improvisation. I could dance, but if I tried to follow dance steps I had a mental collapse, as though imagination had to have free rein or be in complete hibernation. A rock coming at me unexpectedly was something I could work with.

And then, two years later, I was back at a long table on the fourth floor of the Mid-Manhattan Library. I won't pretend to know the exact timing of the expulsion and that call to the New York Egg Cream Company, except that in the spring of 1982 I was a kid who must have felt like there was a rock coming toward him.

3.

For a long time, food on the streets of New York came in two principal forms. There were hot dog vendors, who also sold chestnuts, sodas, and pretzels. And then there were ice-cream vendors, who stood behind orange carts outside playgrounds. These were the yin and yang of New York street food, both accompanied by wafting white smoke of one kind or another: In winter, the steam from the hot dogs mixed with the smoke from the coals heating the pretzels and chestnuts; in summer, the heavy lid of the ice-cream cart pulled open to release the billowing white mist from the dry ice inside. The ice-cream man would put his arm down there as though down the throat of a hibernating dragon, and when he pulled it out he was clutching your ice cream.

Then something changed. And quickly. I don't know what larger forces were at work, but street carts started appearing selling things not usually found on the streets of Midtown Manhattan. In May 1981, the *New York Times* restaurant critic, Mimi Sheraton, wrote a column about the phenomenon:

> Today the peripatetic nosher can choose from Mexican tacos, Middle Eastern falafel, Greek souvlaki, Chinese Fu Manchu stew, Japanese tempura, so-called New York-style steak sandwiches and true New York-style hot dogs and egg creams, Afghanistan kofta kebabs and Caribbean beef or chicken curry. The city's largest and most dazzling permanent summer food festival takes place Mondays through Fridays, from about 11:45 a.m. to 2 p.m., reaching from 46th to 55th Streets along the Avenue of the Americas, perhaps more appropriately called, from now until late September, Avenue of the Street Eaters.[1]

Some of the vendors crowding the sidewalks of Midtown were solo artists with one cart, but most were well-financed businesses with their own logos, fleets of carts, and trucks to deliver the carts around the city.

The egg cream, according to sociologist Daniel Bell, was invented by his Uncle Hymie in Hymie's candy store on Second Avenue.[2] The tone of his claim, in a 1971 piece in *New York Magazine*, is half joking, an acknowledgment that the egg cream is among those cultural artifacts of almost no great commercial value over which there is nevertheless a sense of contentious authorship. It stands alongside those other slightly comic Jewish foods: the pickle and the knish.

I had no connection to the egg cream as artifact or as beverage; its roots were in an immigrant culture that preceded my parents' arrival in America. What caught my eye in the summer of 1981 was the design of the carts themselves, which were handsomely outfitted in brown signage with white letters and topped with a brown-and-white umbrella. It was the design, along with curiosity, that made me get that first egg cream—a chocolate or vanilla soda with a frothy head, a clean undertaste of seltzer—and it was the memory of that egg cream, so pleasant, sweet, refreshing, and cheerful, that I remembered the following spring, when I saw that the company that sold it was for sale. I left my message on Sunday. Uncharacteristically, I called again on Monday.

The owner of the company told me it was a great business.

"Then why are you selling it?" I asked.

The problem, he said, was that he had built more carts than he had room for on the two trucks that shuttled them into Midtown and downtown every morning. Sensing that his desperation was obscuring the fact that he was talking to a high school student, I asked some more questions. He never caught on. By our third or fourth conversation, I had to tactfully explain that I didn't have the resources—which is to say, a million dollars—for the whole operation, but was interested in taking one of the unused carts off his hands. He agreed to lease me a cart by the week and sell me supplies from his truck, provided I stored it myself. I was, in essence, a franchise.

Of the owner himself, I have only the dimmest memory. But Bill, his foreman, assistant, and chief operating officer, I can still see today. He was a huge man with big eyes and lanky arms, all topped by a white cowboy hat. His booming voice had a hint of Oklahoma about it, but at the same time there was an edge of panic, as though he had seen a barn burn down at an impressionable age and that tragic image had stayed with him always.

It was Bill who instructed me on how to make an egg cream: You put an inch of milk at the bottom, add two squirts of syrup, and then run seltzer water in, but not straight in. You put a spoon in there, and turn it so the seltzer falls on its back. I don't know why this is the rule, I don't know what law of physics dictated it, but Bill the Egg Cream Cowboy had made a big deal about the spoon part, and about the brisk little stir at the end, and it seemed to work.

Every morning I pushed my cart from the garage where I leased space on Fifty-Fifth Street and Seventh Avenue down to Forty-Seventh Street between Sixth and Seventh, where I met the truck. From Cowboy Bill I got my ration of milk, my seltzer, my pretzel sticks. I got the all-important ice, which would fall like diamonds into the hull of the cart, keeping everything safe from the heat. I got the chocolate and vanilla syrup, the stirrers, the napkins, and the cups.

Laden with a fresh load of supplies, I would push the cart to a place I had chosen on Fifty-Fourth Street and Sixth Avenue, in front of the ABC building, arriving sometime before eleven. The hot dog man was usually already there. The Chipwich man and the Lebanese guy who sold knockoff Louis Vuitton bags usually arrived around noon. I had picked this spot because it was more than two blocks from the nearest egg cream cart but still in the scrum of Midtown, and because the sidewalk was lined with trees set in huge planters, onto which, with a little effort, you could hoist yourself.

I had spent the spring looking for a school that would take me for my senior year, and at the time that I began working my egg cream cart in June, I still had not found one. That egg cream cart was all I had.

For the first week I shouted, "Egg creams! Egg creams! Get your egg creams!" like a madman. The hot dog man on the corner eyed me wearily. I sold a chocolate, I sold a vanilla, I built up a wad of cash, and still every sale seemed certain to be my last. It was a feeling that never really left me the whole summer. I sold and sold. Other than the few times I had to take off for interviews at various military academies (none of which deemed me suitable), I was always selling. At the end of the long days, when the ice in my cart had melted and Midtown had emptied out, I was still reluctant to push back to the garage, hoping for one last sale.

The June days lengthened, and there was no one to tell me to go home and call it a day. Sometimes I lingered there on the relatively empty avenue, making a few late sales, just for the pleasure of being able to. I was in charge of this little company. I was its only employee. I had gotten a lot of incredulous laughs when I'd told people about my summer plans, and though I was happy to laugh along, there was a part of me that really wanted to make a success out of at least one thing in my life.

4.

The feeling that Midtown Manhattan was a labyrinth into which I could disappear and seek refuge had begun the previous summer, when I had lasted all of three weeks as a bike messenger before I convinced the owners of Speedy Messenger Service to let me be a salesman, whereupon I put on a jacket and used my father's old briefcase to cold-call mail rooms of large corporations, asking for meetings. Now and then I got one. By the end of the summer it felt like I had been inside every office building in the city twice, once in shorts and once in a jacket and tie. Sometimes, in the evenings, I would change into shorts and a T-shirt and coast down on my bicycle to sit on a huge granite bench at the base of the Exxon building, where I would watch the passing parade as the buildings emptied.

Then, with a Walkman on, I would begin to coast among the floating debris that the mass exodus of workers had left behind. The bags and papers and cups drifted in circles, pulled by an unseen wind moving through the grand plazas that sat at the base of the huge glass monoliths of Sixth Avenue. I circled on my bicycle, following the swirling debris like a dancer pirouetting in the dust of a just-vanished stampede. There was something about the enormity of the buildings, the density of it all, that made me seem very small and safe—a solitary molecule pulsing through the bloodstream of the world, present yet hardly noticed—a feeling I very much enjoyed, even craved. Midtown was full of places where you could feel hidden in plain sight.

One of these places, it turned out, was a garage on Fifty-Fifth Street, just off Broadway. It was owned by a Greek man, George, who leased the space from a management company. It was a small garage, with most of the parking in the basement and the ground floor. The second floor of the building had offices that had a separate entrance on Broadway, and an apartment. He could squeeze about fifty cars in the whole place.

His expression looked at almost all times as though he had just eaten something unexpectedly sour. His workers were mostly Greek guys who had immigrated more recently than he had and were now working their way through school. They were young guys, eager, strong. He did the books, took cash, and occasionally parked a car, but mostly he sat out front, in the warmer months, in a dilapidated office chair he had found on the street, one leg crossed over the other, an ankle resting on a knee, one of his sandaled feet shaking and bouncing in the manner of teenage boys and undersexed men whose sexual frustration is obvious to anyone at a passing glance.

One corner of his basement kingdom was awkwardly shaped and no good for cars. He rented this space to street vendors; he could get eight of these carts in there. They had use of a hose. He had a bunch of Chinese guys who sold dumplings, Gyoza, and one souvlaki guy. One day a kid, all arms and legs and a big nose, ambled up and said he needed a spot for his cart. The kid was unclear about what he sold. Something with eggs. George asked for 240 a month. Everyone else paid between 150 and 200. The kid, being an amateur, agreed on the spot. No attempt at negotiating.

At some point, early on, I had the shopkeeper's epiphany that it took about four days each week to earn back my expenses. Only later, usually on Thursday, would I cross into a zone in which every additional dollar I pocketed would stay in my pocket. When the July days began to shorten, I began to stay past dark, moving my cart into Times Square. I worked Saturdays and Sundays, too, taking a spot in front of a famous diamond jeweler on Fifth Avenue. I went to high school with his daughter, was my first thought when I set up there, until it struck me that I no longer attended that high school, or any other.

That summer, I lived in fear of rain. Rain was a killer, emptying the streets of people perusing in a summer mood, flattening the day's receipts. One rainy weekday, when I was doing no business at my usual spot on Fifty-Fourth Street and Sixth Avenue, I decided to check out my weekend spot on Fifty-Sixth and Fifth, in front of the diamond dealer. Four carts were lined up along a corner that on weekends was totally empty. At the head of the line was a hot dog guy, whose name was

George; I set up next to the last cart lined up on Fifty-Sixth street, selling expresso shots. Well off Fifth Avenue, but maybe better than Sixth?

Across the street on Fifth Avenue was a guy named Nicky who did huge business with fresh-squeezed orange juice. Nicky and George were cousins. I suspect I learned this later, though I don't remember. I never had a problem on weekends, because it was just me and Nicky the orange juice guy. But now a couple of young guys came up to me that rainy afternoon, told me they were George's sons, and said they didn't want me selling egg creams on their corner. I knew that by *their corner* they not only meant George's, but also some larger, more tacit family, a family for whom street-cart vending wasn't just a summer job.

"The egg cream customer is not the same thing as a hot dog and soda customer!" I reasoned. I pointed out that it was Nicky across the street who should be most threatened, but he never had a problem with me on weekends. I went on at some length until, perceiving that all the talking was not being accompanied by me going anywhere, one of the guys popped me in the mouth. I tasted blood. Showing my true character, I burst into tears. The puncher vanished into the crowd on Fifth Avenue. One guy stayed behind, though, and tried to calm me down. He handed me some napkins from the side of my cart. Whether he was genuinely trying to console me out of human sympathy, or whether he was trying to talk me down because having a kid with blood pouring out of his mouth while sobbing his head off was even worse for George's hot dog and soda stand than having that same kid selling egg creams, I do not know.

I bled on my shirt. My lip got fat. I pushed the cart all the way back to the garage, went to the hospital, and got stitches on the inside of my lip. Then I went back to the garage, got my cart, still with a good amount of cold milk and seltzer and chocolate and vanilla syrup, and pushed it down to Times Square to pick up some of the lost business. I was nestling in the little ship I had built. Bobbing up and down, encouraged by every beat of my heart and every dollar sale, two discrete things that I had started to think of as one.

Sometime in late June, I had, to the total amazement of my mother and me, been accepted into a good, if unconventional, school in Brooklyn

Heights. They accepted me on the spot, the same day as my interview. It had been pouring rain the morning of the interview, which made leaving the cart in the garage less painful. Afterward, I walked outside into a hard summer shower. The drops melted something in me and I started leaping and waving my arms. At some point during the outburst, a shaft of sunlight appeared, and I remember the unbelievable elation I felt dancing down Montague Street—I had been accepted into a high school, a good school. And also, it was going to clear up. I could take the egg cream cart onto the street. The day was not lost.

5.

The poet Harvey Shapiro remembered the iceman coming down the alley with a big block of ice on his back. In his imagination, in his poem, in my memory of his poem, it is early morning, and the sun finds its way into the alley, hits the block of ice being delivered to Shapiro's home sometime in the 1920s, making it gleam. The meaning of the image, for me, was that a block of ice would be delivered in the age before refrigerators, and this delivery would be witnessed by a child, and then written about long afterward by a much older man, incredulous that he'd once lived in such a world. I could go check that poem and find the precise wording, but the poem, the image, the feeling, exist within me, however inaccurately. Fact-checking memory is perilous.

But that is just what I did recently, when I went online to look at the classified ads in the Sunday *New York Times* business section from the spring of 1982. I was looking for the specific ad that I responded to from a pay phone in the Mid-Manhattan Library. The one advertising the New York Egg Cream Company.

I found the page, and even before I found the specific ad, I was fascinated by the arrangement of words, the density of the type with its cacophony of needs, hustles, pitches, pleas. It all read like a secret code. What it revealed was the world I experienced on those streets: the signs, the neon, the expectant faces. An analog world functioning with the arrogance of the present tense, unaware of how antiquated it would one day seem. These images from 1982 rushed up in my memory, so foreign yet familiar. I may as well have been standing at the refrigerator, recalling the iceman coming up the alley early in the morning.

6.

The headmaster of the high school that had accepted me was a highly eccentric figure toward whom my mother and I had a near worshipful attitude, not only because he had let me into his school, but because he regarded me not as a colossal fuckup but as someone who had something interesting to offer, and he had dismissed the folder that had sent all those military academy people into sighing despair as the claptrap that it was. He seemed to know who I was in reality, outside the folder.

In fact he had a better handle on it than I did, which I discovered when he sat down to help me with my college admissions essay. I was on the other side of his desk when, after a few minutes of conversation, he wheeled around in his chair and burst forth with an alarmingly cacophonous attack on his manual typewriter. When it was over there was a page of writing about getting thrown out of school and starting my egg cream business and how I do things in an unusual way but it's my way and it often has interesting results. I was in total shock. Not only had he resolved the conundrum of what to say in my essay by writing it for me, he had explained me to myself a little, which was ultimately the great coup of my egg cream summer.

Notes
1. Mimi Sheraton, "The Pleasures of Outdoor Eating," *New York Times*, May 27, 1981.
2. *New York Magazine*, March 8, 1971.

Somebody's Mother Is Waiting in the Lobby

I went downstairs to park the car. It should have been a straightforward enough errand, but by the time I came back upstairs I had glimpsed a woman's face, and the face had intrigued me. It was a painting of a woman, not an actual woman. Still, something about her expression interested and provoked me.

The encounter happened at night, during the last act of a lovely summer weekend in New York. That afternoon, my family and I had been at the beach, running in and out of the waves that raced at our feet. There was traffic on the way back into the city, but our mood was somehow undimmed. We found a spot right next to the building, a stroke of luck even if it was on "the bad side."

I asked Christian, the doorman, if he was parked on "the good side." Not only was this the case, he said, but he was parked directly in front of the building. And yes, he said, I could have his spot as soon as he finished his shift. To be parked in front of one's building is a source of childish, irrational pleasure.

So it was that I came downstairs a couple of hours later, just before 11, to fetch my car. The elevator door opened to reveal the stage set of the lobby, its two chairs occupied. Sitting in one was a man around my age who lives in the building with his wife and kids. The other chair was occupied by a woman who, for some reason, I assumed was his mother. Outside, under the awning, an old man stood beside a kind of tote bag with wheels, looking bereft, lost. He wore sandals, slacks, a jacket, and a cap, all of which suggested something out of time about him, like he was an émigré from another decade.

When I rolled up in my car a few minutes later to double-park in front of Christian's car, the old man was still there. It was at this exact moment that I realized I had forgotten my iPhone upstairs. I felt a pang of despair, partly because I would have nothing to read while waiting, and partly because, in this longing for my phone, I'd almost betrayed my own modest pledge to go a few days without looking at the device. I had promised myself to stay away from social media and to try to read on my phone as little as possible. A cleanse, if you will. Now, like any struggling addict, I had to acknowledge my intent to break my pledge less than a day after having made it. That I had simply forgotten the proverbial cigarette in my apartment only heightened the betrayal.

As penance, I paid extra-close attention to my surroundings. The phone cleanse was inspired by the fear that, by having entertainment and information in my palm at all times, glowing hypnotically before my eyes, I was letting my observational instinct, my ability simply to be present in a situation, atrophy. In an attempt to refute this, I stared carefully at the bent tree across the street. I had never noticed how bent it was until that summer.

A strong wind was blowing off the Hudson River, and the bent tree under the streetlamp across the street rustled majestically. This corner has always vacillated between breezy and windy; the wind had blown in the same direction for the tree's entire life, causing this tree, over its decades, to bend permanently away from the river. The cobra-neck streetlamp standing beside it lit its leaves from above like it was an exhibit—the Leaning Tree of Riverside Drive.

I turned from the tree to see that the old man in the cap was advancing toward me, squinting anxiously into the headlights. I suddenly realized that he took me for the taxi he had been waiting for. I waved him away, and, realizing his mistake, he slowly returned to his perch beneath the awning.

I sat there watching cars go by, observing the varied body language of the drivers. They tended to slow down when they saw the empty space in front of the hydrant, only to spot the hydrant, speed up, and a moment later, slow down once more in front of the synagogue, with its empty parking place out front, only to see the No Parking sign and speed off.

The old woman from the lobby appeared, conversed with the man with the suitcase, and came up to my open window.

"Are you access?" she said. Or I think that is what she said. She had a strong Russian accent.

"Not a taxi," I said.

"Are you access, yes or no?"

"No."

She went back to the man and said, I assume, something to the effect of "This is not our cab."

At which point a white car pulled into the empty space beside the hydrant, just across from where I was double-parked. A man emerged and ran into the lobby with a couple of bags. He left his hazard lights on, blinking in the dark.

I have mixed feelings about leaving hazards on when double-parked or parked at a hydrant. It's an attempt to break the law politely, as though acknowledging that you are breaking the law somehow mitigates the fact that you are breaking the law, when, in fact, it just draws attention to it. Nevertheless, I turned my hazards on, too, and got out of the car. I stood in the middle of the street, blinking lights on either side of me.

The street had just been paved, the new tar black and smooth. Its surface reminded me of the day, several years earlier, that something went wrong with my mother's breathing. That, too, was a hot summer night, late, like this. She sat in her chair in her bedroom, with her fingers touching her chest, her mouth open. She had a strange expression on her face, like someone had asked her a question she couldn't answer.

"Mom?" I had said. "You all right?"

"I can't seem to breathe," she said softly.

I called 911. In no time at all, the private space of her bedroom was filled with a pair of firemen and a pair of police officers. Once they ascertained that there was no immediate crisis, they spoke among themselves while waiting for EMS. The discussion turned to how awful it was that Mayor Bloomberg was putting in all these bike lanes. How expensive it was. Meanwhile, there was no money for cops and firemen.

I wondered if they were lobbying us indirectly—We're here when you need us, seemed to be the message, so support us when you don't. Because you will need us again.

My mother and I exchanged glances, smiling at the oddness of the situation. By the time EMS showed up, she was breathing just fine. They took her away in an ambulance anyway. I came downstairs to watch it leave. The street had just been paved and the ambulance drove slowly down the newly paved street with its lights blinking but no siren. On its own the silence of this tableau might have suggested something funereal, as though the emergency were over because the medics arrived too late. But I knew that she was OK. I stood there on the street watching the ambulance as it moved slowly down the block, its lights blinking but silent, like a ship sailing off into the dark sea with my mother on board.

That was five years before my night waiting for the doorman's parking spot. Or maybe seven. Or three? Children ruin your sense of time, even as they grow up so fast that they bludgeon you with the relentless reality of time. All I knew was that the night of the silent ambulance occurred in the summer, that season when I move my family into my childhood home, still occupied by my mother, who is always happy to have us. And now I stood in the same spot, on a similarly unmarked, unfaded, pristinely black street, flanked by blinking hazard lights.

The replacement doorman arrived, though it would be another ten minutes or so before Christian emerged and got in his car.

I went and sat on the metal grate surrounding the flower bed next to the awning. The guy who had parked by the hydrant came out, went to his car, and then returned to the building with a painting under his arm. A framed oil painting, rectangular in shape, unwrapped, tucked under his arm. In the brevity of its passing I perceived the face of a woman wearing a curious, inscrutable expression and a green dress. Or was it a green background? It was evocative of the early, more figurative Picasso, yet there was something midcentury about its style, too.

I didn't recognize the guy with the painting. Maybe he was delivering it to someone in the building, I thought. Maybe this guy was new? It was a pretty big building. But then, I didn't live in the building, either. I was just a visitor, even if I had moved in when I was two weeks old and had been in and out of the place my whole life. Sensing that maybe I would never see him again, and wanting some connection with the painting, or with the story of the painting, I said, as he came out of the lobby, "Cool painting."

"My mom," he responded, without missing a beat, as he hurried back to his car.

Why, I wondered, would someone arrive with a portrait of his mother in the middle of the night? His smile had a sweet, rueful sense of recognition when he spoke the words "My mom." I was suddenly sure that she was dead.

He got into his car and drove off. It wasn't clear from the angle of his chin whether he was driving to a garage, or simply beginning the process of circling, or if he was heading somewhere else entirely, having made his delivery.

After Christian came out in street clothes, waved at me, and I happily inherited his spot, I walked into the lobby, entered the elevator, and turned to see the painting of the man's mother leaning against the bench on the opposite side of the lobby, face out. I glimpsed it at no greater length than I had earlier, and yet, with almost no specific information, it continued to intrigue me. I don't know why.

I went upstairs in the elevator, retrieved my phone, and went right back down to the lobby. The painting was still there, I was relieved to see. The Russian guy in the cap was sitting on one chair, having given up his post on the curb. His son sat in the other chair. The woman who said "Are you access, yes or no?" was on the bench next to the painting.

I walked toward it with my phone and took a picture of it. I made sure to get close enough so as to let the woman on the bench know that she was not in the frame, that it was the painting in which I was interested, not her. Nevertheless, she scooched over a bit—to make room for my shot or to protect her own privacy, I will never know.

The subject of the painting had no choice in the matter.

I went back to the elevator and rode upstairs while peering at the photograph of the painting on my phone. Her expression was wry, amused, a bit insolent—in an appealing way—almost indignant, too, but warm. I was not at all sure of the ethics of having photographed it. In fact, I felt like I had just stolen something. It was a very curious, ambiguous expression on her face. Now it was on my phone. I couldn't help but think that the expression contained, among other things, a question about why she had been left in a lobby where a stranger could capture her image with his phone.

I lived with this ambiguity—wondering if I should just leave it alone. But then I had to start asking questions of the doorman who had been on duty that night. And I found the guy with the painting. I left a note under his door. He called me, very friendly, and told me the two things that I for some reason needed to know. Yes, that was his mother, and, yes, she had died recently, and he had taken her portrait home from the house in Connecticut where she had lived. And, yes, I could reproduce that photograph, if I wanted.

That Time My Band Opened for Blur

Everyone who has been in a rock band has an outlier, that one gig where they glimpsed the rock-and-roll life in another dimension. This perspective shift is common because of the opening act. A friend of mine recently told me that her devoutly Mormon father had once, in his youth, opened for the Beach Boys in Portland, Oregon's Memorial Coliseum, capacity thirteen thousand. His band, Aesop's Fable, had previously only played small clubs. These glimpses always come from an elevation that is higher than one is used to, and they can be profound, even traumatic. Cameron Crowe made a whole movie out of such a glimpse, and his came as a journalist.

My glimpse took place when my band opened for Blur, in 1992. I was the drummer. Our assets were a very talented singer-songwriter guitarist who had been in, or at least proximate to, another band that was famous; a bassist with connections in the music business; and a morose lead guitarist whose mother was going to put us up at her house in Berkeley when we drove out to play the West Coast.

Most of our high points took place on that one West Coast tour, in 1990. We played the Paradise Lounge and the I-Beam in San Francisco. We played the Vogue in Seattle, and met a guy who agreed to do our T-shirts. He also did T-shirts for Nirvana, a fact we proceeded to mention at every opportunity (a habit that clearly persists). Then there was the Los Angeles conundrum: two opportunities on the same night. We had to choose between the legendary punk venue Al's Bar or an industry showcase for a just-signed heavy metal band that no one had ever heard of. We chose Al's. The band we declined to open for was called Alice in Chains.

Our opening for Blur, at the Marquee in New York, was a happy accident—our bassist, Jim Merlis, was the publicist at their American label. He had shepherded them through their first American tour a year earlier. When Blur arrived in America in 1992, the band members surprised him with a tour schedule that included our band on the bill at the Marquee.

I loved the Marquee. It was a dank barn on West Twenty-First Street, in the thick of what is now the gallery/High Line district. At the time, the neighborhood's only art outpost was the Dia Foundation. In 1991 I had worked there as a museum guard. The downside of the gig was standing on your feet all day; the upside was they let you read. One afternoon, while watching people peruse paintings by Brice Marden, I felt the place begin to rumble and shake. It took a moment to realize that this wasn't a passing truck, but rather some kind of music. Then, to my amazement, I recognized it as a Mudhoney song. On our West Coast tour, we had been very excited by all the Sub Pop bands—the Fluid, TAD, L7. We had all gone to see Mudhoney at the I-Beam. It was the second show of two nights. We later heard that they had apparently been great the first night. No matter, it had felt like we were in on something early, something exciting, and everything that had happened since then, the release of *Nevermind* above all, had only served to enhance that feeling. I was going to see Mudhoney that very night. What were the odds that somebody would be blasting a Mudhoney song in Chelsea? Then I realized that the back of the Marquee, where the stage and the speakers are, abutted the back of the Dia building, with its hushed galleries. This was Mudhoney's sound check. The concert that night was chaotic and very enjoyable, but the first seconds of that sound check, when their indecorous music rampaged through the hushed, cement-floored gallery like an earthquake, was one of the great rock experiences of my life.

The Blur show was about a year later. Nirvana, a novelty a year before, were now a template. We were a couple of years away from grunge becoming so prevalent that Marc Jacobs would send models down a runway in silk shirts made to look like flannel, but the famous *Sassy* cover of Kurt Cobain and Courtney Love had already run, and, in general, the incredible sea change in the culture had been effected—the fake was suddenly out, and real was suddenly in, at least in terms of music. One of the fake things that had been overturned was the absurd macho posturing of hair metal bands. This is part of what made the brevity of the Nirvana moment so upsetting—their sound was quickly co-opted by bands who resumed the macho–cock rock posturing of the hair metal bands, but with different outfits. No amount of cardigans and songs called "Rape Me" could turn the tide, even when Kurt was alive. And then he wasn't. But that was later.

When Blur rolled into town in 1992, it felt like their moment had already passed. The musical tension and intrigue of their first record, *Leisure*, had played out in the dialogue between Graham Coxon's intricate guitar licks and Damon Albarn's cheeky vocal melodies. Also, Damon was really pretty. At some point in the midst of the Brit moment in the art world, someone had a show that included a poster of Blur onto which the artist had ejaculated multiple times. Such was the fever around Damon. The prettiness was a visual effect, but it manifested in the very sound of his voice—taunting, naughty, theatrically British—and in the lush enveloping melodies of Blur songs.

For this reason, the Marquee was filled mostly with girls. And I think also partly for this reason, Damon got very drunk and almost killed himself by climbing up to the rafters and hanging upside down by his knees while shouting into a megaphone, a favorite prop of his at the time; it functioned as a kind of manual vocoder. The megaphone vocal was part of the song, but eventually the song ended, and Damon was still hanging upside down. The rest of the band—Graham, Alex, Dave—had mostly averted their gaze while they were playing, but now they joined everyone else in staring upward into the rafters looking worriedly at the drunken man hanging upside down by his knees, forty feet above the floor. The longer he stayed up there, shouting into his megaphone like a deranged gym teacher, the more it seemed like he was really out of his mind drunk and in danger of falling and breaking his neck. This put his many devoted fans in a strange predicament. At first they had stood shrieking up at him with their arms raised, their voices and postures those of worshipful fans. But after a while, the tone became one of pleading and then alarm. They loved Damon, but were they willing to die for him? The answer came in the space beneath him, which began to get less and less crowded. Somehow he got down. The show went on.

By then we had played our set. My view from behind the drums was of a huge room that was mostly empty. But as our set progressed, it filled up. We finished in front of a thousand people. That this surge had nothing to do with us didn't dampen the moment. Backstage the view was a tiny bit different—the trappings of a national act, the bus, the merch, all of it impressed me. But as I said, on some level it felt like Blur was swimming against a tide of American grunge. The other opening act, the real one, was a band of flannel-wearing Brits called the Senseless Things. They were so enamored of American indie rock that their album featured them holding a Replacements record.

At the end of the night Jim and I stood outside and were accosted, politely, by a group of young girls who had seen us play. Never mind that we were the opening act's opening act, they asked us to sign their jeans, and provided a Sharpie for us to do so. As I signed I noticed that a man was sitting in the driver's seat in a minivan up the block. Some intuition, proven correct a moment later when they all marched over to the van and got in, told me that this was the father of one of these girls. His silhouette, a stillness brimming with forbearance, has remained one of the most vivid images from the night, perhaps because I wondered, just then, if I could ever be in such a position myself.

Blur released a second record a year later, *Modern Life Is Rubbish*. It didn't sell, though I loved it. And then came their breakout record, *Parklife*, and their reign as the inventors of Britpop and the era of that Blur poster reinvented as stiffened modern art. *Parklife*, at the time, seemed to me like an incredible comeback, an incredible act of reinvention. But it was nothing compared to what followed their clash with Oasis, two years later, and all that mid-nineties pageantry, a Battle of the Bands on a national scale. It was a rout. It should be noted that it was Damon who picked the fight, moving the release date of their single "Country House" to match that of Oasis's "Roll with It." Which would go to No. 1? Blur won that battle, but the war had already been lost, and for a while it was so lost it seemed impossible Blur could continue to exist. Oasis was the national band. I heard a story about Damon walking down the street in London and people opening their windows and turning up Oasis as he passed by.

I'm not suggesting pity for a rock star. Just that it was remarkable when Blur came back with their eponymous album *Blur* in 1997, which, in addition to having some great songs, "Beetlebum" in particular, also had an incredibly popular one, "Song 2." This tiny little bombshell of shouting and crunching guitars alternating with Damon's boy-in-short-pants voice, besides finally breaking Blur into the American market, has now entered that strange pantheon of British pub songs that fill American sports stadiums in moments of elation. (The king of this genre is "Rock and Roll Part II," aka the British "Louie," sung by a man in a pink jumpsuit, Gary Glitter, who in recent years has entered another, more distressing category: English Pedophiles in Show Business.)

It was around this time that the central dialogue between Graham and Damon became an outright schism: Graham declared an allegiance to the American band Pavement and its low-fi sound while Albarn went off and started a rap-pop group whose physical manifestation was an animated cartoon, Gorillaz, and sold millions of records. It seemed like an ingenious move on Damon's part, staying on the charts while remaining completely out of sight.

Blur didn't flame out. They dissolved like sugar in bitter tea. Their 1999 record, 13, was notable for its song "Tender." I saw them perform the whole album live backed by the Harlem Choir at Roseland. The song from that album that most impressed me was called "No Distance Left to Run," an agonized breakup song whose first words are "It's over." It made a big impression on me at the time, perhaps because I knew that Damon and his longtime girlfriend Justine Frischmann, a pop star in her own right with Elastica, had broken up. In subsequent years Damon put out solo records in which he explored world music. He started a one-off Afro-punk supergroup, the Good, the Bad, and the Queen. Eventually Blur reunited. I'm not even sure I noticed. They played some concerts in England. You can see YouTube videos of a hundred thousand festival goers swaying together and finishing Damon's lyrics. And now they have put out a new album. They came through America for a two-date blitz. LA and New York, where they played Madison Square Garden, by far the biggest venue they have played in America. I witnessed this tour from the distance of New Orleans, watching as they moved left to right across the country, beat-beat and done, like a line in a haiku.

What amazes me about Blur's triumphant return is partly how ancient all this history is. And partly how unexpectedly resilient Albarn and Blur have become. In his youth, Albarn was so cheeky and boyishly beautiful, it was impossible to imagine that he could age, or that, in doing so, it could somehow be all right. But it turns out Albarn and Blur have aged well, or at least it seems so from a distance. This distance is an unexpected pleasure of all one's long-ago adventures—you can see them for their virtues, when the sting of disappointment has faded.

Our band had one single. When Damon went up to the rafters for his extended stay as an upside-down pop star with no net, we were in the midst of recording a follow-up at a nearby studio. Our singer, Tom Cushman, watched the first few songs of Blur's set and then left to record his vocals. The record never came out. We had an offer, but we held out for a better one just on the horizon. When it didn't materialize, everything collapsed. That was the end of the band. That performance at the Marquee is preserved in the raspy sound of Tom's vocals on the song "This One's on Me." I can hear it whenever I want, but only in my memory. I don't have a copy of the recording. You open a drawer to the past for the purpose of moving some old relics around as though curating an exhibit, and then something with life still in it jumps up and bites you.

Death of a Movie Theater

There is something disturbing about a blank movie marquee. It's like a face without a mouth. I don't mean the brief transitory blankness when the lettering for one movie is taken down at the end of its run to be replaced with lettering for the next movie but, rather, a marquee that remains blank, day after day, week after week, month after month. This has been the condition of the Lincoln Plaza Cinemas marquee, on Sixty-Third Street and Broadway, which closed at the end of January 2018. The lease was not renewed. Every time I pass it by, the blankness provokes a feeling that some crime has been committed here. For a while, as though to make the metaphor explicit, some construction equipment beneath the marquee was surrounded by yellow tape.[1] The theater had been at that location for thirty years, but its legacy dates much further back, to a pair of cinema visionaries and entrepreneurs named Dan and Toby Talbot.

In 1934, Broadway had eighteen movie theaters between Fifty-Ninth Street and 110th Street. By 1960, according to Toby Talbot, there were just ten. "Most were 'flea pits' or 'toilets' in movie house jargon," Talbot writes in her book, *The New Yorker Theater and Other Scenes from a Life at the Movies*. In 1960, Toby and her husband, Dan, were just cinema buffs with two little children who had been fantasizing about opening a bookstore, perhaps somewhere up in New Hampshire. On long driving expeditions to scout for locations, they passed the time by making lists of all the old movies they would like to see again. "One day my sister and brother-in-law casually mentioned that their accountant was thinking of buying the Yorktown theater on Broadway between 88th and 89th Streets," she writes. "Maybe we should talk."[2]

One February evening, the accountant, Henry Rosenberg, came to dinner. He gave the Talbots a year to run the theater as an art house, and then they would see. The Talbots replaced the seats in the Yorktown—all nine hundred of them—with seats from the just-closed Roxy Theatre, which had opened in 1927. They changed the name from the Yorktown to the New Yorker, named after the Miami Beach hotel opened by Toby's Uncle Harry in the early 1930s. The first program, in March 1960, was a double feature of *Henry V*, starring Laurence Olivier, and the celebrated French short *The Red Balloon*. Two thousand moviegoers came on opening night. The next program, also a success, was Carl Theodor Dreyer's *Day of Wrath* paired with Marcel Pagnol's *Harvest*. This was followed by Orson Welles's *The Magnificent Ambersons* and Robert Frank and Alfred Leslie's *Pull My Daisy*, which Talbot describes as "a quirky Beat generation riff shot in Leslie's loft in 1959 and narrated by Jack Kerouac of the mellifluous voice."[3]

At some point, a mouthy teenager named Peter Bogdanovich started showing up and pestering the Talbots with programming ideas; he would write program notes and advise the Talbots on selecting films—the Marx Brothers, Buster Keaton, and W. C. Fields were all heavily featured—and soon the place developed a reputation. The book includes a marvelous picture of Dan standing with Alfred Hitchcock in front of the theater's marquee, an atmosphere of toughness, comedy, and erudition crackling between the two men in their rather ostentatious suits.

Dan's father, who had studied language and philosophy at Krakow University but only to end up a textile jobber in New York, did not approve of the enterprise, despite its fast start. "Get yourself some real work," he told his son. "Study to be a pharmacist."[4] In 1962, rejecting this wisdom, the Talbots bought out the lease. It's not hyperbole to say that with both their theaters (they went on to own several after the New Yorker) and their distribution company (founded in 1965 when a twenty-three-year-old filmmaker named Bernardo Bertolucci couldn't find distribution for a film that the Talbots wanted to show), they profoundly affected the fate of cinema in America. But even that observation feels too general to convey the loss around the demise of Lincoln Plaza Cinemas, the six-screen movie theater that they ran from 1981 until January 28, 2018.

It's difficult for me to write about Lincoln Plaza Cinemas with any objectivity because my relationship with the theater is entirely bound up with the Talbots, whom I have known as family friends for what feels like forever. On closer inspection, I realize they came into my life shortly after my father's death. Because I met them as a child, there were tactile, sensory things that stuck in my memory: the smell of

Toby's scarves, the gleam of Dan's shoes, the relaxed, expansive sound of their laughter. It took a while for me to wonder what Dan and Toby did for a living. It took a while longer than that for me to *understand* what they did for a living.

I could grasp owning a movie theater; what it meant that they actually distributed movies, though—this was more abstract. I came to understand that there was a whole world of non-Hollywood movies, often made abroad, whose presence on New York screens was anything but a foregone conclusion, and that someone had to choose to exhibit them. Even then, it took a long while for me to fathom the accomplishment inherent in their choices: their discovery of filmmakers like Bertolucci, Fassbinder, and Werner Herzog, for example, or their championing of Godard, Truffaut, Fellini, and Claude Lanzmann.

Last December, the news broke that Lincoln Plaza Cinemas would be closing. In spite of its reliable profitability, the landlord had declined to renew the lease. Howard Milstein, patriarch of the family that owned the building, had, after an initial period of discussion, stopped returning the Talbots' calls. For much of the past year, Dan had not been well. But what about Toby? Before that question could even be answered, and shortly after the news that the theater would close, came the news of Dan's passing.

A friend of mine who once worked in a bookstore told me that whenever the building put up scaffolding, customers whom he hadn't seen in years would rush into the store in a panic, asking if it was going out of business. Told no, they would vanish again until the next panic. But that was not the case with Lincoln Plaza Cinemas, which did good business until its very last day. A petition was circulated in the run-up to this closure with the tagline "Save Lincoln Plaza Cinemas." And though it seemed at first to be a purely symbolic gesture, it generated more than twelve thousand signatures. Surely, it is important to raise a fist in protest against these plunderings. The same grief that propelled all of us to sign a petition protesting the end of Lincoln Plaza Cinemas led to the creation of a group called New Plaza Cinema, which hopes to continue the programming of the Talbots somewhere on the Upper West Side.[5] It has Toby Talbot's blessing, if not direct involvement.

As soon as I heard about Lincoln Plaza Cinemas' imminent closing, I rushed to the theater as often as I could, as though to visit a loved one in intensive care. I saw the Churchill movie *Darkest Hour*, and I saw the new Haneke movie, which I found to be hilarious at times, though I seemed to be the only one laughing in the dark. I saw the previews for my own mother's film, which, in a further complication, opened at the theater on January 5. There was a memorial for the theater, a kind of closing ceremony, held at Lincoln Plaza Cinemas on January 28. It was open to the public. Clips from movies that had been shown there over the years (*Tampopo*, *Aguirre, the Wrath of God*, *Shoah*, to name just a few) were interspersed with commentary from filmmakers and writers (Wallace Shawn, Molly Haskell, Phillip Lopate, Michael Moore, among others) and the theater's employees.

I couldn't attend, having just returned home to New Orleans, but later I wrote someone in attendance—my mother—to ask about that last day. It felt like a terrible loss, I said. But why?
She responded:

It is not so much the physical place as it is the atmosphere. The level of the films. The world of the films selected that created, in turn, a world of its own that encompassed us. The physical space became dear to us. I want to hug it so it could not be taken away from us. But it is not hug-able. It is the elusive very special and unique something created by Daniel and Toby, by their personalities, humanity, special taste, intelligence.

The way that the end of the theater so neatly coincided with the death of Dan has made the entire experience seem emotionally perverse. Dan was ninety-one. It almost feels as if the whole thing had naturally come to an end. But it did not have to end. Now that it is gone, I have been thinking: What was this entity that could not be hugged?

I was hired as an usher at the theater shortly after it opened, in 1981, when I was sixteen. It was one of my first jobs, and therefore it was one of the first jobs from which I got fired. I lasted all of two days. The firing infraction was that I kept getting into conversations with people as they waited in line about what else was playing. Some of these films were good, I felt, and some were not, and I had a lot to say in either case. The manager politely told me to look for a job where freely expressing my opinions to customers would be appropriate, or at least tolerated. I didn't feel at all bitter about this. I had so enjoyed the two days of talking with, and to, the captive audience in line that it hadn't even felt like a job, really, which I knew, even then, meant I probably wasn't doing it right.

In its early years, after it opened, there was something sleek, even a bit opulent, about the place. The seats felt cushy, the polished metal of the two escalators churning in opposite directions had a glitzy, show-biz quality. Over the years, that faded. The concession stand sold some unusual things—salmon sandwiches, hard pretzels, pieces of cake. The staff had been mostly unchanged. At some point, maybe a decade in, a huge mural by the Talbots' daughter Nina appeared on one of the walls. It depicted faces talking. This only added to the feeling of mom-and-pop-ness, of idiosyncrasy and taste. In the thirty years of its run, the movies changed but the place didn't. The quality and taste of Dan and Toby Talbot never faded.

It was toward the end of high school or early in college that I started going regularly. I liked to go to the late show, ideally on a Sunday night. If the movie was a hit, I would wait until the second or third week of its run, when the crowds had dissipated. The theater would be mostly empty, or at least empty enough that I could properly spread out. For a long time, I got a popcorn and a soda, but then I started experimenting with the bags of hard pretzels. By the end, thirty years later, I was a pretty staunch hard-pretzels guy. I liked the quiet, nondescript nature of these late shows, and how, when I came back aboveground afterward, somewhere near the midnight hour, the city had quieted. It felt like I'd been hiding out down there while the whole world above me shifted.

I saw many movies there but recall very few specific instances of the act of seeing. One vivid moment I do recall involved Jim Jarmusch's *Stranger Than Paradise*. I suddenly became aware, in the theater, of myself, and of what was on the screen. I remember the moment: The film's protagonists are about to embark on a road trip. One of the characters, a woman, says something in a foreign language. Or maybe just a foreign accent. There is snow on the ground, and this accentuates the starkness of the black-and-white footage. There is an old car. Are they going to go on a road trip? Or not go on the road trip? That is the question. One of the guys is wearing a hat. Or both of the guys. Nothing much is happening on-screen, not even talking. Yet I remember feeling this tingle of excitement, of discovery. Or was it just boredom? I remember discussing this with myself as I came out of the theater. I may even have stopped to read the review posted near the box office. It felt as though I had discovered something, some way not only of seeing, but of being.

Central to a movie theater's somewhat paradoxical charm is its anonymity—a public place where people do private things: kiss, cry, laugh. This is captured in such book titles as Nabokov's *Laughter in the Dark* and Pauline Kael's *I Lost It at the Movies*. Roland Barthes writes of how, after leaving a theater, it is as though he has emerged from hypnosis, with its inevitable association with psychoanalysis. I agree with this characterization and its suggestion of moviegoing as self-discovery, though perhaps one feels, upon leaving the theater, not just like a patient after a session but also an analyst.

The best representation of a movie theater as a setting for epiphanies is Delmore Schwartz's short story "In Dreams Begin Responsibilities." The narrator goes to a theater and sees, up on the big screen, his mother and father in the act of courtship, before their wedding and his birth. He watches the developments with increasing ambivalence. Eventually, his father proposes. At the key moment, the narrator can restrain himself no longer and begins to shout, "Don't do it!"[6]

At the back of *The New Yorker Theater*, Toby Talbot lists notable films shown in each year of its existence, and one title recently caught my eye: *A Flash of Green*. I have thought of a scene at the end of that film for many years. The movie came out in 1984 and centers around a small community in Florida that is trying to resist the development of a power plant on the Florida coast. There is one man in particular who fights it. The fight is lost. The movie ends with the man standing at the edge of the water, a bay of some kind. It's night, and he is peering at the newly built plant in the distance. There is a bitter comedy in the moment, or, rather, sadness leavened by something else. Something ever so slightly redemptive in this simple act of witnessing the built power plant glowing in the distance, emitting its poisons. Is it the simple act of testifying to a fight that was intensely fought? But there was also a sense of devastation in this plant glimmering in the distance, a devastation that would be felt for a long time. In my memory the light it emits is green, a kind of grim echo of the green light at the end of *The Great Gatsby*.

I'm not sure how, but this scene, and the feeling of ambiguity it provoked, got into my head and lay dormant there, only to surface now and then, often when some seemingly hopeless environmental battle is on the verge of being lost. Here in New Orleans, there is a drama unfolding in which the local electric utility, Entergy, is trying to build a gas plant in New Orleans East over the objections of the community. The company was caught hiring actors to pack a city council hearing on the subject, leaving actual citizens outside. An act of grotesque civic malfeasance for which there were few meaningful consequences.

Reading about this, thirty-three years after I saw the movie, I thought of *A Flash of Green*. There is so much in art and life that you don't know about until people like the Talbots create a space where you wander in, open-minded, trusting that you might encounter some revelation, something that might stay with you.

Notes

1. It seemed logical that the construction equipment was for the purpose of removing the marquee, but after a few weeks the equipment was gone and the marquee remained. This piece was published in 2018, at which point the marquee had remained in place, and blank, for nine months. Seven years later, the marquee remains in exactly the same state.
2. Toby Talbot, *The New Yorker Theater and Other Scenes from a Life at the Movies* (Columbia University Press, 2009), 4–5.
3. Talbot, *New Yorker Theater*, 8.
4. Talbot, *New Yorker Theater*, 7.
5. After some false starts, it has for years now been showing art house and repertory programming in a small auditorium at the Macaulay Honors College at 35 West Sixty-Seventh Street.
6. Delmore Schwartz, *In Dreams Begin Responsibilities and Other Stories* (New Directions, 1978), 6.

A Few Words About Jerry Stiller

Jerry Stiller has died at the age of ninety-two. For the last few years of his life he made a habit of sitting in a little folding chair in front of my mother's building and greeting people who came in and out. I always enjoyed seeing him, especially when my kids were with me. Jerry was one of the grown-ups in the building whom, when I was a kid, I would sometimes see in the elevator, or in his apartment, where he might come upon me staring into his fridge before I retreated to his son's room. I didn't spend a whole lot of time with Ben, but we had the same babysitter and were part of a gang of kids about the same age in the building who started spending time together, now and then, starting at the age of six.

When you are a kid, the parents of your friends, classmates, and neighbors are not distinct. They are more like benign features of a local scenery that might otherwise be unfriendly, even harsh, as was the Upper West Side of the late 1960s and '70s in which I grew up. But these parents occasionally distinguish themselves in some memorable, lasting way, which was the case with Stiller and me.

The Stillers lived on the fifth floor. We lived on fourteen. I first grasped what Stiller and his wife, Anne Meara, did, and what they were about, while visiting another friend, on fifteen. The parents of that household hosted a regular group that included Mel Brooks, Zero Mostel, Joseph Heller, and some others. It was on the fifteenth floor that I first heard Mel Brooks and Carl Reiner's 2000 *Year Old Man* comedy albums (the reanimated caveman's favorite inventions of the modern world are Saran Wrap and the nectarine) and through those voices I grasped the tones of the Borscht Belt comedy-circuit sensibility and its manifestations on television. Also on fifteen, I heard some of Stiller and Meara's comedy records, which seemed of a similar cast to Brooks and Reiner but organized around the husband-and-wife dynamic. At that time, Stiller and Meara were like the married Crazy Eddie of wine, because their radio ads for Blue Nun were on heavy rotation.

It was from these comedy roots that Jerry drew the over-the-top performances for which he is well known—on *Seinfeld*, primarily, but elsewhere, too. A rube, a man of appetites, insistent, confused, but also innocent—that was the vibe of his characters. I don't wish to take anything away from the qualities that make him beloved, but I valued him for other reasons. Jerry was for me a figure of nearly spiritual solemnity and warmth, on account of what his face was like at rest, the deep lines. I know him, and cherish him, most of all for an exchange that we had when we were alone in the elevator shortly after I turned ten, when my father had just died.

I was going down. The elevator stopped on the fifth floor. Jerry got on, turned to me, his face very still, and looked at me. I had no sense of how much he did or didn't know my father. They certainly weren't close, but who knows? Maybe they once shared a cab. The sheer camaraderie of raising kids who were the same age in the same building would have meant something. Perhaps my father's status as a refugee from Vienna added to Jerry's feelings about him. After a moment of looking at me, he said, "Your father's death is a tragedy. A tragedy."

I saw a tear coming down his cheek. I was shocked by this show of emotion, not because I didn't think of Jerry as emotional but because I had never much thought of him. This tear and the words consoled me enormously and move me still. It meant a lot that another dad, a grown-up in the building with some sense of my life and my world, would recognize the gravity of the situation. I don't recall my response. But even as I was brought anew into my grief about my father as I stared into Jerry's face, I felt powerfully that I had an ally who could participate in the impossible task of remembering my father, or at least remembering that feeling of loss.

The second phase of my relationship with Jerry and, to some extent, Anne began after I moved out of New York, because that is when I started spending a lot of time at my mother's apartment. During the summer and over winter holidays, we would pile into her apartment on fourteen: my pregnant wife and I, at first; then Elizabeth, baby, and I; then a second baby—all of us setting up in my childhood bedroom. Most of the parents of the old gang were still in residence,

Jerry and Anne included. To my surprise, I made friends with Anne. She had always frightened me a little, so brassy and direct! But one day I escorted my brassy and direct five-year-old daughter on a trick-or-treating mission in the building, and Anne opened the door dressed as a witch, or was it a nurse? Evangeline and Anne had a kind of conversation in which Anne gave the kid as good as she got. I was thrilled to have found someone who could at last stand up to my daughter.

At some point, Anne wrote a personal essay about her childhood for a publication that I edited. It was called "Old Nuns." It toggles between the present and snatches of past memory, including a reminiscence about her and Jerry's infrequent experiments with pot:

> I was one of those straights who inhale a joint and announce to everyone around me that, "I don't think this is working ... I don't feel anything." Then one of our friends would say something innocuous like, "Let's leave the kids with the sitter and eat dinner at Scandia." I would immediately burst into uncontrollable laughter: "My God, that is so hilarious, the wit, the insight!" Jerry would get very Hasidic and claim he was allergic to marijuana, that it infected his gums or something.[1]

That tossed-off line about Jerry getting "very Hasidic" jumped out at me as both funny and familiar somehow. Once, as adults, Ben Stiller and I went back to his childhood apartment to look for some of the Super 8 tapes he had made as a kid, which were the basis for a project that we were working on. There, I passed a framed drawing of Jerry done by Al Hirschfeld, with the "Ninas" that Hirschfeld drew into his compositions. It was very spare and had that Hasidic lion quality that I associate with Jerry, a different note than the ones he struck in his acting.

After Anne died, in 2015, Jerry began to spend time sitting outside the building in a chair, a kind of mayoral position, greeting people on their way in or out and also the occasional passersby, some of whom would recognize him and respond with excitement. Naturally, I would stop and chat, and my kids would, too. Jerry had become foggy by then—you were never sure if he recognized you or remembered you—but he carried it lightly, and was always able to keep a conversation going. The front-door sidewalk encounters were precious.

But there is another moment that stays with me, nearly as vividly as the elevator scene. It took place a few years earlier, when Anne was still alive, late one Saturday night. I was walking up to the newsstand on Broadway to buy a copy of the Sunday paper, which had something of mine in it, and who should I see coming in the opposite direction down the hill from Broadway but Jerry Stiller. It was a balmy night, but Jerry had on a long winter coat, and he was pulling a carry-on suitcase along on two wheels. Although it was after midnight, he was wearing a huge pair of Anna Wintour–like sunglasses. I suppose it's possible that he had flown in from somewhere and asked the cab to stop on Broadway so he could walk the last few blocks. At the time, this possibility did not occur to me. I just assumed that Jerry had decided that he wanted to take a walk at midnight in sunglasses, and had brought a carry-on bag. We greeted each other warmly, and before I could ask what he was doing, he asked me what I was doing.

"Going to get the paper," I said. "I have a piece in it. I suppose I just wanted to see my name in print."

Something about the bashfulness with which I conveyed this provoked him.

"Have you ever heard of the word *nachas*?" he asked, pronouncing it with the harsh sound at the back of the throat that one hears in Hebrew and Yiddish.

"No," I said.

He launched into a long disquisition, explaining how it was a Yiddish word that meant being proud of somebody.

With his fist raised he said, "Sometimes you have to have *nachas* for yourself!"

I found this quite uplifting, and we parted ways with a wave and in good spirits, me up to the newsstand on Broadway, and Jerry in his sunglasses, dragging along the carry-on bag, which zigzagged this way and that behind him, full of life.

Note
1. Anne Meara, "Old Nuns," *Mr. Beller's Neighborhood*, June 8, 2009, https://mrbellersneighborhood.com/2009/06/old-nuns.

Loitering with Intent at *Manet/Degas*

Near the end of the *Manet/Degas* exhibit at the Metropolitan Museum of Art, there is a small drawing by Edgar Degas of a bearish man with a beard. At first glance, you might think the man in the drawing is Édouard Manet, but in fact he's an author and critic named Edmond Duranty. Nine years before this drawing was created, Duranty wrote something critical of Manet, in response to which Manet, encountering Duranty in a café, slapped him. Duranty demanded that Manet apologize. Manet refused. Duranty challenged Manet to a duel. The duel, by sword, took place three days later. Manet was unscathed; I guess you could say he won. Duranty, the man in the Degas drawing, "received a wound in his upper chest," as the museum text accompanying the drawing states matter-of-factly. I stared incredulously at the text's last line: "Surprisingly, the two men remained friends after the incident."

By the time I really noticed the Duranty drawing, I was on my sixth or seventh visit to *Manet/Degas*. I'd been dipping in and out of it ever since it opened, arriving at odd hours and lingering. There are public spaces where, if you stay long enough, you start to feel like you own the place or at least belong.

I used to do this when I was a teenager—I'd come to the Met, decline to pay the "suggested" admission, hand over a penny (which was the prerogative of locals), and then proceed to the same few spots over and over. It wasn't sensitivity to art that brought me to the museum; it was more like curiosity and comfort. These visits were, I think, a form of self-soothing about money and, to use a modern term, inclusion—there was some unconscious and irrational feeling that if I went often enough, the museum would become my own private club. There was some equation of occupancy and possession. An irrational and legally unsound principle that nevertheless is a primary tool by which many New Yorkers survive the city. It's why I sometimes get so happy when parking a car or sitting on a park bench.

Back then, my spots were the black sarcophagus next to the glass wall in the Temple of Dendur and Jackson Pollock's *Autumn Rhythm*. Now, new membership in hand, it was this *Manet/Degas* show that I returned to, over and over. I usually arrived shortly before closing time when there were no lines, an experience not unlike showing up at the airport and finding that there is no wait to get through security. You still have to walk through a long maze of ropes, but you get to the start of your trip right away.

The show for me offered a fascinating narrative of a friendship, and in every gallery there lay coded clues and submerged hints about the intense feelings that the two painters had for, and about, each other. The fact that Degas had done a drawing of a man whom Manet wounded in the chest made me feel that Manet was part of the story Degas was telling. It's a story both amazing and faintly familiar to anyone who's read Greek tragedy, the Bible, or Shakespeare, or watched the evening news. As grandiose as it sounds, it also felt familiar from my own experience.

I recognized in the story the excitement of adjacency that comes with certain friendships that border on rivalry—when you have a friend who inspires feelings in you, some admiring, others confusing or even unpleasant, even hateful, and all of them as intense as love. It's a love that can turn readily to rage but can also be rocket fuel to keep you going creatively, out of both a need for your friend's approval and a fear that, with his accomplishments, that friend will leave you behind. Rivalry and affection become so intertwined as to become indistinguishable. When you add ambition to the mix, it creates a complexity that ultimately can make these friendships deeper and more valuable, the most treasured friendships of all, especially after they are lost.

The *Manet/Degas* trip begins with a pair of self-portraits arranged side by side with a slash of white paint between them at a rakish angle. Their names on the wall above are so large as to make the paintings seem like small portals of light. The slash suggests opposition, and also that they are two halves of a whole, their own ecosystem. The two men confront you, and you confront them, in a kind of mutual appraisal. Manet stares out at you with an alert, vibrant expression. The effect of staring at him is not unlike gazing at one of those giant, dazzling bouquets of flowers one sometimes finds in the lobby of fancy hotels or restaurants, or, for that matter, in the Metropolitan Museum itself.

If Manet is a magnificent bouquet, Degas's self-portrait is muted, almost sultry, his expression in the inscrutable space between indifference and judgment. When I thought about this pairing, I always imagined Manet's portrait as brighter and more vivid than Degas's, but then I would stand before them again, on yet another visit, and be reminded it was Degas whose face is rendered with more crisp precision, whereas Manet is all gestural brush strokes, almost a blur. Manet is painting himself in the act of painting, which I suspect is another way of thinking. Degas paints himself in the act of thinking, which may be another way of painting.

My conversations with other people who have seen the show—augmented by some eavesdropping in the galleries—confirmed my sense that Manet is the favorite of most people. He has the wow factor. Everyone loves him. To look at his paintings is to see a burst of light and possibility. Degas operates in a dimmer light, an undercurrent of alarm or distress ever present in his compositions.

At first, the pleasure I took in the show came from the juxtaposition between the two men which made it a kind of game in which you got to choose the winner, as though it were a high minded, nineteenth-century version of Hot or Not. On these terms, Manet is definitely the winner. But the show is greater than the sum of its impressive parts. It tells a story, and that story is about a friendship. A complicated, interesting friendship that played out over many years, up to and beyond the death of Manet, after which the friendship lived on, with Degas as its custodian, collecting and in some cases restoring his friend's work.

Early in the Met exhibit, you encounter a pair of engravings, accompanied by text that details the origin story of Degas and Manet's relationship. They met at the Louvre, while gazing at a Velázquez. Degas was drawing directly onto the waxy surface of a copper plate without having first made a preparatory drawing, a style Manet found unorthodox. Manet approached him and paid him a compliment for his audacity.

Contemplating this moment in which a heartfelt compliment was the spark of a complicated friendship, I thought of my friend, the writer Robert Bingham, who died of a heroin overdose in 1999. At a gallery show in New York in the early 1990s, Rob, then a stranger, came up to me and told me he'd read a short story of mine and liked it very much. The story was about a young man whose father died young. I would later discover that Rob was a guy whose father died young, as had mine, though this affinity was something we never actually acknowledged in words. Rob later got involved in a literary magazine I'd started and we had various adventures at home and abroad; he got married and then he died. Now it all seems to have taken place in the blink of an eye, though the exact span, gallery to funeral, was about seven years. In the spring of 2000, we both published novels, his posthumous.

We had a strange dynamic with our writing: outwardly supportive but not involved in the particulars. We talked about literature all the time, but we didn't read each other's work or offer notes. We were each a source of anxiety for the other, but also of confidence, in equal if fluctuating measures. To say we were competitive is surely true, but it would miss something more interesting: Rob and I wholeheartedly wanted the best for each other, while also feeling stressed out by the prospect of being exceeded by the other.

Vivid in my memory is an answering-machine message he once left that starts with the exultant but gently delivered news that he had placed a story at a magazine of note, where I had also published, suggesting we get together to celebrate. Then, as though he had run out of things to say but didn't want to put the phone down, he concluded with what almost felt at the time like a taunt: "How about that, Jack?"

Rob's death was so abrupt that I still remain stunned: the swearing off drugs, the drunken relapse, the overdose, the discovered body, and suddenly, the groomsmen at his wedding reassembling six months later to be ushers at his funeral. These days, my friendships with other writers are more cordial, even delicate, as though we have seen enough people burst into flames and then go up in smoke that we appreciate the fragility of the other person's presence. I have never been able to write properly about my friend Rob or that time in my life. Instead, I smuggle mentions of him into various pieces of writing, as I am doing here, as though I can only see him in memory through eclipse glasses.

It might be this dynamic, above all, that prompted my visceral response and repeat visits to *Manet/Degas*. The mysteries of the artists' friendship were most conspicuous in a gallery devoted to two paintings, side by side, one by Manet and one by Degas. They are variations on a theme: In each, the same woman is seen in profile playing the piano.

The woman is Manet's wife, Suzanne, and the living room is in Manet's home, the atmosphere cozy and domestic. In Degas's painting, Manet himself is lounging on a sofa behind her, his mood ambiguous. The most conspicuous difference between the paintings is that the one made by Degas is missing a third of its canvas, the victim of a violent, if very precise, excision—by Manet, it turns out. He had sliced out the portion of the canvas in which Degas had painted his wife's face. But why? These unanswered questions about the slashed Degas are complicated by the other painting, in which Manet depicted the same scene, with the same woman, at the same piano, this time with her face visible. What is missing from Manet's version of the scene is Manet.

"He was greater than we thought," Degas said in the aftermath of Manet's premature death.[1] In that line, I recognized the shock and confused self-reproach of the stunned, surviving friend. The survivor is in the position of making inside jokes to a room in which he is the only occupant.

I thought of this when looking at another image exhibited not too far from the sketch of Duranty. It's a small photograph of Degas taken late in his life. Photography was brand-new and Degas was now old. The tiny black-and-white picture needed to be squinted at, and I brought my nose right next to it, rudely boxing out everyone else.

Once close enough, you can see Degas sitting in his studio. On the wall behind him is the painting of Suzanne at the piano that Manet had slashed. It's a mischievous, moody, in some ways depressing souvenir that nevertheless feels like a touching act of love and a totem of longing. Suzanne's face is gone but Manet himself is there, in that tiny photo at the dawn of the twentieth century, serving the double purpose of evoking that long-ago salon and Manet's rage and passion in the excision of his friend's painting.

There is speculation that Degas had planned on restoring the painting. Both that wish and the fact that he never acted on it seem true to life, and to death—a longing for resurrection yet settling for the pulse of life that comes from the longing itself. Degas had become a custodian of his friend's work and a de facto custodian of their friendship. In some ways, this seemed the most profound echo of my own experience, or that of anyone who has had the experience of having loved someone he or she then outlived.

Note
1. Ashley E. Dunn and Stephan Wolohojian, "Manet/Degas: A Podcast," The Met, December 8, 2023, https://www.metmuseum.org/perspectives/manet-degas-audio.

The Rights

1.

Summer in New York, and Evangeline, age two, is dressed for a party. A grown-up party. She likes parties. This one was at the National Arts Club on Gramercy Park, near where Elizabeth lived when I met her, and where she took me, with her key, late at night on our first date, to sit on a bench, talk, and kiss. Another life. Except then, as now, it was May, the air newly soft.

This was a party for my magazine, *Open City*, and I didn't want to be late. We drove. I took an unusual route. A gamble which I lost. The traffic was bad. I wore a jacket and tie. The tie was, I was pretty sure, an old tie of my father's. I did everything I could to suppress the anxiety and free-floating exasperation that comes with being stuck in traffic on the way to a party. The traffic finally let up. We arrived. Like magic, a parking space materialized. We got out of the car, all of us dressed up, and I started to hurry to the party with Evangeline in my arms.

"How do I look?" I said to her. I didn't like myself for asking. It sounded needy. A father shouldn't be needy of a two-year-old. I don't know at what age a child should be before a parent can start being needy, or showing it. Not two.

"Concerned," she said.

"I do?" I said. "Really? Wow! Where did you learn that word?" And then. "And how do *you* feel?"

"Confused!" she said, and laughed.

2.

I once knew a florist who was like a pharmacist; he didn't sell flowers so much as prescribe them. He was a big guy cloistered in a tiny shop on Bleecker Street filled with exotic flowers. They were very expensive. Most of his business was doing fancy restaurants and private parties, but he sold to whoever wedged themselves into the store because he liked the theater of the random encounter.

Sometimes he would take huge bunches of dazzling flowers that had moved slightly past their prime and dump them in the trash can on the corner. That was how I first knew his store had opened; I came across a courtly old man rummaging through flowers in the trash.

"They're like abandoned pets or lost children," said the old man as he gently plucked a few of the better stems. "Wounded but beautiful. Go ahead, take some."

After picking through the floral orphans a couple of times, I ventured into the store itself, and it was not long before I developed a kind of rapport with the florist, David Browne. I bought a stem at a time for reasons of economy. Gradually, I turned the matter of what to buy over to him, like I was visiting a psychic or an astrologer.

"I've got a twenty," I would say.

"What do you need?" he would say.

One day I said, "It's for a girl."

"A girl or *the* girl?" he said.

"*The* girl."

He sent me off with a small bouquet of roses tied with rough twine. I had never seen roses like these before—velvety, dark red, almost purple; held up to a black light, they probably would have glowed. Their petals were well open, and, in the manner that roses have at a certain point in their progression, there was a lewd, almost panting quality to the outermost petals, which hung down somewhat labially. Sex and romance wrapped in string, a discreet calling card for my particular needs and wishes.

I delivered this smart little bundle to my girlfriend, who greeted me at her doorstep. She was my new girlfriend at the time, very new, in fact, but I thought we had safely crossed into the boyfriend-girlfriend column. She blushed a little when she took the bouquet, pressing her nose into the bouquet's velvety mouth as we walked into her house. Her brother would shortly be visiting, she told me, and proceeded to hurriedly put the flowers in a vase with anxious, surreptitious gestures, as though her brother shouldn't know I was the one who had brought them for her. I didn't know what to make of this; it didn't seem that auspicious. And indeed that relationship didn't end very well for me.

In its aftermath, wandering the landscape of singledom, I was out of sorts, and when Valentine's Day rolled around I asked the florist to put together several bouquets. This wasn't as promiscuous as it may sound—only one of them was meant to be romantic, the rest offered in the spirit of apology, I suppose, or condolence. The florist, sizing me up, avoided roses and made the bouquets out of ragged-edged pink and white tulips, as though to comment on my clearly frayed state of mind.

This was all a long time ago. Since then the florist has closed his shop. I met a woman who did not seem conflicted about the flowers I offered. I tended to buy her roses that were, like her, a cool, pearly pink. Elizabeth and I married, as you know, and eventually, not all that long after my long campaign to get her to move into my place, we moved out of it—of the place, the neighborhood, the whole city.

In New Orleans, our front yard is adorned by a small but productive rosebush. Evangeline, a toddler with rosy cheeks, always marches straight over to it and reaches for the petals. The flowers to be found on a rosebush are so different from the coy, coiled, secretive stems in flower stores. On the bush the rose opens and expands and then expands further, effusive and fragrant. Like a baby's emotions, it holds nothing back.

Moving to it with her customary urgency, Evangeline reaches for the lush flowers, and I stand above her, bent over, like a house enclosing her, and tell her to be gentle with the beautiful flower. I love these kinds of moments, when I am an unseen structure to my daughter's explorations. I am not the subject of her gaze so much as the context for that subject.

Her fingers move from the petals to the thorns. I tell her to be careful of these. I can see her breathing and contemplating these opposing forces as she stands before the rosebush, sorting out the ecology of beauty and danger while breathing in the unmistakable fragrance of a rose.

3.

I have an agent who handles all of my business affairs connected to writing. In the rest of my life I manage, often with some difficulty, to take care of the business of living, but in the realm of my literary affairs, I am a cosseted and innocent babe protected from wolves. An example of my innocence in these matters—which must be a kind of schizophrenia, because I edited and published a literary journal and ran a small press, so I do have a clue about the world and its machinations—is that I think the issue over which people butt heads is usually money. But this is not always the case. A lot of the head-butting in negotiations concerns fine print that is itself concerned with things entirely abstract.

Film rights, for example. You write something for a magazine or newspaper, and in addition to printing it, they might want the rights to make a movie out of it. This is different from actually wanting to make a movie out of it. For one thing, at the time of the signing there usually isn't any *it*. *It* is all in the realm of the hypothetical. So the dispute is about who owns the movie rights to the thing which does not yet exist. Evangeline does exist, though. When I include some tidbit about her in a piece of writing, this hypothetical takes on a new twist. For if I am selling movie rights to something that includes a tidbit about my daughter, what exactly does that mean?

My agent holds a firm line—she doesn't ever give away film rights. She is a tough cookie, my agent. She reads the fine print. She takes care of it. The whole matter of who owns the "rights" provokes so many questions. What would a movie based on this essay look like? Perhaps the question arises because Evangeline's remarks are strewn over various things I write. Has she given her consent to be quoted? What's the fine print on that?

4.

My father resides, or perhaps I should say is buried, atop a gorgeously landscaped hill in Westchester in the company of recognizable names like Guggenheim, Gershwin, Sulzberger, Lortel, and Strasberg. "That which dies acquires a life of its own," wrote Isaac Rosenfeld, and physical truth of this finds expression on top of this hill, where my father took up residence after his death and which has become for my mother and me a kind of luxury time-share—a lovely place we visit once a year, in spring. There are dogwoods and azalea bushes, flora of incredible variety and delicacy, huge looming oak and pine and weeping willow, and a perfectly manicured lawn. I like to joke, on our annual visit on the anniversary of his death, that this is the most prestigious address with which I am affiliated.

Every year since he died, or ever since he started dying in a visible way, which was around three or four months before he actually did die of cancer, just when I was about to turn ten, there has been this tension in me between wanting to make jokes and the plain unadorned feelings of sadness and fear.

It's no joke to be perched on the side of a very steep hill watching your mother crouched down beside the open hole in the ground, a kind of halo of grief surrounding her and shimmering above her in the unseasonable heat, while your father's best friend Arnie bends down on one knee and holds her shoulder patiently, patting it and holding it. In hindsight I see this gesture of Arnie's as both consoling and, perhaps, given the odd kind of crouch my mother was in at that moment, and the force of her grief, a precaution against her falling into the grave. It was a scalding hot day, unusual for May. Everyone else who was just standing at the perimeter of the empty grave into which the coffin had been lowered was now retreating down the hill to the road.

Back then, in 1975, the section of the cemetery my dad is in, high on top of the hill, was mostly empty. Now, four decades on, it's getting full. Every year new people arrive. Some have little headstones flat on the ground, and some, fronting the road, have giant stone mausoleums, the equivalent of the generic glass towers that have been built on Riverside "boulevard," south of Seventy-Second Street, bulky interlopers. We are still at the top of the hill with an unimpeded view. Right next door are Don and Helen Meyers. An exquisitely sculpted, highly realistic, life-size ham sandwich is affixed to Helen's grave, though because it is a Jewish cemetery it is not identified as ham. There was a dogwood tree planted next to my father's grave, but it died a few years after he did. It is survived by the azalea bush, which lives. My mother always asks the people who maintain the cemetery, keeping it manicured and in a state of perpetual gorgeousness, not to trim this bush. She wants it wild. Every year, though, we arrive and, halfway up that hill from the road, she looks up and catches her breath. "They trimmed the azalea," she says, sighing, at once disappointed and faintly amused, the remark itself a ritual of our attendance.

We are always laden with picnic supplies. My mother, a champion picnicker, brings a basket, a blanket, strawberries, cherries, grapes, peaches, cold cuts from Zabar's, baguettes, bread, mustard, orange juice, water, chocolate, and a copious amount of white flowers. This last visit she looked up and said, "Oh, look at that."

I looked. The azalea bush had not been trimmed. It rose from its place in the ground, bushy and wild, crowding the simple granite stone with my father's name on it—Alexander Beller—and directly beneath it the austere, familiar numbers, "1922–1975."[1]

Why, having started off thinking about my daughter, am I going on about my father's grave? And not even my father himself—his pensive humor, the feeling of his arm dangling around my shoulders, pulling me close, his blue socks tipped with gold thread pointed upward during one of his mysterious naps—but simply a piece of ground within which, if you think about it literally, which sometimes I do and sometimes I don't, is a box within which is a badly decomposed body. Why should that drift into my thoughts?

In becoming parents, I suppose, we meet our own parents again, in a way for the first time. And if you didn't really know one of your parents that well, then the dialogue that now springs up—what you were like when I was a kid, what it was like to stand in the place you now find yourself standing—becomes not so much a reunion on different terms, but an entirely new acquaintance.

The visit to the cemetery a few days before the party at the National Arts Club was unusual. It was just my mother and me walking up the hill, which is how it always had been until I met my wife. When I first brought Elizabeth along to visit, it felt like a kind of momentous intimacy, a slightly macabre version of introducing your spouse to your parent and vice versa.

And then we had a baby. Did we bring our tiny infant her first year to the top of that hill? We did. The following year, too, when she was a year and a few months, we brought her, and I balanced Evangeline on top of the headstone and made her hand trace the name carved into the granite. This year, though, the year of the bushy azalea bush, we had a live wire on our hands, a person who spoke and remembered and asked questions. A person who could see, hear, talk, and think. What to tell her about why we were taking her to the top of a steep hill to have a picnic next to a stone with a name and numbers on it?

For the first time I could see how being religious might be helpful in raising a kid. We could roll out the heaven concept, right?—say he was up there somewhere, looking down, and then eat sandwiches while Evangeline frolicked, confining our graveside anxieties to the worry that she would tumble down the steep hill, perhaps smacking into one of those proud new mausoleums at the bottom. But we are not religious (though it is a Jewish cemetery, which brings up all kinds of thorny questions about Elizabeth and Evangeline—can they be buried there?), and so this option was not suitably available to us.

Should we bring the baby? The baby who, at two, was now a little girl?

Whatever benefits there might be in a nice picnic could not compete with the negative possibilities of opening up in my daughter the cavern of horror and dread associated with death. The person underground in the dark was my father, after all, and to have her grasp that would be to make her consciously aware, for the first time, that her mother has two parents she has met and her father only one. And the absent person was the father of me, who is the father of her. And if my father could be dead and underground in the dark with no air to breathe and no one to talk to, then . . . her father could also be there, too. Couldn't he? Which was not a thought I wanted to rush into existence, for her, as it had been for me. All these considerations were compounded with the arrival of Alexander, as it was his name carved into the stone.

Up on the hill, in this year of the bushy bush, I had drifted into one of those meandering ruminations that I allow myself in the company of my mother, thinking about how different it would have been if that scale of possibility—two to twenty-five years—had slid a bit further toward the deeper end.

"If he lived even just a few more years," I suggested, "it would have been so different."

"Yes, very different," my mother said, nodding.

"But you know, even two more years, I would have been, what, twelve?—so it's not like it would have all been nice and good. He would have had the money I wanted for things; he would have been the one to say no to things. He would have been my problem!"

"And your strength," said my mom.

I got married when I was forty, just a year later than the age at which my father had married my mother. Evangeline was born when I was forty-two, the age of my father the year I was born.

The last time I saw him, I was summoned to the hospital by my mother. I went with a terrible sadness, not because my father was in the hospital but because I was going to miss a boxing match I'd been looking forward to featuring Muhammad Ali. What I remember from this moment was the night ride in the taxi, where the fight was on the radio, and then the sight of my father lying in bed, asleep or unconscious. Ray Raskin, my "Gum Uncle," standing on the other side of the bed, looking . . . It was difficult to decipher Ray's expression.

Ray had been a figure of lightness and comedy for me, as a kid. He was mostly bald, the hair at the rim of his head always a bit unkempt. He wore bifocals that hung low on his nose, like a jeweler, which he was, on the side (he was a psychoanalyst), polishing topaz into shiny shapes and affixing it to watchbands and bolo ties. That night at the hospital, he peered down at my father. When he looked across the bed at me his eyes peered over the rims, and his eyebrows rose, as though to acknowledge that this situation was, well, not too hot. He made a comic grimace at me, *tough break, kid*, he seemed to say, only he wanted to lighten it, to make it kind of funny.

I still recall the sound of Ray, at the funeral itself, breaking into sobs in the silence of the chapel, or whatever it was, and this seemingly out-of-character behavior signaling to me that the situation was, indeed, dire.

I had done everything in my power to keep it from being so, had kept an almost manically light tone on that last hospital visit, and throughout his illness, really, jumping around and calling my father "Pops," when I had previously only called him "Papa." My mother had bought him an electric razor—an act of optimism or denial, though if your husband is dying of cancer, what is the difference—and I took it out to the hall to try and plug it in and use it. Norelco. White. Three heads. It's still in my mother's apartment somewhere.

And what about this boxing match I was missing to be with my dying father? I remember clearly a promo image from the network—ABC, I would guess—and it featured Muhammad Ali. It wasn't that I was a huge Ali fan, but I very much wanted to see this fight. And now I could not. Looking into it now, I see that Ali had a fight on May 16, 1975, and that must have been the night in question, because it was early in the morning of May 18 that my father died.

It was Ali against Ron Lyle. Ali won. I spent the weekend with family friends—Jerry and Jason—on Fire Island, and when I returned, my mother, ashen-faced, came to their door and summoned me to our apartment. I did not want to go. But I did eventually. We walked down a flight of stairs and sat together at the kitchen table so she could tell me the news. "Oh, but I prayed!" I cried out, and banged my fist on the table. Then my head lowered to my arms and I sobbed. My mother comforted me, and when I looked up she was crying, too.

I rarely write about this. Yet I am moved to put this down by the most incredible sensation I had recently while playing with Evangeline. She was on the bed, just after her bath, and I was on my hands and knees above her, doing something to make her laugh, I forget what. At some point she started demanding that I "make a house." She wanted to get in "Daddy's house," which meant I had to arrange myself on my hands and knees with my arms on either side of her, or if she was standing, that I had to bend at the waist to make a kind of A-frame above her—an exaggerated version of the thing I was doing while she stared at the rosebush. At some point she gave it a name and made it a game of ours.

"Close the door!" she would tell me, after I made the house, and then, a moment later, she would demand, "Open the door!"

We had been playing this game, but then something else happened—she kicked me in the nose, and I retaliated by shoving this enormous feature right into her chest and ribs; I'm always roughhousing with her, you know, throwing her around, and, as usual, she was laughing uproariously.

There was one moment, though, that seared itself into me: Her eyes flashed as she was looking up at me and laughing. There is something in a child's laughter that opens you up to the universe in its totality, shooting you into its mysterious depths. Sometimes you can go along for the ride. And sometimes you can't. And sometimes you think you are on that ride up and into the totality, that highest plane of unbridled laughter, and then, at a certain altitude, consciousness returns, and it's like a dream—how did I get all the way up here? And what is all this I see?

A spear of pain moved through me, which was also kind of delicious, delivering a blunt truth—this person needs me. Pretty obvious, I know, simple, goes without saying—but this was an understanding that bypassed the intellectual, even the emotional, to plant something very heavy in my chest; it encompassed a fantasy of my absence, and what that would do to her, how it would hurt her, how the ongoing absence could hurt even more than the departure itself, as my father's absence, an absence that could not be challenged, only endured, had hurt me.

Looking down at her looking at me looking at her. The spear in my chest said, *She would be hurt! That laughter would be ended!* The laughter, and the person, would evolve and reappear, but it would be different, its shape changed, her shape changed, as mine had been. And then I imagined, or felt, my father grappling with that same thought, though not of the hypothetical variety, but rather the cold facts of the blood test, the cancer, the absurd and arbitrary spectrum of two to twenty years to live. It turned out that he had eight.

I saw myself at two, laughing and looking up at my own father laughing; and I saw myself at two, laughing, through the eyes of my father, at forty-two, recently diagnosed with cancer, told he could live somewhere between two years and twenty-five, having already begun rounds of chemo and radiation, keeping it a secret from his colleagues, his patients, his friends, his son. Memories of my laughing mother. My laughing father. Now tinged with the question of how I would carry the knowledge *they* carried.

In that moment I had a recognition of what my father must have been going through as he enjoyed playing and laughing with me, and how I must surely have seen this, seen something, picked up on something, however subliminally, and that something now registered somewhere in my eyes as they looked at Evangeline laughing at me, picking up the faint echo of that register.

How would you film that, let alone apportion the rights?

5.

Evangeline has invented a new game in the elevator of my mother's building, which they have fancied up a bit, but which is more or less the same as when I was growing up. I used to get into the elevator and turn to say goodbye to my mom, who would stand on the landing as the door would close and I would make my descent. Every now and then, when I was a kid, I would shout, "Bye!" really loud, even after the doors had closed, and my mother, too, would call out, "Bye!" really loud, which would come down to me ever so faintly. I remembered this when Evangeline found herself in my arms, in the same descending elevator, having just watched the door close on my mother. Her face lit up with mischievous delight and she yelled, "Nana!"

And I heard my mother's voice call out her name.

"Nana!" she yelled again. And again the voice came to us, fainter now.

She yelled out "Nana" every floor on the way down. Long after we stopped hearing the response she was still yelling the name. When we got to the lobby, just before the door opened, she yelled her grandmother's name one more time. Usually, this is the moment she squirms free from me and bolts out into the lobby and then the street, screaming hello to whomever is there. Now she turned to me and said pensively, "I don't think she can hear us anymore."

Note

1. The regularity of these annual visits, once inscribed onto the calendar, tapered considerably after we moved to New Orleans. But it's possible that the incentive to visit was slightly diminished by the fact that my son's name is the exact same name as the one on the gravestone. Now that he is getting to be his own man, this seems like less and less an impediment, but when he was a little kid, it did give me pause.

Evacuation

At the beach in Florida, a heron was quacking, or doing whatever a heron does when it makes its quacking noise. If indeed it was a heron. We had taken a walk at dusk to see the ocean, Evangeline and I, having spent the previous day in the car, and then today in the rented condo, glued to our phones. We walked on the wet, white sand, peered at the rough waves, and then took a seat on a wooden bench. She had started high school at the beginning of the week.

It was Sunday night. We had flown down from New York a week earlier so she could start high school. It was the confusing COVID season of autumn 2021. Things had begun to return to normal over the summer, after the vaccines rolled out. And then came the August spike in cases in the Southern states. Alexander was too young to get a vaccination. He and Elizabeth stayed in New York.

That first week was as normal as was possible, just me and Evangeline in our house in New Orleans, driving her to school in the morning. Halfway through the week, Hurricane Ida formed in the Gulf. When I dropped her off at her sleepover on Friday afternoon, I talked with her friend's parents about their plans and we agreed it wasn't worth leaving. No one I knew planned to leave. But the forecast had begun to shift over the course of Friday, and with it the city's mood.

We had arrived the previous night after midnight. For almost the entire twelve-hour drive, we were surrounded by cars with Louisiana plates. A traffic jam across several states which I didn't mind at all. I found it comforting. The solidarity of evacuation, even if each car was its own small ecosystem of panic, grief, and merriment. Some cars were full of people, some were crammed with stuff. For over an hour I was eye to eye with a droll white hound, sitting in the rear of a hatchback, facing me with a black splotch on one eye like a pirate. I will never forget his utter shock and mystification when the rear windshield wiper suddenly came to life, swept back and forth, and again became still.

These cars were each their own world; above all, the parade of evacuating vehicles felt austere. "We took what we needed," each vehicle seemed to say, "our phones, our loved ones, and ourselves."

On Sunday, we woke up and spent that day waiting for the hurricane, obsessed with our phones and the news they brought.

This walk at the end of the day was meant to cleanse the palate. Yet as the sky went from pale purple to deep purple, and in the presence of the roiling Gulf of Mexico, we again looked at our phones. First, at my phone, looking at images of the fallen trees, fallen houses, and the map that indicated that power was out in all of New Orleans. Then she showed me her phone, with her friend's "snaps," the ones who were still in New Orleans, "hunkering down," in the parlance. "Riding it out." A picture of water coming into the house, under a door; a picture of the cookies that were in progress when the power went out.

Then we walked back to the condo where the blue pool was empty. And all the palm trees blew gently in the breeze. And the sound of the ocean waves nearby. Off to the side: The hot tub glowed like some strange aquamarine jewel. And I realized that Evangeline, who had reluctantly acquiesced to a walk to the beach, and who had gone upstairs, was in a situation to do me a favor. I was feeling very much in touch with the favor economy.

For example, as we returned from the beach a woman had asked for my help. "Do you know anything about cars?"

"No," I said honestly. "But maybe I know more than you."

I sent Evangeline ahead and the woman took me to inspect her brand new white BMW, whose headlights would not turn off.

Ten minutes later it was established that I could not in fact help her turn off the headlights—no matter what button was pushed. She was also from New Orleans, "Old Metairie," she explained when I asked what neighborhood. That's the place that elected David Duke. Her husband was back there, in their house, she said. It had started taking on water. We commiserated about the city, the storm, and I marveled at the sleek and powerful curve of the new car's body. But what would all that power and elegance mean if the battery was dead?

She said she had called the maintenance guy from the condo. "Call BMW," was my advice. We wished each other luck.

Evacuating from a hurricane is like being asked to leave a room where your friend will soon be beaten up. You step into the adjoining room and can hear the blows, the cries of pain. A house is not a friend, exactly, but maybe a city is. You hear it all, but you can't see it. Or you see it but you can't stop it. Even before the lights go out, you are powerless. You simply have to endure it. Just things, you say, or people say to you. Possessions. Not as bad as actually dying and suffering. But it is very strange. Imagining the roof of your house blown off, the windows blown out, walls moldy and wet. I thought of all the people in New Orleans who don't have to imagine because they lived through Katrina. I arrived three years after that event, when you could still smell the vapors of PTSD, and, as in "The Topographical Soul," made the association with Phnom Penh. Two cities with the rare distinction of being completely emptied.

That it was sixteen years to the day between Katrina and Ida was both beside the point and also overdetermined. Major weather events were punctuation marks in the life of a place and the lives of the people who lived there, but what kind of punctuation was never known in advance.

"Those that can leave should leave," is how the mayor defined the voluntary evacuation for which she had called on Friday. As Jarvis DeBerry, a local columnist, quipped, this was also the definition of a mandatory evacuation. In either case, those who can't leave don't. This moment in time in the late summer of 2021 echoed, slightly, the moment in the spring of 2020, specifically late February and early March, when everyone in America began to brace for the arrival of COVID. I shouldn't even bring this up; it's apples and oranges, contagious virus on one hand, weather on the other. But they share the quality of realities to which individuals can respond but that they cannot control. In both instances, there were those who could evacuate, if they chose to do so, and those who couldn't, regardless of what they wanted. In both situations, people relied on magical thinking, wishful thinking, and had confused and genuinely ambivalent feelings about how best to proceed.

On Thursday night and Friday morning we were a city full of Hamlets—to go or not to go, that was the question.

Evangeline slept over at a friend's house Friday night. The first sleepover of the fall. She had finished her first week of high school. As I had so many times before, I picked her up in the morning at the big, Spanish-looking house on Newcomb Place with the white steps out front. I had a brief chat with the parents while I waited for her to appear. This interval was usually an occasion for being annoyed. "I am on my way," I would text, sometimes more than once, as I began what was a seven- or eight-minute drive. Then I would wait with mounting incredulity for five or ten minutes once I arrived. Now I was glad for the interval. They were leaving, too. From there I took her home, explained the plan.

"Why is it always sunny before the storm?" Evangeline mused on the way out the door, on that bright and pleasant Saturday morning. I had told her to throw some clothes and toiletries in a bag, and had done so myself. I carried two plastic grocery bags from the house. Those flimsy, sometimes useful things. I recall how light they felt in my hand, each with just a few possessions, a toothbrush and so forth. A couple of transient packages to cover a brief span of time. I will always remember the feeling of coming down the front steps to the car with those plastic bags. The air was so calm, the light so pleasant, everything felt so manageable and exciting. We were going to have an adventure. I could not have imagined that those moments were the last moments my family lived in that house. But that is what happened. The house survived and so did the city. But the hurricane's initial impact was severe enough to make the front page of the *New York Times*, which made it seem like the city had been destroyed.

Elizabeth made calls around town, and some schools in New York, no doubt depleted from COVID, took us on short notice, at refugee rates. A temporary arrangement. I was on leave that year and didn't have to be in New Orleans.

And that is how things proceeded—first a temporary solution for a week, then a month, then a semester. That August, Alexander had asked to take trapeze lessons. I took him and watched him swinging and turning upside down high above the West Side Highway. Letting go of one thing and catching another. It didn't occur to either of us that there was some metaphor in this.

A few weeks into this new arrangement, Evangeline started high school yet again, this time in New York. Alexander started fifth grade in a new school, where he walked around wearing its uniform of polo shirts and khaki pants in a daze. I wrote to a friend, the New Orleans native Tom Sancton, who now lived in France, and reported that my family seemed to want to stay in New York for the whole semester. He responded, "So your life has reached one of those big turning points. Sounds like you're on the way to sloughing off the New Orleans phase and (re) becoming the New Yorker you've always been at heart."

I was offended by this. Six weeks after the hurricane, I couldn't accept or even fathom the idea that we would no longer live in New Orleans. And yet he was right. It's been over three years and I still do not believe it. But when I walked out of the house Saturday morning with Evangeline and our plastic bags of clothes, that was the end of our sojourn in that city. As dislocations go, ours was as measured as such a thing could be. It was, most of all, a choice we made. Still, thinking of my family and in particular my son's dreamlike relationship to the place—it's too primal and irrational to be actual nostalgia, he was only ten when he left—it occurred to me that it echoes very faintly other dislocations that my father's family experienced. But it immediately seems absurd to make such comparisons. Decisions about what American city to live in are not the same as decisions to leave Vienna, Austria, in 1938! And yet the thought occurred to me. In childhood, these changes mean so much.

We got a late start on the Saturday we left New Orleans; we drove down St. Charles Avenue slowly. The city had emptied out. I looked up at the live oaks' lattice of branches above and thought they were like beautiful lace that might soon be torn.

We woke the next day in Florida, lived vicariously through our phones, flinching privately the moment we learned that the power in New Orleans was out. Then we took our walk to the beach.

By the time we returned to the nameless, faceless condo, it was dark. I went and sat by the pool and realized I didn't have a towel. So I texted Evangeline and said, "Could you do me a favor?"

And as a fourteen-year-old will say, even in the best mood, she replied, "What?"

"Throw me a towel."

Our room was on the third floor. She came out onto the outdoor hallway overlooking the pool with a towel.

"Roll it up like a football!" I yelled. She did. There were some little palm trees at the base of the building. I worried that she would throw the towel and it would get stuck on the palm trees—not only would I not have a towel but there would be this flapping towel defacing the pleasant landscaping. A white flag.

But Evangeline has a good arm. She flung the towel out. The sky was very black. The white towel unfurled against the black sky. I raised my hand up in anxiety that I would drop it, like it was a pass thrown in football or a pop-up fly ball, something that, as a kid, I would have bungled. It later occurred to me that this moment echoed the ending of a novel I love, *The Leopard*, by Giuseppe Lampedusa, which ends with the image of an inanimate object falling through the air and suddenly taking a recognizable shape, suggesting something from long ago. In this case the effect was the opposite: The past vanished into the present.

I caught the towel. But in the moment of panic as it opened and fell, it took the shape of a bird's wing, a white wing against a black sky, and I had the first moment of relief from worrying about this hurricane.

The Frozen River (Reprise)

The last time I saw my Uncle Kuno was in Vienna, in the summer of 2010. After years and years of asking him about my father, and his evading the topic in one way or another—sometimes offhandedly, other times ferociously, or with varying degrees of indignation—he'd finally agreed to show me the apartment where he and my father grew up.

He was in Vienna in connection with work and intended to continue, by train, to a conference in Budapest, before returning to his home in Berlin. His son, Dan, a musicologist, had flown out to be a kind of aide-de-camp on this journey from one conference to another.

It was when I called Dan a few months earlier to say we were taking a trip to Vienna that we discovered that, by complete chance, he and my uncle would be arriving in the city one day before we did. All the tickets had been purchased. All I had to do was change our hotel reservations to the Hotel Papageno, where they were staying, and ask for a room next to theirs. If this serendipity undermines the idea that what took place was a family reunion, it also gives everything that happened in Vienna an aura of the providential.

I had seen the building of my father's youth once, long ago, while traveling after college. I remember peering up at the building's face, which was quite plain, especially by the standards of Vienna. All the windows reflected a cloudy sky; they told me nothing. Neither did the street or the neighborhood.

As soon as Emperor Franz Joseph made it legal to be Jewish in Vienna in 1867, the city's Jewish population began to rapidly increase. The second district, in particular, near the famous Prater amusement park, was the destination for thousands of Jews fleeing pogroms of the early twentieth century and then the carnage of World War I. This group included my grandparents, who arrived in 1918. This fact, however, was static and cold, if I even knew it at the time of this first visit.

Which I suppose I didn't. I simply peered at the four- or five-story apartment block and tried to remain calm, take it in—to open myself to the emotional impact this place might make while steeling myself against getting, I suppose, overwhelmed.

Wanting something you can't have provokes a feeling not unlike claustrophobia. But what did I want? Standing there on the street, I suppose I wanted knowledge, or at least facts—a sense of what had once been there, and who had been there, to better appreciate what was lost.

And what is claustrophobia, once you think about it, but a fear of the grave, where my father went when I was nine. It is because of this that I can't know all the things I wish to know, sort of, half-heartedly; none of this knowledge, after all, could ever properly substitute for the feeling of pressing against him, his body, his cheek. For a long time, this feeling was abstract, a memory, a mood. Then I had children and felt them pressing against me. I pressed back, the friction and the support a gift both from me to them and from them to me.

My mother once told me a story about my father having come back to the building he grew up in sometime after the war. A woman he knew from childhood apparently leaned out of one of these windows and shouted down at him that he wasn't wanted there. Standing before the building as a recent graduate, I felt nothing of my father, but I did feel something, some vestigial hatred, for this woman. My vigil that day was brief. But I held on to this feeling about the shouting woman in the window. A connection between the world before and the world after—the ambiguous complicity of all the people remaining. After a few minutes spent peering at the building and into the bottomless well of wishes concerning my father that would forever remain out of reach, I went on my way.

Several decades later, on the same call with my cousin Dan in which the accidental family reunion was revealed and negotiated, I learned that the people who moved into the apartment after my father's family had left in 1938 were, incredibly, still there. At least, one of them was. A young girl at the time, she and my uncle had since corresponded. A year earlier, Dan told me, she had received him and his father as guests.

At some point between this excited first phone call and our arrival in Vienna, my Uncle Kuno had offered—or did I ask? Or was it Dan's idea?—to reprise this return visit for the purpose of showing me the place where my father grew up. That I would have him as a willing guide, interlocutor, and translator seemed as significant a development as my sudden ability to enter a space about which I knew so little.

My uncle, I should mention, has an almost violent allergy to telling stories related to his family's escape from Vienna in 1938, and has seemed wary of telling stories about himself, in general. Or maybe he's just wary of telling them to *me*. After I published a work of fiction that touched, glancingly, on his life, and less glancingly on his sister and older son, he wrote me a long letter, the upshot of which was that he was severing relations with me. I should never again write about him or his family, he instructed. It wasn't the first time we'd gone into a long period of noncommunication. He was a champion severer, my Uncle Kuno.

Having arrived at the Hotel Papageno a day earlier than us, Dan and Uncle Kuno were already established in a spacious corner room with an espresso machine by the time we got to Vienna. We put our bags down in our room next door and immediately piled into their room. Evangeline, three, a whirlwind, leaped around between the beds while Dan made espressos. As Elizabeth warmly greeted my cousin and uncle, I observed Kuno taking pleasure in this pretty, blonde wife of mine, not Jewish, a bit high strung, demonstrably well mannered and well dressed. Did she remind him, I wondered, of his first wife, Anne?

"Your father came to me towards the end," Uncle Kuno told me that first day. "He said, 'You have to be a father to Thomas when I am gone.'"

I didn't say: "And what did *you* say?"

Nor: "Please don't say that, it reminds me both that you were never around, and for that matter how *lucky* I was that you were never around."

I didn't say: "Shut the fuck up about my father!"

The indignation I felt just then at my Uncle Kuno talking about my father was, after all, complicated by the fact that whenever I was with my Uncle Kuno, I did little but try to get him to talk about my father.

And so I didn't say anything.

Into this moment of silence Dan interjected, rather perceptively, "Well, he was living in a different city, that's important to remember."

This was addressed to me, as if to say, "Don't be mad. Don't be angry." And, I imagine, "There's no point in being angry with him, nothing good comes from it, I happen to know." Whether this wisdom of Dan's reflected qualities specific to his father, or simply his experience as a child of divorce in general, I don't know.

At the time of this visit, 2010, Uncle Kuno was ninety-two years old. The last surviving member of my father's family, he was the portal to the entire kingdom of facts about my father—trivial and not—which would disappear once and for all when he was gone. And yet he was such an unreliable narrator, I could not stand to hear him talk about it. It was maddening. I needed him to talk and I hated it when he did so. Maybe that is why he'd always been so reluctant to indulge me in any of it.

If not that, why, then, did my uncle have such a hard time talking to me about my father? Perhaps the resistance was, at least in part, vanity—a resistance to moving the focus of the story from himself to his younger brother. But as I said, he was reluctant to tell stories about his own experiences, too—the months of Nazi occupation in Vienna, the family's scattered flight into Italy and eventual reunion in New York. Much of this I would later piece together from documents, from scraps of narrative obtained from my mother or cousin, or one of my uncle's wives.

Perhaps some of his apparent sudden willingness to engage the topic was that he was ninety-two and in failing health. But then, in that airy hotel room with the espresso machine, he had mentioned in passing that he had been enjoying his psychoanalysis, and mentioned the phrase, "leading a volitional life." I was impressed that my ninety-two-year-old uncle was, in this final stage of his life, returning to the couch. As for what he meant by that rather abstruse turn of phrase, the OED defines volition as "An act of willing or resolving; a decision or choice made after due consideration or deliberation; a resolution or determination."

I was fifteen when Uncle Kuno moved to Berlin. He had been a professor at Temple University's psychology department, lived in a big house in the suburbs, raised two sons with a beautiful wife; but all that had fallen away in pieces. His younger brother, my father, died in 1975, his marriage fell apart a couple of years after that, and then the sons went to college or at any rate moved out of the house. Now that I am approaching the age he was when all this came to pass, I can see what a flat, childish view of these events I had back then, how complex the relationship with his wife, Anne, and his two sons must have been. But this is how I experienced these events at the time, to the extent I was aware of them at all: my rather remote uncle being uprooted to a place even more remote than Philadelphia.

It was 1980. The University of Berlin, as I understood it, gave him a good deal. This reflected his accomplishments as a developmental psychologist and also, perhaps, a desire on the part of a German university to have a Viennese Jew as a member of their faculty.

And so, in the face of all the difficulties of the last several years, he picked up and left it all behind. A clean break.

I remembered visits to their large, many-chambered house as a child, the lively chaos of my two older cousins—in particular a large, cathedral-like room that had been built onto the back of their house overlooking a deep green garden.

"Do you miss the house?" I asked him one day while sitting in his room at the Hotel Papageno. "Do you think about it?"

"Bad air," he remarked, waving his hand in front of him. "Bad air."

Letting go of the house was one of the smartest things he had done, he insisted, by which he meant, I think, that by handing my aunt the house, he had bought himself freedom from all further obligation to her or to his former life.

For a long time, I talked to Anne rarely, if ever, but knew from communications with her sons that she was still in that house, renting rooms to itinerant graduate students. It was a kind of labyrinth through which she moved, the house, sustaining her even as it sapped her. It was near the town's main street, which was good, as she chose not to have a car. She would walk for groceries, or anything else. His past, then, remained her present, the life of their family—the furniture, the rugs, the old boxes of receipts and letters and photos—still all around her even in his absence. Perhaps especially so.

Late in her life I re-met Anne. It was the death of her older son that brought us together, at first, and then my friendship with her remaining son, Dan, and then the easy grace of how she took to Elizabeth. But above all it was that she was, it turned out, a lovely, interesting person. She was tolerant of my curiosity about my father. It might have seemed a bitter irony that she should be peppered with questions about her ex-husband's family by his nephew, but she had liked my father and seemed to like me, as well, and so she offered what she could. She was a writer, too, in fact; had published two books. I guess I'd known this and at the same time *un*known it. When she died, she left a manuscript in my care, which I have tried, without success, to get published. Its opening is magnificent—all of it is, actually—and says a lot about that house Kuno left behind:

> "Houses are like animals: They're born, they grow old, and then, if you don't take care of them, they die." So said Ames the engineer, speaking gently, like a doctor preparing you for worse to come. Or am I reading too much into them: that I've been a bad caretaker; that the walls are already beyond repair; that houses are no safer than stocks and bonds or money in the bank, and nothing lasts forever anyway?
>
> I think about Ames as I sit bagging old newspapers for kindling, attracted to the random headline as it goes flashing by; war in Rwanda; a newborn gorilla in some high security western zoo. And this: a pizza delivery man who has just saved three women stuck at a railroad crossing somewhere in California in 1988; but not the fourth, who spoke no English and didn't understand his plea to leave the car. In the picture above this story the unlikely hero looks out at us with puzzled eyes. He's saved a total of three lives out of four, it's true; but is it the lives you've saved that count or only the one you didn't?

My father's older sister, Aunti B, lived a mere twelve blocks away from us on the Upper West Side, but it might as well have been another world. It was a dark, large one-bedroom in a prewar building she lived in, but the neighborhood was rougher than ours. The lobby was very long, I remember, and the walk to the elevator seemed to take forever, the light growing gloomier with each step. Reaching her floor, you had to walk to the very last door at the end of the hallway. The sound of three locks being unlocked. And then, at last, she'd pull open the door, to stand there, all at once revealed: hair cut short above a broad forehead, ferocious blue eyes magnified behind thick glasses, a wide expressive mouth. That big, brazen face supported by a body that seemed slender and frail.

For a moment, as she looked me up and down with wide eyes, she would seem almost angry at the sight of me, or somehow mortified. But then she'd begin to laugh. I never understood why.

"What's so funny?" I would say, sometimes tentatively laughing along with her, as she stood in the doorway, laughing at the sight of me. It wasn't until many years later, when, looking into the face of Evangeline or Alexander, that I started to feel an inkling of understanding regarding her laughter. Both of their faces reminded me, a bit, of both my aunt and my father—the round monkeyness of their shape, the attractiveness, and also, most intensely, the outrageous sense of expectancy! For life, love, justice, candy, sweets. The casual way in which they seemed to take for granted life's very existence. It all made me want to laugh. Their innocence was comedic, their presence a kind of ongoing miracle, at least when I was in the mood to see it. I would sometimes look at them and think: "Oh, what you don't know!"

What was it, exactly, that my Aunti B knew? The childhood in Vienna, the Nazis next door—by which I mean next door in Germany, but also literally. The Nazis spilling over the border, to be greeted by crowds of Nazi enthusiasts who had been living in the same city, the same neighborhood, maybe the same building, all cheering the Nazi parade.[1] Vienna a sudden hell. And then the escape. The frantic attempts to get visas—the five of them were to get their visas in Genoa (my grandfather), Zurich (my Uncle Kuno), and Naples (my grandmother, aunt, and father). Then the travel to the ports. The boats to New York City.

When I burst into laughter for no reason at the sight of one of my children, I can't really explain the initial spark, but once it gets going I know that part of it is the incredible comedy of their very existence. My laugh is not the same manic, steam-from-a-radiator laugh that powered my aunt at the doorway. But it must come from the same place. For isn't it the charming, goofy hopefulness of Evangeline's and Alexander's faces that makes me laugh?

At some point, as a teenager, Evangeline perceived something immoral about my laughter. It was always stoked by her own displeasure, she said. "You are taking pleasure in the suffering of others!"

There was some truth to this. For example, I am in possession of a short account my Uncle Kuno wrote about a visit to an academic conference in Vienna that took place when he was ninety. It is a rich, interesting document, but early on, in the first few paragraphs, he describes the taxi ride to the conference. "The taxi driver... refused to drop us off directly at the entrance of the university because it would be too much of a bother to drive through several busy traffic lights. So we had to fight our way against a cold, rainy wind to the entrance of the audimax at the university. I was quite exhausted. I had to hold my walking cane with one hand and my hat with the other hand in this unpleasant walk."

Something about this line, the last two words in particular, caused me to burst into laughter. Maybe Evangeline has a point. But it's something else, the formality and indignation of his complaint. Something so true to his voice. Maybe it's the Viennese in me that makes me laugh. But I also think my Uncle Kuno, who like my aunt, his sister, had a temper, would have softened up at my laughter and joined it. They were very angry people whose laughter came easily.

Once, when I was a teenager, I visited Uncle Kuno in Berlin. He was living in a loft, with his new girlfriend, in a section of Berlin where there were cobblestone streets. At night the streets were lined with prostitutes, their stylish raincoats shiny with the thin drizzle as the headlights raked across them. All those cobblestones slick with wet.

He and his girlfriend, Bärbel, lived in a big, old building in the center of town. The door to the street was a heavy wooden thing that towered over you, big enough for a carriage, with a smaller, human door set within it, which itself contained a small cut for the mail slot. Shapes within shapes. A great, wide staircase led up from a courtyard, with broad landings on every floor. The front door to each apartment, formidable in its width and height and massive hardware, seemed towering. Years later, when I read *Crime and Punishment*, I pictured this building, these landings.

Kuno, in those years, wore a long gray leather coat. There was a grandeur to this coat. The sleek heaviness of it. A very German coat. Not so dissimilar from the long black leather trench coats of the Nazis themselves, when you thought about it. These were my nineteen-year-old impressions, at any rate. Nazis, hookers, the epic courtyard of my uncle's building, the broad stairway up to the second floor, the great wooden planks of each step a deep forest green.

Bärbel, his girlfriend, was tall, formidable, her skin pale, her expression severe, with a straight nose and a broad, sensual mouth. She wore a red lipstick that was striking against her pallor. Fine brown hair fell in straight lines around her face in a way that went well with her own long leather coat. She seemed temperamental to me, volatile, but I never saw this firsthand. Maybe it was her very Germanness that seemed to me charged. Or the fact that she was not in fact married to Kuno. Or maybe it was just Kuno's own volatility that I was responding to. When she got pregnant, my uncle demanded she abort the child. Apparently he had made his desire to have no more children plain from the start, and she had agreed. Only then she got pregnant. And now she wanted the baby. He objected.

I say this without judgment. Who knows what goes on in a relationship? And this information all came to me secondhand. The story I heard was that he was against the child and made it clear to Bärbel that the relationship would end if she went through with it, a position he held firm right up to the moment in the hospital when the child was placed in his hands. A daughter. His first. Jessica. Whereupon everything changed. A conversion experience on the occasion of fatherhood, a third time, at the age of sixty.

There followed an episode of relative harmony, as I understood it, the three of them living as a family in that large loft. And then, when Jessica was six or seven, it all blew up between my Uncle Kuno and Bärbel. In the vicious custody battle that ensued, the loft was, for a while, divided, with Jessica moving between two separate but adjoining apartments. And then Bärbel moved out altogether, taking her daughter with her. I heard all this through my cousin Karl, a highly unreliable source but my only one, as my mother and Uncle Kuno had by then had a falling out and I was in the midst of a thirty-year stretch of not being in touch with Dan, who had recused himself from the affairs of his family as fast as he could.

The fallout between my mother and Kuno, at least on the surface of it all, seems to have involved paper towels. My mother had been Uncle Kuno and Bärbel's guest in Berlin while researching her first film. Over the course of her stay, apparently, she used too many paper towels.

Bärbel expressed her displeasure. Kuno felt obliged to pass this along. My mother packed her bags and left for a hotel, leaving behind a fresh roll of paper towels on the kitchen table, or maybe a tower of them, by way of a goodbye. They didn't speak again for twelve years. And so, for a long time, I saw and thought of my Uncle Kuno but rarely, a function not only of circumstance but also, perhaps, self-preservation.

It was in my early thirties that I had my first adult reunion with my Uncle Kuno, visiting him again in Berlin. I was on a mission, of sorts: I wanted to learn things about my father. I didn't know exactly *what* things I wanted to learn; when you lose a parent so young, something gets torn inside of you and with it, your sense of coherence. Narrative coherence, that is. This I made up for by sheer desperation. My aunt had died by then. And so my uncle was my only living source for information about my father's youth. The narrowing of opportunity, then, the sense there was but one door to go through, strengthened my resolve.

We made plans for lunch. I went to meet him in the offices of his institute on the university campus. "Everyone thinks things are easier in university life than in the corporate world," he'd once remarked to me. "But it's not so. You always have to fight for your rooms." Now I had a chance to see these rooms he'd been fighting for.

I entered a space filled with desks, printers, file cabinets—an office, in other words. It should have been unremarkable, and yet my first impression was that I had entered the house of a sultan. I saw several young women, one of them with a head of frizzy blonde hair, and a bright blouse of metallic teal above her short gray tweed skirt. Everyone there seemed busy with files, with papers, on the phone. Taking my eyes off this glittering young lady, I saw that everyone else present was also female and only somewhat less striking. It's possible that what I was reacting to was European style; everyone dresses up more in Europe than in America. But I am also open to the possibility that I was embellishing what my eyes saw in front of me, the better to fit a fantasy I had of my uncle living in lascivious splendor while my father lay dead in the ground. Maybe I was projecting fantasies and anger and jealousy I would have felt toward my own father onto my uncle, because, in the absence of my father, he was the closest man for the job. What I do know for sure is that many of these women were graduate students, and it was from among this cadre that he would find his third wife.

Emerging from his inner office to greet me, my uncle introduced me around to some of his colleagues, and soon we were walking out to his car, a big blue BMW. There was a richness to his silk scarves and tie, the heavy blue overcoat that had by now replaced the leather one, and, as he settled into the driver's seat, the car's sumptuous interior seemed a natural extension of his tasteful opulence.

He turned the ignition and put the stick in reverse. The car began to beep. "It beeps," he said, as though discovering this for the first time. What is it about this Viennese Jewish accent that can imbue the most banal statement with comedy? As he slowly backed up, the beeps became faster, more frantic. His eyebrows rose in mock surprise. For all his severity, he had a beautiful, easy smile that started in the eyes. He knew how to laugh, and his particular brand of Old World merriment, which often began with a beat of deadpan humor before opening out into the laugh itself, was what most reminded me of my own father.

Finally, putting the car in drive, he eased us forward. Only now the beeps began again, first slowly and then rapidly, as the front of his car approached the back of the car in front of him. A standard feature today, this cutting-edge technology seemed, in the early 1990s, like some futuristic nightmare. We went back and forth like this for what felt like quite a long time in an increasingly Chaplinesque mood, until we had at last eased our way out of a not very tight parking space.

Our destination, for all this drama, turned out to be quite nearby. Most of our time was spent getting out of one parking space and then getting into another, to the accompaniment of all those beeps, like an EKG machine gone haywire.

My memory of this lunch at the faculty cafeteria, done in tasteful shades of gray, makes me feel as though I must have dreamed it, or experienced it in a Stanley Kubrick movie, which is to say the atmosphere felt very particular and specific while also being in some way off—gray carpet, gray chairs, white Formica tables. In the distance, gray walls that seemed lit from below, as though they were glowing, the light brightening through shades of silver until on the ceiling it became a crescent of white. The table at which we'd sat felt as though it were on a riser, the two of us up in the air, facing each other. Uncle Kuno's hair, bristly, a bit long and side parted, made him look like a Viennese version of George Washington on a dollar bill.

At some point during lunch, I asked him about the period of time when he was at the University of Iowa with my father. I had no idea how or why these two Viennese teenagers had made their way to the University of Iowa; indeed, I didn't know how they had made it from Vienna to America in the first place. My father never had a chance to tell me such things, and I never had a chance to ask.

My uncle could have offered me crumbs and I would have cherished them: the aid organization who helped them immigrate to America; what it was like arriving in New York City and learning English; what it was like being dispatched to the Midwest for college; what their sister was doing at the time; what it was like to leave her, and their parents, in New York; how his parents adjusted to America, or didn't; what it was like to read about the war as it unfolded in the following years; what it was like to read about the concentration camps. Had he ever met his paternal grandparents? His maternal grandparents? What I most wish I had said: "Tell me about your mother."

So many questions I could have asked that might, in their indirection, have brought me closer to my goal!

But it took me years for the alternate approach to dawn on me. The sense of missed opportunity ever since has been so strong that years later, as a father, I went through a period of barking at my children, demanding that they ask their grandparents—there were three, after all, to choose from—for some details about *their* childhood: to gather some concrete image or detail, as though my kids must be on the same detective-like mission that I myself was. It was absurd, though I think on some level they came to understand what was driving the sentiment. And they understood, as perhaps all children do, on some level, a central fact—whatever troubles had preceded them, they were, by their very existence, the good news, representing the latest chapter of the unfurling tale. They were proof that the story was ongoing.

They were proof and also a key, for it turns out that to understand what questions I should have asked my Uncle Kuno at that lunch in Berlin, and at the subsequent confrontation for which it was merely an overture, I needed to have children of my own.

Our lunch at the faculty cafeteria began casually, but soon enough a negative magnetism began to assert itself; I would try and steer the conversation to my father, only for the conversation to direct itself back toward my uncle. In that still room, I sat as still as possible, as though not to spook him or alarm him with any sudden gestures. As though he might run. And now my Uncle Kuno was telling me of the time they both took a psychology class together at the University of Iowa.

"We took an exam and we both got C's," he said. "And we were very upset about it. So we sat down and studied very seriously."

"And then what happened?" I asked, suspended at this table floating above the gray, glowing room.

"We went and took our next test. And when the grades came back, I got an A." There was a pause. "Your father got an A minus."

The subject of my father—his life, his loss of it, my loss of him—was for a long time a force so overpowering and unresolvable that I could no more take in its circumference than I could stare for any length of time at the sun.

The image of my Uncle Kuno looking at me so directly now, the outline of his hair imposed against that glowing halo of gray behind him while saying, "Your father got an A minus," has stayed with me like a retinal burn. After a beat, surely in response to my facial expression, though perhaps because of some inner prompt, a call to order, the imagined voice of his mother or father (but probably his mother) yelling at him to be nice to his younger brother—or in this case the only child of his dead younger brother—he added, "but you want to hear about your father, not about me."

He said this with a matter-of-factness that resists interpretation, his mouth set in such a way that suggested displeasure but also held a comic self-awareness just barely discernable, like vermouth in the very driest martini. I can't help but wonder, now, if there was some longing on his part to have his own sons, with whom he had intense, fraught relations, asking these questions of *him*. He did have sons. But they, too, were kept at a distance. And not just geographically. They were still back in the old life, after all, breathing the bad air. For all I knew, they may have been the bad air.

Kuno was healthy and in good spirits at the start of our serendipitous encounter in Vienna, but as the trip unfurled from one day to the next, his energy seemed to flag. Perhaps it was Evangeline's bouncing up and down on his bed, and then on him, on that first exuberant day; or maybe it was all the dinners and meals together. Maybe it was the conference he attended.

While he attended to his business in the company of Dan, we moved through the city. We took Evangeline to the Prater amusement park, rose up high on the famous Ferris wheel. There was, around the corner from the Hotel Papageno, something called the Third Man Museum, dedicated to the movie based on the Graham Greene novel. There were old movie posters framed on the door. I was curious, but it was never open. Still, as we rose up on the Ferris wheel to take in the view of the neighborhood and the whole city, I wondered if my father had gone on this ride, or if it had been too expensive for him, as it nearly was for us even now. Intruding into these thoughts was my memory of the monologue Harry Lime makes from this same vantage at the end of *The Third Man*, describing the faceless anonymity of everyone down below when seen from this height, a bunch of ants, a rationale for his dastardly machinations selling tainted penicillin on the black market.

Surely, I thought, my father had seen this view as a child. That was the easy part. But had he read the book or seen the movie? And if so, what had he thought about it? And if not, what was it like up there on the giant carousel with its commanding view of the second district and the rest of Vienna beyond, when he was a kid? What had he thought about it, then? That part was much harder to imagine.

On the day of the visit to my father's childhood apartment, we meet for lunch nearby. I try to stay calm. Eventually it is time. The day had been overcast, but at some point during lunch the sun comes out. The street where they lived is narrow and straight, the blank faces of the apartment buildings lining it as low and forbidding as I remembered, only now I have a guide to lead me inside. At my uncle's suggestion, Evangeline and Dan remain downstairs, perhaps because Evangeline has demonstrated a great enthusiasm for saying *"mit Schlag!"* whenever we order anything at a café, and a special talent for completely ignoring the withering looks her noisiness generates in these same cafés.

The front door is plain yet somehow well designed. The steps are deeply worn marble. The balustrade has a pattern of metal leaves, elegant, stylish, the Jugendstil at its most appealingly modest. These are the same stairs my father had walked up and down as a little kid and then as a teenager. Sunlight now falls on them softly.

"At the end of the block was a candy store where your father used to buy candy he'd share with his friends," my uncle says. "He was always very proud of this." A tossed-off remark that, observing the habits of my own children, and of myself, I have had frequent reason to ponder.

The bathroom, I was told, was in the hallway, which had always suggested a certain squalor to me. But the first impression I have now is of a kind of shabby elegance. Reaching the second floor, we move down the hall. My uncle points to the door that contained the bathroom; the apartments have long since been renovated to include bathrooms of their own.

The apartment's front door opens and we are greeted warmly by the elderly couple who now live there. It is just me and Elizabeth, and my Uncle Kuno. The tour of the place does not take long. The apartment was once two apartments. Initially, this couple moved into the one next door to my family's apartment; only recently have they acquired the other one, where my family lived, and combined the two.

My family's part was small enough that it takes all of a minute to tour it. What had once been a bedroom is now a bathroom, and not even a particularly spacious one. This was my aunt's bedroom, a prize of privacy, because the old place held just one other room: a pleasant, spacious one with windows out onto the street. There is a large wooden dresser in the corner, and a full-size bed. A nice bedroom for one person or a couple. But this is where my father and my Uncle Kuno slept on cots, along with their mother and father in the main bed. From the time they were babies, all the way until the fateful events of 1938, they all lived in this one room. It took a while to grasp what this must have been like for the two boys, especially once they became teenagers. I still can barely manage to imagine what it must have been like for the husband and wife.

I suppose I should say something about my father's father.

Some people have grandfathers that loom up in their lives, enormous and vivid. My mother's father would fall into this category. Some people have grandfathers who are barely there at all, even as a myth. My father's father, Salomon, falls into this latter category.

He escaped with his wife from a shtetl named Bobrica, then located in Poland, in the aftermath of a pogrom at the end of World War I. Descriptions of this pogrom speak about charred bodies scattered on the ground. He and my grandmother arrived in Vienna, had three children, and must have assumed this would be their new home from here on out.

They waited until 1938 to leave, after all—though even as I write those words, I catch myself; the impatience in the word *waited* is so fraught, so filled with the clucking, empty virtue of hindsight. Yet it's the word that first came to mind. For a long time I had thought they "waited" until Kristallnacht, in November 1938, to leave. Later, I discovered they sprang into action in the aftermath of the Anschluss—the curfews, and all the other terrible harassment that came with the arrival of the Nazis in the spring.

In any event, finally seeing what had to be done, Salomon rushed into Italy on his own, to Genoa, trying to make arrangements for his family, who in the end scattered to Zurich and Naples. From these different locations, and not all at the same time, they convened in New York City in early 1939.

He had two professions that I know of, my grandfather, and they sound like the setup to a joke—butcher and matchmaker. (I once shared this with a professor of history, a very sharp cookie at a well-known university, who nevertheless understood the remark to mean that my grandfather had a business that made matches of the sort of that you light candles with—a confusion that attests to how thoroughly the idea of this profession has been relegated to ancient history.) My grandfather may also have been trained as a rabbi. It's unclear. But the matchmaking is verified from several sources. I found testimony from a woman named Minna whose marriage he arranged in the shtetl back in Bobrica. She described him as handsome and surreptitious. He was anxious to receive his fee, she said, having made the match.

It later turned out there was a reason for this anxiety: He had set her up with his cousin, and the custom of his profession forbade taking a fee when the match was with a family member. Certainly, he made enough from his commissions to spend a great deal of his time in the cafés, though, perhaps I have it backward in regarding the café as a place of leisure. Viennese cafés were where he conducted his business. The details of how he made a living in his field of expertise after arriving in New York are lost to me. In the end he would die on an operating table—a botched stomach surgery—in 1954, in New York City. The funeral, my uncle told me, was attended by many Hasidim whose marriages he arranged. I never met him.

When I first heard of my grandfather's propensity for spending his days, and not a few nights, at cafés, I felt a pinch of judgment. "What about your family?" I'd wanted to ask. Now, though, standing here in this constrained space—what the alternative would have been—those cafés made all the sense in the world.

I try to process the fact that I am standing in the room where my father, in the company of his brother and parents, his sister in the tiny room next door, had spent his childhood. In between these two rooms, my uncle explains to us, was a kind of hallway where the cooking was done. I don't talk or ask questions. There are very light curtains over the windows. They filter the light outside, and also hold it, and I try to imagine the room that held my father and his brother and mother and *his* father. Standing in the soft light of that room trying to imagine the arrangements that lasted from my father's birth until they all left Vienna when my father was fifteen, trying to fathom the conversations, the going to sleep and waking up that occurred there, I've become very subdued.

Suddenly I hear Evangeline's shrieks of laughter coming in through the windows, blown on a soft, sunny breeze that ripples the curtain in a way that allows me to imagine what the street sounds would have been like when it was my father down there running around with his friends. Dan is very good with her—patient, kind, completely uninterested in his own grandeur or even his needs, and he has all these funny voices. It's a mystery to me, frankly, how he stays so chipper. Here he's flown all the way to Vienna to chaperone his father to Budapest and then Berlin, and this father isn't even particularly nice to him.

We all sit down on the sofa in the living room, and our hosts serve cappuccino and pastries. While my uncle and our hosts chat in German, I hold Elizabeth's hand on the couch and stare at the many gorillas in this apartment. They are everywhere. Little furry gorilla dolls attached to bookshelves, arranged on the mantle, on the coffee table. Sitting here on the couch, still and quiet, trying to gather my thoughts, I find myself staring at the gorillas on the coffee table, the shelves, trying to locate the emotion within me, just beneath the surface. To identify it. Self-pity, perhaps. Or maybe just pity, in general—for my father, and his family, what they must have gone through. In the years since, as my children have grown, I have become more and more cognizant that what had for years seemed like my uncle's withholding may also have been an attempt to protect me from poisons he must have wanted to avoid transmitting, to whatever extent possible.

The visit concluded, we all piled into the car Dan had rented and drove to the famous pedestrian mall known as Vienna's Goldenes Quartier. The sky, milky earlier that morning, had by now opened into a clear blue, and the streets were filled with people exulting in the sunshine. The broad pale cobblestones reflected the cheerful afternoon light. We all got ice-cream cones and strolled. Someone walked by holding a huge number of colorful balloons. Someone else made giant bubbles that shimmered and undulated in the air like underwater creatures. Uncle Kuno pointed out the coffee shop where he used to go with my father and his friends as a youth. Under other circumstances it would have felt like a momentous detail, but on this afternoon it was packed with people sitting in the café outside, and for once I could not make out my grandfather or my father moving through the sepia-toned world of pre-Nazi Vienna; just this busy, festive crowd of young people living in their time, a bright summer day in 2010.

Abruptly announcing that he was tired and needed to sit down, Uncle Kuno lowered himself with some urgency to the nearest steps of a fountain while Dan hurried to fetch the car. It occurs to me now to wonder if part of my uncle's strength, his stamina in life, was the force with which he projected himself away from that old life, away from that tiny apartment he shared with his parents, away from the Ringstrasse and the faces of Vienna. Now, here on the boulevard in the sun, it was as if he felt the warmth of the day but could not get warm himself. Or maybe it was that he was ninety-two, and no longer up for traveling across the cities of Europe.

The next morning I woke at dawn and hurried outside to walk the Ringstrasse. My uncle had mentioned that he and my father would walk from their home in the second district to the opera—the last stretch along the Ringstrasse—to sit up in the cheap seats. And then, when it was over, they'd walk home in the dark.

My own stroll along the majestic avenue was in no way leisurely, however. Such solitary expeditions always felt, in the years of babies and little children, like a form of playing hooky. Leaving the hotel room, I had paused to glance at my wife and daughter, asleep in the large bed, the dawn light just touching their cheeks and hair. Soon they would be up, so if I was to get in this walk I had to hurry.

In spite of the Ringstrasse's being a great circle, I managed briefly to get lost. The dawn had started chilly and overcast, but soon the sun was out. The morning commute had begun. The sense of having the city to myself was already evaporating when I first felt something peck at my head. It felt like an acorn or branch falling from a tree, but there was something alive about the touch, and I wheeled around just in time to take in the open beak of a black bird shrieking toward me on a kamikaze mission for my face. I ducked, and then, as I stood back up again, spotted a trio of villains perched in a nearby tree. I was being attacked by crows.

There is no great science or skill involved in a situation like this: Should you find yourself harassed by crows, or anyone else, really, the thing to do is simply to move away. Leave. You have other things to do. But no, out of some idiocy, I decided to stand my ground. If the crows wanted a fight, I would give it to them. I had a right to this sidewalk in Vienna. Never mind that there was a monument outside the university to the mayor of Vienna under the Nazis—himself a party member—that, in spite of protests and petitions in recent years, the city had declined to remove. There was a proposal from a Jewish group to tilt the base of the statue one degree, the result of which would have been imperceptible. Even this suggestion was declined. So . . . let's just say I wasn't going to be pushed around by these fascist crows, all right?

Several times they dive-bombed me while I flailed at them with my jacket. At some point I picked up a stick and hurled it at the crows where they had taken a perch in a tree. They peered at me scornfully, clearly unimpressed. Nothing to do but slink away, touching the top of my head, worried they might have drawn blood or shat on me, possibly both. The malevolent crows of Vienna! I tried to make it funny for myself, but the truth was that I was upset. A trolley full of people had rolled by in the sun, commuters, who did nothing to help. Although what could they have done? But this only occurred to me later. At the time I thought: The fucking Viennese. "Beautiful buildings, terrible faces," my uncle had remarked. Or maybe it was Helen Meyers. Someone who had seen those faces in 1938.

Later that morning I bid Kuno farewell. He was checking out of the Hotel Papageno, and so were we. Dan and he were off to Budapest. We were going to the Hotel Intercontinental for the remaining two nights of our stay. He did not approve of this when I told him.

"Your father would never stay at the Intercontinental," he said acidly.

What was that supposed to mean?

I played it off, thanked him for showing me the apartment. I was invested in a nice ending. But I felt antagonized. The previous day he had been so generous taking me to the apartment and then walking up and down the Goldenes Quartier. Crowds. Bubbles. Evangeline dancing around. A feeling of festivity. I didn't want to end on a sour note. And why let my experience be darkened by his mood?

A few weeks later I would hear from Dan that Uncle Kuno had not been well on the train to Budapest. He had hardly arrived when he declared himself unable to attend the conference and flew back to Berlin with Dan. It was his heart. Two months later he died. I was astonished to discover, later, that he had left me money in his will. It was divided equally between Dan, Jessica, and his third wife, Simone, but four percentage points had been shaved off and bequeathed to me. Four percent, a curious number. Maybe because I was the fourth heir? It came to over fifty thousand dollars.

It took over a year for the outrage at Uncle Kuno's jibe about the Intercontinental to fully sink in, followed not long afterward by fantasies of how I ought to have responded: "You're going to tell me that my father would approve or not of my choice of *hotels*? And yet I can hardly drag out of you a single thing about your childhood or how you escaped Vienna, not after years of trying?" But then, what would such a response have achieved?

The Intercontinental *was* a bit pricey. He and my father had both grown up poor; could he have been warning me against profligate spending of the inheritance of which I was not yet aware? Perhaps. Still, the fact that he invoked my father to make the point is infuriating. Why bring him into it? And yet the advice itself, if that is what it was, can only be called fatherly—annoying or even maddening in the moment but . . . ultimately worth following.

As it turned out, the Intercontinental Hotel would not even prove to be the most extravagant expense of the trip. The expense that really stung had already been incurred without our even knowing it. Evangeline had been watching videos and movies on our phone throughout the trip. We were not naive about data charges in foreign countries and had downloaded several movies in advance. And so, upon receiving the exorbitant bill a month later, I immediately got on the phone with AT&T in order to correct what was surely a mistake. What followed was an epic customer support session. After a forensic analysis of how, exactly, such a bill could have been run up, it was determined that we had streamed an entire movie on the phone. Streamed at a cost of eighteen hundred dollars, to be exact. (If there was an irony to the specific entertainment in question, I would have noted it; all I can offer was that she was three years old so it must have been a Disney movie of some relatively recent vintage.) As if this weren't bad enough, the streamed movie was one of those we had already downloaded onto the phone. The cost of this error, foreshadowing by a year the cost and circumstances of the two-thousand-dollar Popsicle, was almost enough to fly two adults back and forth across the ocean. It was a mistake, I protested; we had the same movie already downloaded on the phone, I explained, as if this was of any interest to AT&T. I was beside myself.

After extensive lobbying, pleading, expressions of outrage, being put on hold, I got the bill down to close to a thousand and gave up. Nothing to do but pay. It haunts me still.

And so, from the sacred to the profane, the lost childhood world of my late father to the minutiae of extortionate data streaming charges. Though I do wonder if part of the paradox of my dynamic with my Uncle Kuno—echoed in the research, genealogical and otherwise, that has become a national pastime in America, with a specific subset for the descendants of Holocaust survivors—is that the Uncle Kunos of the world sense that we, the searching descendants, the genealogical sleuths, are on a kind of treasure hunt. The treasure, in this case, being their pain: the anguish of being uprooted, the terrible encounters with the prejudice and hate, all coming from people among whom you have lived, the visceral terror of all that murder, all of it sitting beside the endless, anxious hustle of escape, the getting out, the making of "arrangements," the frantic assembling of visas and tickets, letters and passports. All those stamps to be affixed to all those documents. The most awful customer service session of all time. And that was what it was like for the people who actually *made* it out.

Thinking about it now, there is something ironic about the entire expedition—about all my efforts over the years, really, to glean facts about my father from my uncle, or my mother, cousins, aunts, or from documents, from stories of others who knew my father, from state archives, from Viennese stairs rounded smooth by the footsteps of a thousand souls, one of them my father. For isn't all of it just an attempt to gather and import into myself some essence of my father that is already there? As it is inside my children, too, I realize. A most unexpected gift.

Note
1. My old professor's remark while sitting in Bryant Park comes to mind: "The Austrians, they never acknowledged that part of their history. It's as though their entire self-image is: We make the world's best chocolate. About their Nazi history, they have nothing to say."